THE LONELY WAYFARING MAN

EMERSON IN ENGLAND, 1848
From a daguerreotype taken in Liverpool
Courtesy of Mrs. Louis Pirsson

THE
LONELY WAYFARING
MAN

Emerson and some Englishmen

BY

TOWNSEND SCUDDER

They reckon ill who leave me out ;
  When me they fly, I am the wings ;
I am the doubter and the doubt,
  And I the hymn the Brahmin sings.

OXFORD UNIVERSITY PRESS

LONDON · NEW YORK

1936

INTRODUCTION

'THE lonely wayfaring man'—that is how Carlyle described him when, as if dropped from the clouds, young Ralph Waldo Emerson came to Craigenputtock one August day in 1833, paused for twenty-four hours, then departed to resume his quest. Carlyle learned that the wayfarer was in search of men possessing the talisman of self-sufficiency. That, and the sudden visit itself, introduced him to the traveller from America. Hence Carlyle's phrase, and his phrases have a startling capacity for truth and error. This one was both right and wrong. Emerson's quest was indeed to be unfulfilled and never ending. In his unassuming way, he entered and probed many men's lives. But what Carlyle could not see then was that it was Emerson's destiny, by the very failure of his search, to become that which he sought for. He built his own fortress of security, and his stronghold of self-reliance turned into a temporary stopping place or a permanent refuge for other men. They came, and he left his presence with them. Some were disciples. Some liked him exceedingly but could not accept his ideas. Some attacked him and his supposed doctrines, when these emerged, with a crusading zeal. From a few he drew hatred. All took notice of him intently. Their diverse perceptions should form a composite picture and furnish a looking-glass to reflect his personality as his age knew it.

What is a man? Is he what his contemporaries make him? Not entirely. No period, though by its observation it shapes its noteworthy figures, can see an undistorted image. The crude mirror is too recently cast. Perhaps only the action of time can add sufficient polish to the surface.

v

The present book attempts to give a portrait of Emerson through persons, and a reading of his life by means of the attitude of his generation. I have sought in it to show him through the eyes and in the actions of some of the note-worthy men and women who crossed his path, but with an effort towards a synthesis not permitted them because of their closeness to him. For these ends I have tried, how-ever imperfectly, to summon to life and speech those of Emerson's contemporaries who, I felt, helped to mold that personality by which he was recognized among them. Because British observers of Emerson, it seemed to me, ex-plored him with an even keener curiosity than did his countrymen, and because their geographical position gave them perspective, I have paid most attention to the re-sponses of his acquaintances in England and Scotland. But I hope that Emerson's compatriots will not be found to have been neglected, nor America. I have centred many of the episodes not on Emerson, but on those who shared the occasion with him. Since even the most unselfish of men are subconsciously more interested in themselves than in those about them, I believed the emphasis on the observers was justified. The oblique glances towards Emerson, per-haps, may be of greater use in revealing a three dimensional figure than would direct concentration. Furthermore, these watchers are for the most part men and women of such vitality or distinction that they cannot be crowded into the background. Yet ultimately their function was to portray Emerson, and I have sought to terminate an episode when he ceased to be a figure in it.

Few ages have written themselves down more fully than the nineteenth century. It was a day of scrutinizing curi-osity and of scribbling vigilance. Humanity was its pas-sion, but humanity as individuals rather than collectively. The urge to keep diaries, the zest for letter writing, were manifestations of this inquisitiveness concerning life and living. A letter, in the nineteenth century, was no commonplace thing. It was a lively recording in miniature of the acts and emotions, the thoughts and opinions, of a little world of people.

Believing that the witnesses should speak for themselves, I have sought to borrow the clothing of their diction and to pilfer their manner of thought. But in a book which tries to show Emerson through personalities and in a setting of specific episodes, tissues are essential to draw the whole together and there must be a beginning to the history. Those initiated in the story of his life will find themselves travelling over familiar ground in the account of his first journey abroad, and of the years immediately preceding. This preliminary excursion seemed necessary as an approach to less mapped regions. Yet fresh material used in this section may lend it some novelty.

I have tried throughout to include essential landmarks for guidance — indications of the spirit of the age — both for Great Britain and America. I have done this because I hoped the book might be not a mere series of portraits centred on Emerson, but in a modest way a biographical study of the man and of his time. In America, Emerson moved in an atmosphere filled with boundless hope for the future. Thoughtful Americans realized that disappointments might come, that checks on the upward way might occur, but these they felt could be surmounted. The hugeness of their country, her bountiful resources, her vigour, her youthful spirit, vouched for that destiny. In Britain, pained awareness of Europe's past disasters, the turmoil of industrial and financial maladjustments, the crowded cities where young men saw the portals to advancement shut cruelly in their faces, permitted no such optimism — made it, indeed, somewhat irritating and very

juvenile to the more sophisticated spectators of the day.
Yet even these managed somehow to feed their hope.   The
century was too full of living for despair.   In spite of ripe,
cautioning wisdom, these observers sustained that vitality
and that air of confidence which were characteristics of
their times.   Some, like old Henry Crabb Robinson,
lawyer, man of the world, and intimate friend of the famous, existed in London society as pleasant, knowing dilet-
tantes — persons who found life good because they held
the keys to their own gratification.   Wordsworth had his
trust in the soul of nature, the shaping spirit of the Universe, and could not fall into a true pessimism, even when
'his increasing conservatism modified his pantheistic philosophy.   Coleridge, who once felt some of this, but had
seen it dimmed, could at least retire to an orthodox God.
The turmoil of the city, the fret of London life, the argumentation of his friends and acquaintances, evoked a cor-
responding liveliness in Carlyle, if indeed he might not be
called an instigator in the bustle.   And for him there was
always the quiet of Cheyne Row, when guests had departed, or a temporary retreat from activity to his beloved
Scotland.   In his fullest years, notwithstanding all his
querulous complaint, Thomas Carlyle throve on the
strength of his outpourings — powers commanding attention as much through his marvellous gift of incisive speech
as through his writings.

   And the spirit of the times worked in men and women
less known today, but impressive in their own generation.
George Gilfillan was an example, and Harriet Martineau.
From Dundee, the town of his ministry, Gilfillan taught
Scotland not only what it should lay to heart in religion,
but instructed all England on what it was to read, and what
to believe, for he was a masterful critic of wide influence.
Harriet Martineau was proficient in many fields, and wrote

on all with a sureness of touch shocking to a more timid and uncertain posterity.

But many of the younger people of the times, who sensed more sharply the failure of liberalism and who saw, at mid-century, the defeat of revolutionary movements which had seemed vital with hope of better things, were not so fortunate. The young artist, the young poet, the young thinker or reformer, did not find the afternoon of his day so promising as morning light. Some, like John Sterling, wavered in uncertainty at the branching of the ways that led, respectively, to the church and its philosophy or to a more unconfined intellectualism, and died like strayed wanderers, their hope frustrated, their promise unfulfilled. Or there was David Scott, a youthful artist of promise in Edinburgh, who fought for the renaissance of painting and the merging of art and life. He could not bring realization to his soaring aspirations, and perished a victim to himself and to his age. William Allingham, who spanned the years from Carlyle's maturity in the middle of the century to the time when the great Victorians were gone, hovered on the threshold of many careers — an unwilling subordinate official in government service, a reluctant though fairly successful editor and hack writer, a minor poet. When Carlyle and Emerson were dead, when the age of which they were a part was ended, perhaps his surest claim to fame lay in the single fact that he had known them. These were some of the men and women surrounding Emerson, and such was their day.

It has been my purpose to base my work on discoverable facts, and, unless I have done so unwittingly, I have not called on fancy even to fill in unimportant gaps. The book is derived from the contemporary records. All conversations that appear are given as they were written in the original sources save that in a very few, designated instances, I have turned indirect discourse into direct. The century was peculiarly rich in memoirs, biographies, and letters. Journalism, both in London and the provinces, flourished, and its reportings have been of the greatest service to me. I have been most fortunate in benefitting by the liberality of owners and custodians of manuscripts bearing on Emerson and others. In the appendix is given a bibliography of the materials from which this book is made — a list of sources both for the work in general and for each chapter. There I also render my thanks for personal kindnesses and help extended to me in the writing of this biography. But there is one courtesy for which I want to make present acknowledgement. To Mr. Charles E. Lauriat, Jr., of Boston, Massachusetts, and to his family, I wish to express my deepest gratitude for providing a sanctuary for the composition of this book. In memory of their delightful hospitality, I take great pleasure in dating this preface,

Hull, Massachusetts,
29 August 1936

T. S.

CONTENTS

PAGE

PRELUDE

The Seeker   1

CHAPTER I

Right Fellows and Wearisome Americans   32
Terrestrial Red-Herrings and an Unborn Soul . . .   38

CHAPTER II

The Yankee's Virus   50
The Earnest Young Men   60

CHAPTER III

Belshazzar's Feast   74
The Banquet of the Half-Gods   86

CHAPTER IV

A Harmless Stranger-Son of Genius   96
Miss Gooseberry of Manchester 108
A Point of Sympathy 111
The Hale and Comely Englishman 113
Full of a Great Desire 117

CHAPTER V

A Spray of Wild Currant 127
Old Crabb 135
'Poor Emerson !' 144

CHAPTER VI

Incredible Recoil 154

PAGE

CHAPTER VII
'From Old Years, a Human Friend to Me' 168
The Road from Craigenputtock 176

EPILOGUE
Explicit 194

Acknowledgements 197
Bibliography 199
Index 221

PRELUDE

No common illness caused his friends to advise him, in his twenty-ninth year, to seek health through travel. Not just his body was sick — life itself was sick within him. By a sea voyage, Ralph Waldo Emerson was to prepare himself for a new existence. So his advisers hoped.

But how make a fresh start when there had been no previous true beginning: only false moves which had ended in frustration and catastrophe? Ill health, poverty, deaths, his own indecision as to a career, were shadows haunting Emerson's rearward path, though he had sought bravely and with intelligence to keep his way in the open sun. The Emersons were not a robust race. A racking, persistent cough, a sharp, clawing pain in his chest, had forced Ralph Waldo, when he was twenty-two years old, to forsake the Divinity School at Cambridge, Massachusetts, and to quit his damp first floor room in the dormitory. Glowing, oxygen-consuming stoves in winter, inadequate ventilation, and a scant appreciation of the virtues of sanitation, made 'lung-complaint' the scourge of New England.

Checked by sickness, checked by lack of funds which made necessary an interim of not very remunerative school teaching, Emerson began to entertain misgivings over the career — the Church — toward which family tradition impelled him. Uncertainty as to one's life course can be a desperate disease. Waldo did not lack ambition; if anything, he possessed too much of it. But ambition unsure of its direction is capable of turning on its possessor, rending him with pangs of doubt and persuading him that he has faults of character which in reality are nonexistent.

The young man sought to cheer his heart. He told himself that, once in, the Ministry would prove to be his starting point: the medium for his regeneration. But his avocation belied his hopes, for he found more pleasure in quiet walks in the country, in reading the new books and journals, or in scribbling in his diaries, than he felt in all has interrupted gestures of assuming the cowl.

But he completed his training, and, in the spring of 1829, when he was twenty-five years old, was ordained minister of the secure, established, highly reputable Old North Church, Boston.

Surely this was a fair augury, and the young incumbent did indeed feel encouraged. Better still, he fell in love. This experience, when he looked back on it, was revolutionizing, vitalizing. The passion rebuilds the world for the youth. It makes all things alive and significant. The lover becomes a new man, filled with new perceptions and a keen purpose. Fortunate, promising year, that of 1829, year of his marriage, year of sanguine beginnings! Could the felicities which it brought endure? Emerson at times found his mind haunted by the old misgivings. And well might that be. Ellen Tucker Emerson shared the fate of so many women of her time — consumption. In spite of every care, she would not get well. A southern journey one year after the marriage brought only temporary relief. January of the succeeding year found the young husband planning another flight to the South. 'My poor Ellen has been sadly sick,' Emerson, writing beside her bed, informed his brother William living in New York. 'Nurse is rubbing her cold hands this moment to quicken her circulations.' In New York, the house was to be prepared to receive the invalid on her way southwards. But there was no need. Eight days after the letter was dispatched, she was dead. Where now was the significance and life in all things?

The year following this catastrophe, Emerson resolved to give up his pastorate. In September, from the pulpit no longer to be his, he announced his resignation to his congregation. He was too ill, later that winter, to bid them the personal farewell he had intended. His decision gave him a momentary sense of freedom and release; a feeling which, with his natural courage, he seized on and expanded. Surely the world was a bountiful, boundless field from which to gather harvest! But his brother Charles, whose personal experiences with infirmity made him a shrewd judge, wrote to Mary Moody Emerson concerning her favourite nephew: 'Waldo is sick. His spirits droop. . . I never saw him so disheartened.' The moment, the final instant, for wise counsel had come.

A month after Charles's letter, Ralph Waldo was on the sea, bound for the Old World. 'My narrow and desultory reading had inspired the wish to see the faces of three or four writers, — Coleridge, Wordsworth, Landor, DeQuincey, and the latest and strongest contributor to the critical journals, Carlyle; and I suppose if I had sifted the reasons that led me to Europe, when I was ill and was advised to travel, it was mainly the attraction of these persons.' These men were now to teach him how to rescue life; they were to help him become the saviour of himself.

The wish to meet these thinkers face to face had been dominant earlier than Emerson himself realized, dominant though unformed even while he was making his slow preparations for the ministry. While he was still a Harvard undergraduate, he was acquiring an awareness of horizons far beyond provincial Boston. His diaries were filled with notations on modern and ancient history, on current British reviews, and on contemporary poetry. His jottings mentioned not only Byron, whose spectacular career and virile writings were magnets that attracted the fancy of

many young men; they also recorded opinions on 'the
experiments of Mr. Wordsworth and Mr. Coleridge.'
'What is poetry?' he asked himself. 'I would go to the
farthest verge of the green earth to learn what it was or
was not.' Why not put the question to Wordsworth, to
Coleridge and Landor? Their writing had borne him
company through the difficult years; why not seek to
know their living minds? In spite of his professed dis-
belief in the advantages of travel, a minor voice of Emerson's philosophy whispered to him that there were realms
of intellect which could only be found through an actual
journey. In the autumn of 1832 this conviction was
strengthened. It was then that Emerson discovered the
new writer in *The Edinburgh Review*. Presently he
learned his name — Thomas Carlyle.

In the *Review* he read of Carlyle's determination to give
his life to thought and literature; to develop a style which
would be true vehicle to the inner man. When Emerson,
groping along his own uncertain path into the future, came
on Carlyle's *Life of Schiller*, he found there a searching
analysis of the possibilities offered by a career as writer.
And in the *Life* were echoes of Waldo's own first years of
manhood. There Emerson's newly discovered critic
presented the 'sturm und drang' of the German poet's early
days, his dedication of himself in childhood to the Church,
his shifting purposes, and his final discovery of himself as
an author. Why, these words seemed written expressly
for himself! 'If Carlyle knew what an interest I have in
his persistent goodness, would it not be worth one effort
more, one prayer, one meditation?'

When nothing is left to cling to, self still remains: self
and the universal soul of which it is a part, of which these
encouragers and teachers — men like Wordsworth, Landor,
Coleridge, and Carlyle — were also manifestations! With-

out narrow egotism, one could swear fealty to one's self, a self which contained in it all the world and all intellect.

Rarely has a half-annihilated human atom launched forth on a journey such as young Waldo's to Europe with a firmer resolve to clutch and hold its independence. Self-preservation demanded it. Emerson's sickness, the whole series of arrests which had stopped his course, made him fight the harder for the strength to be won through self-dependence. He flung himself as a gage at the Old World. Let its sights instruct him, and, at the same time, let them serve as a test. He would not permit himself to be swayed into unthinking admiration. The sanction of his own convictions must first tell him that the spectacle be truly admirable. See Naples and die? No! Rather, see Naples and ask why it is beautiful, and gain strength through independent judgment. And these wise instructors whom he hoped to find, surely they would help him to fortify his belief in himself. Were they not far greater than that crowd of little folk who lived not as themselves but as puppets fashioned by stale convention?

Emerson was winning his right to life. He had his formula for success and he had marked the men who were to help him accomplish its actuality. He could not realize that his defensive self-reliance might erect barriers between his wishful receptivity and the words of the teachers he sought. Yet intuitive sympathies might surmount even these walls.

The young adventurer landed at Malta on the second of February, 1833. No need to seek England in order to view Landor's face. England, for certain poets of the day, was a stale land, narrow in its views and confining, and they had left. Byron and Shelley, fugitives of swift, brief passage over the earth, paused at Florence and Venice twelve years before the American traveller came to those cities. Keats, in 1821, had lived three agonizing months at Rome, then died there. These men were gone for ever. But Landor, whose haughty spirit would not tolerate the thought of association even with them, remained in Florence, a patrician who sought to maintain himself independent of the petty frets of his nineteenth century world and to live with dignity, in the classic spirit which he revered, among his cypresses and roses. True, rumour averred that his calm was not infrequently shattered by towering rages; that, unmindful of the tranquil violets below, he was capable of hurling his cook out of the window. But what isolated rock in the stream of existence is not jarred at times by the flotsam in the torrent rushing past? 'I strove with none; for none was worth my strife.' That was the ideal; what mattered the occasional lapses?

In 1829 he had secured, in an old, legend-haunted villa, a well-nigh perfect setting for the patrician life which he desired (Roman, was it to be, or Renaissance? Landor himself was not quite certain); and there, two years later, on Wednesday, the fifteenth of May, Emerson found him. The Villa Gherardesca, embowered in its vines and olive trees, faced north, towards the ancient town of Fiesole, three-quarters of a mile away. Beyond, below, lay Florence and the Arno. From terrace and housetop, all Italy, as Landor's friend Charles Dickens expressed it, was melted down into the glowing landscape, where blue hills dreamed in the enchantment of the Italian Spring. Beautiful names — Valdarno, Vallombrosa — here made music of commonest speech, and mighty traditions lent glamour to the countryside. The house itself had belonged to the venerable family of Ugolino, the Ugolino of Dante's tragic tale. Boccaccio's Villa Gherardi stood within view on ground where that poet's imaginary company of the Decameron sought refuge from the plague and death in Florence, to enjoy the calm security of gardens, streams, and fountains. On the left was the house where Machiavelli once lived, and beyond that drowsed the white-walled village of Settignano, birth-place of Michel Angelo. For the Italy of the present, Landor had slight regard, but symbols of the magnificent past he loved, and by these he lived.

Before leaving Boston, Waldo had inquired concerning letters of introduction. He was told that usage permitted the traveller to call and pay his respects to celebrated men, and of this privilege he meant to avail himself. He would seek out such persons as his own tastes and interests gave him a right to visit; they could accept him or pass him by as they saw fit. But with Landor he was able to make use of the kind offices of Horatio Greenough, the American sculptor, then in Florence, who obtained for his fellow-countryman an invitation to dine at the villa.

When the young traveller presented himself at the gate, he was prepared through rumour for outbursts of Achillean wrath, or, one might better say, of temperamental petulance hardly in the Greek tradition. Instead, he found the poet the most patient and gentle of hosts.

Landor was like a gladiator of the Coliseum. Erect, ruddy, muscular, a leonine man, he stood ready to give or receive a blow. Yet for all this, when he chose, he could muffle his explosiveness, subdue his resonant voice, and show himself essentially chivalrous and tender. He was conscious of his slashing temper, and sought to curb it in the presence of those whom he favoured, although he bridled at argument, which indeed few dared attempt with him. Perhaps the mildness of the season, perhaps the flattery of a visit from one who even in the New World had discovered and read his *Imaginary Conversations*, influenced Landor to check somewhat his arrogant spirit. He

talked freely, unguardedly, without the defences of an-
tagonism or too harsh contradiction. Indeed his present
mildness was possibly the reflection of a temporary lull in
his more customarily turbulent existence. His sojourn at
San Dominica di Fiesole was the happiest period of his
Italian life; even of his entire span of years. Here he could
take delight in his gardens filled with myrtles, pomegranates,
and mimosas. Here the conflict of the classic ideal with
his romantic and stormy temperament was subsiding into
comparative truce, and the ideal was in command. Here
he could be proud of his children, not harassed by them,
and his love of animals surrounded him with cats and dogs
and other creatures — even to tame nightingales. He was
in the midst of his collecting of pictures by old, unrecognized, neglected masters, and his confident opinions on art
gave a ready topic of conversation for the present guest.

If proffered hospitality is a gauge, then Landor enjoyed
his chance visitor. On Friday, two days after dining at
the villa, Emerson was again at his table, this time for
breakfast in the company of Greenough. Once more
the poet was courteous and noble, but he liked to surprise,
and took pleasure in impressing his English whim upon the
immutable past. Landor talked chiefly of men: their arts
and accomplishments. He spoke like a king on his travels,
with his court about him. Greek sculpture alone could lay
claim to greatness. After the Greeks, John of Bologna
might be counted, and he outranked Michel Angelo.
True, Raphael was a great painter, but Giotto and the
early masters were not to be scorned. Of mighty men,
Phocion and Timoleon topped the list, yet in their company was Washington. Did Emerson notice the simi-
larity of termination in their names? The host made
much of this. As for Socrates, Landor had little use for
him, and Emerson felt that he undervalued Burke, extolling

instead Lord Chesterfield. Landor's judgment, it appeared
to his auditor, was undiscriminating. Most things modern
were under his ban, or unknown to him. He spoke con-
temptuously of entomology, yet said that 'the sublime was
in a grain of dust,' and the second thought should have
condemned the first. He talked with spirit and learning,
touching now here, now there, and his guests, before they
left, were given wide opportunity to sample his qualities.

But Emerson, thinking over the experience in solitude,
felt disappointed in his man. He could not suppress the
suspicion that his host had been showing off. Perhaps the
Englishman had been too unguarded. Surely he could not
realize by what a scrutinizing eye, by what a retentive and
critical ear, he was being analysed. Fifty-eight years are
prone to be dogmatic in the presence of twenty-nine, and
Emerson had found Landor hard as steel in his opinions.
The conversation had assumed much the nature of a monologue, and the young man's attempted participation had
been brushed aside. Landor possessed a reckless indifference of statement. His thoughts flew at random in all
directions, like sparks from an anvil. He had no care to
ascertain that what he said one moment should harmonize
with what followed, and he never stooped to explain. He
was a creature with an unmanageable mind: with a great
deal of knowledge, a great deal of pride, and a profound
contempt for what he did not choose to understand. Such
a person would not remember a fact two hours after it
was told to him. He was buttoned in English broadcloth
to the chin. And, since he was too much at the mercy of
his own talent for epigram, and the slave to his partialities
and dislikes, he could not qualify as philosopher or critic.
His eccentricity was so marked as to diminish his greatness,
and his wilfulness was so large that he could not abandon
himself to his genius. How disappointing to discover these

failings in him! His ringing, sledge-hammer voice had power to shatter the tranquillity of his writings and fracture the quiet statuary of his verse. One small matter fairly shocked the young guest: 'He does not aspirate; drops his h's like a cockney. I cannot understand it.'

But more serious to Emerson's mind was Landor's unwillingness to reason or to preserve an open mind. 'Sir James Mackintosh he would not praise, nor my Carlyle.' It was not so much the view that mattered; what bothered Emerson was the suspicion that the opinion of the moment was not honestly expressed. 'I love real men & therefore I meet continued rebuffs & disappointments. . . Sincerity, in the highest sense, is very rare. Men of talents want simplicity & sincerity as much as others. . . Mr Landor dared to tell me . . . that "Socrates was a vulgar sophist, & that he could not pardon vulgarity even in a man of genius." Out upon his assurance!' Was such exhibitionism all that could be expected of these Half-Gods whom he sought on this pilgrimage? 'I should think they would sometimes be pinched with curiosity to know what a fellow-traveller in the same regions of speculation had found or thought. So obstinate indeed is my own conviction that in minds of the first class this hunger for truth from others must exist that I rather deny that I have met any wise man than admit that any such can be indifferent to the topics which interest me.' And Emerson, writing to his brother Charles, sadly remarked that Landor did not show the same calibre in his conversation as in his books, and added, 'I hope better things of Carlyle.'

Emerson resumed his tour of Italy, an eye on the wonders about him, but half of his attention ranging ahead to England and Carlyle. His health was returning. Travel gave iron and steel to his constitution. He had not felt so well, so keen and forward looking, for years. He was a restless tourist. When some American friends decided to leave Florence for Venice, he went with them, but not without a word of gratitude to his late host. 'Permit me, Sir,' he wrote, 'to thank you for your ready hospitality to a stranger, and, at the same time, to acknowledge a very deep debt of pleasure and instruction to the author of the Imaginary Conversations.'

By hired carriage, by diligence, even on foot, Emerson made his way across Europe. Perhaps to his surprise, he left Florence, the pleasant city, with regret.

Landor had praised the works of John of Bologna. At the sculptor's native city, Emerson and his American acquaintances paused to inspect the renowned statue of Neptune. 'Good enough,' he thought, 'but why so famous?'

At Ferrara there were faint tracings of a vigorous hand, a hand that had released its nervous grasp on life a scant nine years before. On the wall of the dungeon where Tasso once lay imprisoned, Byron's penknife had scratched his name. Emerson gazed at it, fascinated.

Between Ferrara and Rovigo lay the Po, which the travellers crossed by ferry. The young American, with the naïveté of the provincial, noticed that it flowed with steady power and was about as wide as the Connecticut at Hartford. And when he and his companions took the boat from Mestre for Venice, that city, five miles distant across the lagoons, looked to him like nothing but New York. In the evening, however, when the Piazza of St. Mark was flooded by opalescence, Emerson surrendered to the spell. 'It was all glorious to behold. In moonlight this Arabesque square is all enchantment, so rich and strange and visionary.' By day, it was another matter. Ralph Waldo felt pity for the natives, who were not beavers, yet were compelled to live there.

He and his friends approached Switzerland by easy

marches, twenty to thirty-five miles a day, through towns whose past was legend, whose names were poetry. Through Vicenza, through Verona to Brescia, and thence to Milan. From Brescia, Emerson and Wall, a young American dabbler in art, sauntered into the countryside; and while his companion sketched, Emerson sat on a bridge that arched a brook. He listened to the silences of the olive trees, the vineyards and fields. Surely that bird's song was a nightingale's.

At Milan lived the Conte dal Verme, friendly towards Americans, and from his carriage the travellers could study the historic city. But Emerson learned something of the present, too; of the rapacity and blindness of Austrian rule, which held Italy down by the cannon's mouth. It was pleasant, some days later, to observe the free Swiss. Yet Emerson's admiration went out also to Napoleon and his chief engineer, Ceard, who had built that marvellous artery, the Simplon Pass, across the barrier of the Alps. The traverse, begun with the sun's rising, was a thrilling adventure, but by evenfall was safely accomplished. Emerson, to lose none of it, held an outside place on the diligence, a circumstance which later forced him on his high perch to endure the cold for two nights as the conveyance rumbled past Sion, past Martigny, past Clarens and the Castle of Chillon, to Lausanne, where the cramped passengers enjoyed the luxury of a night in a hotel bed before the resumption of the journey, next day, by boat to Geneva. Here the trip was broken for a space, presently to be resumed — and on Thursday, the twentieth of June, Emerson first saw Paris.

How many voyagers have humbled themselves before that seductive metropolis, where the phantom chariot that carries the fates of humanity has turned corners with breath-taking abruptness, where mankind has used its most

exquisite skill in arts, where civilization comes to flower.
But the young man from the New World refused to
relinquish his stiff-necked independence, even though his
stubbornness shocked his companions, who grumbled at his
qualified admiration. Aside from the motive behind the
attitude itself, however, there was some excuse for the
mood. 'The gardens of the Louvre looked pinched and
the wind blew dust in my eyes, and before I got into the
Champs Élysées I turned about and flatly refused to go
farther. I was sorry to find that in leaving Italy I had
left forever that air of antiquity and history which her
towns possess, and in coming hither came to a loud, modern
New York of a place.'

Nevertheless, he remained in Paris almost a month, then
passed on by diligence to Boulogne, for the Channel and
England, where were Coleridge, Wordsworth, and Carlyle,
who might receive and instruct him.

Samuel Taylor Coleridge, Emerson found, lived on
Highgate Hill, which rose gently, somewhat apart from
the heart of the city, above the smoke and uproar of London. Thither, on the fifth of August, the young enquirer
went to make the acquaintance of the man whose critical
and philosophical prose, diligently studied by Emerson at
home, seemed to assure that its writer must be the very
fountain-head of universal knowledge.

Waldo was somewhat taken aback to discover that no
one at Highgate seemed even to know the philosopher's
name, much less where he lived. At last a porter to whom
Emerson put his question answered, 'You mean an elderly
gentleman with white hair?' Elderly gentleman! White
hair! Why, his reader had found him such a vitally living
soul! How could he be aware of what the devastation of
the years had done to Coleridge? Coming from America,

he could hardly be expected to know, what Coleridge's friends themselves were reluctant to acknowledge: that he survived largely because Dr. Gillman had taken him into his house in 1816, when the poet in Coleridge was dead, and the splendid mind, injured by self-inflicted abuses, lingered almost miraculously in a half-waking slumber, a life in death, among the pleasant surroundings which his benefactor's loving care had provided.

At noon Emerson knocked at the door of Number 3, Highgate Hill. But Coleridge was still in bed, and the visitor had to cool his heels for an hour before gaining admittance to the rooms where the poet lived, in the upper portion of the house. 'A short thick old man with bright blue eyes, black suit & cane,' Emerson wrote in his diary, '& anything but what I had imagined.'

Since 1830 his friends noticed that the poet's health, miserable at best, had visibly declined. His sufferings were great. Though he was not yet sixty, Harriet Martineau, who saw him in the year of Emerson's visit, thought that he looked eighty, and noticed that his lower lip quivered with the pitiable weakness of infirmity. Yet Emerson observed that the old man's face was clear: almost childish indeed because of its fine, rosy complexion. His mind was still vigorous, and his feeble, snuffling voice had sufficient power to give vent to a cascade of words.

No sooner was the caller admitted than Coleridge, taking command, asked if he knew the American artist, Washington Allston, whom the old poet had met at Rome, and the train of thought thus introduced put him in mind of another acquaintance from America, William Ellery Channing. Coleridge, in his last years, no longer talked; he flowed in phrases. Given a mental impulse, his brain would pour itself out in a tremendous monologue, dealing

— with solemn emphasis, and learnedly — in all phases of the subject, great and small, interesting and dull. It was an unspeakable misfortune, he said, that such a man as Dr. Channing should have turned out an Unitarian after all. With that he burst into a long and indignant declamation on the folly and ignorance of Unitarianism — how highly unreasonable it was. Yes, he knew: he had once himself been an Unitarian; he was through with all that business now. From a near-by table he picked up a volume by the eighteenth-century polemicist, Bishop Waterland, and read with vehemence two or three pages of manuscript notes which he had himself scribbled on the fly leaves. Emerson, watching, could not hold back the thought that the act was pre-arranged. 'Laid there I think for the occasion,' he remarked in his diary of the opportunely placed volume. Although he passed more than an hour in the poet's chambers, he was able to divert the flow of Coleridge's talk but twice. Once, when the old man stopped to take breath in the tornado of his harangue on Unitarianism, Emerson interposed the remark that he himself was born and bred in that sect. Yes, yes, said Coleridge, and went on. Once he managed to insist that Coleridge's books were read with pleasure and profit by many Unitarians in the New World who did not subscribe to his theology.

The dissolution of the meeting left Coleridge's auditor confused and uncertain of what, if anything, had been said. 'I have put down the least part of the conversation or rather discourse of Mr. C.' Emerson, attempting to recapture the thread, wrote in his journals, 'much of the discourse was like so many printed paragraphs in his book, perhaps the same, not to be easily followed.'

He was not the first visitor to retire baffled from the presence of the elder Coleridge. Wordsworth and Samuel

Rogers, after an evening with the metaphysician at Highgate, were discussing the conversation on their way home.

'I did not altogether understand the latter part of what Coleridge said,' hazarded Rogers, with circumspection.

'I did not understand any of it,' said Wordsworth.

'No more did I!' replied Samuel Rogers, obviously relieved.

As for Emerson, the whole amazing adventure, judged solely on the basis of an opportunity for the exchange of thought, was a failure. He realized, when he pondered it, that Coleridge had become the parrot of his books, and that his conversation ran to effervescence of formulas. Regretfully he chid himself for having entertained the hope that it might be otherwise. Yes, the creative, experimentative Coleridge was dead; the old man who still animated his body could no longer escape habitual grooves of mind to think with a new companion.

Yet it was a misfortune that it had been thus. Given other circumstances and other topics, these two thoughtful and reflective men — the young and the old philosopher — might have met, recognized, and greeted each other, although not on the mountain tops. Coleridge still loved certain common joys, and was capable of sharing them with others. He still loved sunsets, and often called his friends to the upper casements of his rooms to experience with him the benediction of such beauty. He liked to watch the little children who played on Highgate Hill. Flowers were a passion with him, and he could himself be a child and listen to birds outside his windows. As Carlyle testified, Samuel Taylor Coleridge, quite unconscious of what he was doing, generally treated an auditor as if he were a passive bucket to be pumped into, releasing a confused, unintelligible flood of utterance, threatening to submerge

all known landmarks of thought, and to drown world and
hearer alike.   But he still knew the meaning of the word
tolerance, though his infirmities, if plethora of talk may be
so characterized, did not often permit him to exercise that
awareness.   In his *Table Talk*, for the very year in which
Emerson sought him, stands recorded a long discussion of
the bright prospects which lay before America. 'How
deeply to be lamented is the spirit of hostility and sneering
which some of the popular books of travels have shown in
treating of the Americans!   A very little humouring of
their prejudices, and some courtesy of language and de-
meanor, on the part of Englishmen, would work wonders
. . . with the public mind of the Americans.'   Had the
men but met in that spirit!   Even so, Coleridge may have
been more considerate of another's ego than youthful Ralph
Waldo Emerson realized.   He *had* admitted him.   Visitors were warned not to stay above half an hour, lest they
tire the sick old man; Emerson's call took twice that time.
Thursday was the day set aside for the reception of Coleridge's friends, and the stranger had been received on Monday.   Emerson was an unsought, perhaps an unwelcome
guest.

But if Coleridge the man had failed him, Coleridge the
writer never did.   Emerson learned more and more to
appreciate the subtle distinctions of his terms of classifica-
tion.   Through Coleridge's aid, he formulated his own
critical appreciation of Wordsworth, and on those founda-
tions he built his own system of criticism.   And Coleridge
helped him to reconcile Platonism with Transcendental
Idealism, paving the way which Emerson's thought was for
many years to follow.

July and August were given over to England and Scotland.   The traveller, inspecting dutifully the proper sights,

gradually worked his way northward. But Carlyle was not to be found in Edinburgh; there he passed only occasional winters. So, after a vigorous trip in the rain through the Highlands, Emerson came, at the end of August, to Dumfries, whence, as he had been informed, he could reach his new-light writer's habitation. Now eight months from home, the young explorer had been more alone during his British wanderings than in Italy. More and more his thoughts turned wistfully to New England.

Carlyle lived at Craigenputtock, in the parish of Dunscore, to the northwest of Dumfries. The place was within carriage reach of the shire town, and Emerson, who had the grand American indifference to petty distances, was not deterred by the prospect of a score or so of barren miles of moorland. All one needed was an adequate conveyance.

The Carlyles, Thomas and Jane, had set up their domestic establishment on their upland farm in the spring of 1828. They were then less than two years married. Live among barren rocks? Preposterous notion! Such had been Jeannie's first half indignant, half hilarious reaction when Thomas first looked toward the hills. Jeannie loved town ways, and company. She sparkled in urban surroundings, if her health, ever precarious, permitted, and even a new and clever husband might prove insufficient foreground to mask the loneliness of the moors. Why, she could not live a month at Craigenputtock with an Angel, and, to be sure, as her loving but mischievous heart told her, her husband was perhaps scarcely qualified to bear wings.

Yet the experiment in rusticity turned out more successfully than she had anticipated. Jeannie found herself actually enjoying the freedom and quietude of her breeze-swept home. The house was adequate: not even their poverty deprived the young couple of the necessities of subsistence.

And Jane derived much amusement from feeding her hens, or cantering her little horse over the heather, her black hair flying in the wind, her dark, mocking eyes alive with excitement. There were petulant spells, of course. But for the most part, life was good, and Tom had cause to rejoice in the Jeannie he loved — not the Jeannie of mocking, graceful laughter, the derisive Jeannie who saw too clearly, and with sarcasm, the ridiculousness of man. No, he now lived with the earnest, warm-hearted, affectionate, enthusiastic girl he adored. The other Jane — clever, witty, brilliant as she was — he could at best only admire. He was still a very new husband.

As for Thomas, the Laird of the Manor, he was accomplishing wonders. A great amount of reading, and some writing, was getting itself done. The brilliant reviews which, all unknown to him, were attracting the eyes of a young man in distant America, were flowing from his pen, and the French Revolution, with its phantasmagoric puppet-show of shifting human figures, was beginning to reveal to him here and there a modern hero.

When writing or study were over for the day, one could play at farming. Carlyle took pleasure both in the 'improvements' he made at the Craig and in the ridiculous failures which not infrequently resulted from his conflicts with the ribs of the earth beneath his homestead. He gravelled the walks: he transplanted fruit trees outside the garden-dike: he made escape-proof pens for his pig from which that sagacious beast presently escaped. Cabbages flourished briskly under his care, and he even persuaded roses to bloom, three petals of which he sent to his brother, John, as proof of triumph. And, on every side, eternal symbol of immensity, lay the tranquil, mighty landscape. There he could saunter on the Glaisters hillside in the warm dusk, his pipe glowing like some mythical Titan's eye.

The moors surrounded him, a wilderness all vapoury and silent, save for the cry of a curlew, the tutelary spirit of the place.   Above was the great heaven.   The lone man, lifted out of himself, felt the presence of the ghosts of the distant, of the dead.

Yet though solitude is good, one cannot live on solitude alone.   Carlyle, in 1833, after five years of it, was beginning to find that out.   Even occasional visits to Edinburgh, a city which, while he had lived there in semi-permanence, seemed at times a noisy prison, did not now fill him full enough with the breath of intelligent society.   He admitted to himself that the experiment of a country hermitage would not serve its purposes for a lifetime.   'This place, with a little company so very pleasant, does ill, very ill for me, without it.'   During a brief stay in London, he had met one or two wise men ('How few articulate-speaking mortals there are!' he mused at the time); now he was urging them to visit him in his retreat — they must come, they positively must!   John Stuart Mill: surely he.   But Craigenputtock was far away, and the guest room, as the summer of 1833 wore on, stood empty.   True, brother John, fresh from Italy, had filled it for a time in the late spring, much to Jane's delight, who spent whole days reading Italian with him.   But now he was gone, and Thomas Carlyle, musing in doubts, perplexities, and loneliness of soul, wrote in his journals, on August 24, 'I am left here the solitariest, stranded, most helpless creature that I have been for many years.'

On August 25 — Sunday — Ralph Waldo Emerson, in a somewhat weather-beaten old gig hired for the occasion, set out for Craigenputtock.   What Gods devise our comings and our goings, and juggle so humorously with the eternal unfitness and fitness of circumstance?   Over Buccleuch Street Bridge rattled the ancient equipage, through Maxwelltown, and on along the Dunscore road.

Like lowland Massachusetts is the country which surrounds Dumfries — fields a lush green, with occasional boulders shouldering through the brown soil. A region full of echoes and suggestions for a home-sick New Englander. Its familiarity almost takes the place of companionship. Of course there is also a novelty and variety in it which makes its exploration an adventure. There are the stone walls. They are not the tumbled, reckless heaps to be found in Connecticut and New Hampshire; instead, they are neat, narrow, economical fabrications of reddish sandstone. And hedgerows, which are not customary sights to the eyes of the New World, also do duty as boundaries to the fields. Oaks and plane trees of good size stand massive in the drowse of summer, but the occasional elms are fantastic-limbed — not the erect, plume-like sentinels that stand guard over the peace of the American meadows and intervales. About five miles before the way enters Dunscore, the lowlands, flat back towards Dumfries, alter perceptibly — again a startling reminder of home, but this time of upland New England. The walls change in texture to granite boulders, giving an impression of rougher workmanship and more rugged life. Armies of small trees, in single file, march along the hedgerow-bordered fields, with here and there a larger hawthorn, its gnarled trunk losing itself in tumbled branches and dark green confusion of leaves. The land is still a cattle region, but higher up, on the more barren hillsides away from the road, are sheep, like dirty quartz boulders against the green-grey slopes. The tops of many of the hills are wooded, with now a predominance of evergreen: chiefly spruce and pine. Even the farmhouses, more than in any other section which

Emerson had visited, reflect New England. Built low, of native rock whitewashed over, with for the most part but a single story, they have something of the appearance of the wooden dwellings of New Hampshire, and it is largely their thatch or slate roofing which startles the American beholder from his musings of home. The out-buildings are frequently joined to the main dwelling, in Massachusetts fashion, with the farm yards trampled, dangerous underfoot from cowdung, and with ducks and chickens wandering about.

Now more frequently the way passes through groves of trees, with here and there masses of holly for undergrowth. As the region becomes more hilly, tinkling brooks thread their way down larch-filled hollows, the light green sharp against the darker hue of maple and oak. At last the road dips into the little village of Dunscore, surrounded by long and rolling hills. Then left towards Milton, and up the glen, like a path laid in the trough of two giant sea waves, goes the way towards Craigenputtock, the hills visibly larger, more bare, with only at long intervals a cottage. The district has become sheep country, the moors rough and strewn with boulders, retrieved from utter barrenness by occasional clumps of spruce and bursts of yellow from random tufts of gorse. Cleared spaces are patchy with low growing heather, and here and there are fronds of stately ferns. Strange, heavy birds sail away on curving wing as the carriage rolls along. As they soar, they utter a gurgling cry, a call beginning gradually, reaching a crescendo, then fading away like a sound detached from all earthly experience. Where a short time before the world seemed old and familiar, now all is strange and exciting, portentous of some great adventure.

The road, as one climbs little rises of ground, reaching the heights, becomes no road at all: merely a double track with grass between, save for the exact centre where the beat of horses' hooves has cut a channel of pale grey, dusty soil. Surely the prophet lives in a far, strange land. Yet not the dreariest imaginable spot. Superficially the landscape might appear rugged and bare, but there is the beauty of wild freedom in it; beauty in the granite outlines of the hills against the sky or dark banks of storm cloud. The swirling mists breathe deep with beauty: the rush of the wind through the pine needles is a vibrant, complete music.

By now, as the road creeps towards the high point of the glen, Carlyle's solitary house at upper Craigenputtock is almost in sight. Paralleling the slope of the Craig goes the way, then over a gap in the ridge through a grove of trees to the dwelling, which commands a long view of a new valley. The house is a large enough structure, much larger than New England eyes might expect to find in such a place: a real manor or grange in comparison with the few poor little farms tucked away near the beginning of the glen, in lower Craigenputtock. To the left stands a big plane tree, grateful to sit under towards evening. Rising in front, to the northeast, is the massive shoulder of the Craig. Back of the house stands a cluster of outbuildings — a wing to the rear, containing the 'new kitchen' (years older than the occupancy of the Carlyles), links the main building with one of the sheds. Beyond, stretching westward towards the hamlet of Monybuie, opens a fan-shaped valley, falling away in broad and swampy moorlands. The house, two stories high, is built of whitewashed stone, the larger windows recessed in the thick walls.

Within, the householders were at dinner when the 'lonely, wayfaring man' — so Carlyle described him — like an apparition from the blue, announced his presence. When their first surprise was over, the Carlyles insisted that the pilgrim, who had crossed three thousand miles of

land and water to seek them, spend the night, and the gig in
which Emerson had planned to return to the world was
sent off, to come back next day in time for connexions with
the evening coach from Dumfries to the South.

Emerson scrutinized the tall, yet gaunt sinewy form of
his host. Here was a man! Here was youth — eager as a
hound on the scent! This fellow human being would not
lecture at him, as had Coleridge and Landor. The two
found each other instantly. Both were hungry for talk,
and talk was the order of the day and night. A legend
runs that on the one evening passed by Emerson with the
sage of Craigenputtock, Carlyle handed him a pipe, lit his
own, and the new-made friends puffed silently through the
gloom, at last rising in silence to shake hands on the pleasant
night passed in each other's company. Far otherwise
was the reality as the shadows crept down the glen and
evening thickened into night. The great Carlylean doctrine of *silence*, never lived up to by its promulgator, was
not as yet a byword, and the conversation, for the four
and twenty hours, flowed like an Alpine stream. There
was so much to say that the many words skimmed lightly
over the surface of intellectual depths, like skaters hurry-
ing over thin ice, and the strong contrary currents beneath
were robbed of their power to drown. It did not matter
what the two talked of. Their opinions might be poles
apart. What counted was that in each other the two men,
hungry for fresh and honest minds, found sincerity and a
mighty curiosity for truth.

Emerson was quick to perceive that he could speak freely
of his own brief career — the early difficulties and Ellen's
death — while Carlyle, whose capacity for sympathy and
understanding smoothed the blunt edges of his manner,
listened by his side. And when the conversation turned
to less intimate matters, hovering over the little absurdities

of life on the moors, the irritating corruptions and ineffi-
ciencies of those who sold books, or the young traveller's
adventures in Italy, then it was gay to listen to Carlyle's
broad northern accent, rolling like thunder over the earth
and filled with the lightning's stroke, and to hear the unexpected gusty laughter with which he punctured the bubble
of his abusiveness. Emerson was wary of laughter. Smiling is better: it does not strip from the individual the
armour of self-possession. But who could resist Carlyle's
heartiness? Emerson knew that he loved the childlike,
brilliant man.

Jane flourished in company. Never since Noah's flood
had so long a pilgrimage been made on such a mission, and
she shimmered before the pilgrim, her slight figure, airy
and graceful, making sensitive response to the liveliness of
her words. Here, she said, touching a chain which en-
circled her throat, was a gift from the great Goethe himself, sent as token of approval of her husband's translations
from *Wilhelm Meister*. Whatever irritability a too long
association with solitude may have roused in her was now
dismissed: her pale, intense face was gay and animated:
she checked the mockery of her tongue: and the traveller
was convinced that not the least of the treasures possessed
by his friend was this sparkling wife, who had, with all her
brilliance, the knack of domesticity, so that at all times her
neat house was beneficent to its inhabitants and ready to
receive its guest.

As Emerson looked about him within doors, he must
have observed that the general ground plan of the dwelling
was much like the homely colonial architecture of the
Eastern United States, except that the ceilings were higher
and the thick walls were heavy with a sense of age and
stability. One entered a hall, flanked on either side by
living room and dining room, at the rear end of which a

circular staircase of stone mounted to the bedrooms above. Such were the quarters in which Emerson found himself. And Carlyle, who was deeply interested in America, and had, indeed, in his reading of history, included that of the New World, sought first-hand enlightenment from this ambassador who had so providentially dropped, as if from the clouds, at his portals.

But not all the time was spent at home. While dinner was preparing, Carlyle took his guest for a walk over several miles of hills to the summit of the Craig. A fortunate stroke, this, to weld together the iron ties of brotherhood. Had Emerson come upon Carlyle two years later, when the latter was imbedded in the huge mass of London, there could have been no genuine amalgamation, and there would have been no equivalent stimulus for both, pregnant with those subtle essences which give life and breath to friendship. In the hills, Emerson's sympathies were quickest; cities made of him a cold, if interested, spectator. Whole-heartedly he approved of the setting where he found his friend. Its familiarity was that of his own homeland; its strangeness that of genius and inspiration. And in the hills, Carlyle was free from the shows and distractions which captured so much of his attention in murky London.

Up from the front of the house, in long, gentle undulations, rises the Craig. There is no established way up it, save random sheep-paths, which begin nowhere, lead purposefully on for a brief space, then vanish deceivingly in sweeps of grass-tufted moorland or small bogs soft with quaking sphagnum moss. Here and there little irregular shallow lakes of close-growing heather, rosy in August tints, cover the hummocky ground. It is least confusing to follow the corrugated spine of the hill, which rises into three little culminations of weather-worn granite, the highest being most distant from the house. Emerson, at home, had traversed similar ridges of the earth, patched, in place of heather, with unkempt blueberry bushes.

As one mounts higher, one presently sees, in a valley to the northeast, a smallish body of water with weirdly convoluted arms and miniature peninsulas — Loch Urr — whence come, most unexpectedly, flocks of sea birds, that catch grasshoppers on the heath, or, in the sparse patches of cultivation, follow the plow and spade for grubs, like snowy crows.

From the second summit the eye sweeps on either side of the ridge over the long undulations of Dumfrieshire — flattened ancient hills, rounded and wide, worn by count-less centuries of beating rains, of cutting winds that bear down from the north, of snows. The panorama of these great hills, like ocean waves on a calm day after storm, is majestic and far-flung, of a vaster presence though lesser height than the magnificence of New Hampshire's White Mountains.

At last the third summit is reached. Round about, in huge circle, slumber the broad uplands — untrammelled, sublime, life-giving, a place of confidences and lowered voices. 'May he never have to leave these hills of wild freedom,' thought Emerson, glancing at Carlyle, who seemed rugged and strong as they, 'to cheapen himself in the stir of little men in London.'

The two companions sat on the moss-covered rocks fac-ing the valley up which Emerson had come in his gig: the valley which was presently to swallow him again. When the moment for that arrived, Carlyle preferred not to follow the carriage to the crest — rather to see it mount from the house and disappear among the clouds, bearing his friend away as if he were indeed a visitor from some heavenly sphere.

Emerson, who had stood by Ellen's grave, had taken the opportunity suggested by the silence of the hills to ask an imperative question. But Carlyle was wary of conjecture on immortality, and, gently as he could, parried the interrogation. Emerson felt in his heart that he had met men of far less powers who had yet greater insight. No help, then, in that direction?

Perhaps the prophet had failed as a prophet, but not, surely, as a friend?

The two men came down from the Craig.

It was a new descent from Pisgah. One wayfarer was like a man looking to the east, and new dawn; the other to the west, and night. Emerson hurried into the future of the days, and turned his hopeful face towards the promise of America and her democracy — young, crude, ignorant America, materialistic America, yet an America full of infinite possibility: a nation marching like a blindfolded giant, but sure to find the truest way once thinkers plucked the bandage from its eyes. Carlyle, with slower steps, turned his back on the dawn, to find himself at last in a world troubled with the puny spectres of the present. He sought giants, the giants of the mighty past, before whom contemporary men were dwarfs. If there were any escape for man from his shallowness, it lay through these. These ancient ones should guide the degenerate world.

Yet though the roads diverged, neither traveller could forget the rendezvous of their friendship. It was a compass bearing — a common point.

It had been a white day to Emerson. To Carlyle, it brought cheering word that his name was known in America. It was also to bring the feeling that in a village called, appropriately, Concord, there dwelt a man (Carlyle thought of him as a beautiful, transparent soul; he did not then suspect his genius) who was pleasant to think of in the smoke and roar, the stimulations and irritations, of London.

Carlyle hastened to write to his mother of the miraculous visit. And a year afterward, when he received his first letter from Emerson, a letter 'sincere, not baseless, of most exaggerated estimation,' in praise of 'Sartor Resartus' which was in process of appearance in *Fraser's Magazine*, he sent it also to Ecclefechan, for his mother to share his delight. 'Precious is man to man!' he exulted.

Emerson by this time should have known better than to seek out old Wordsworth, now in the hundredth cycle of his years, though the calendar insisted on only sixty-three. He found 'a plain, elderly, white-haired man, not prepossessing, and disfigured by green goggles.' The poet was indoors when the stranger called, but his daughter, Dora, brought him forth into the light, and the old gentleman, his inflamed eyes blinking in the glare, conversed with his visitor with good-natured simplicity. Goethe's *Wilhelm Meister* he abused with might and main. Was it not all manner of fornication? Why, it was like flies crossing each other in the air. But on Emerson's speaking for the better parts of the book, Wordsworth, with a display of magnanimity, promised to look at it again. He was now far past the stage of his life where new writings interested him: mostly, they repelled or angered him. Therefore he ignored them. His great mind was beginning to ossify, hardening into fixed ideas. 'Was not Carlyle a maniac?' But Emerson stoutly defended him.

Here was another shut mind. Yet when Wordsworth, standing on his garden path, recited three sonnets which he had just composed on Fingal's Cave, Emerson was disarmed. He felt the second and third to be 'more beautiful than any of his printed poems,' and expressed the hope that Wordsworth would soon publish them. Not till years later, when he was reworking his early recollections to fashion *English Traits*, did the unworthy thought crystallize that this had been an almost comic situation — the old poet chanting his lines in the garden walk, like a declaiming schoolboy. But even so, Emerson did then make some amends. The 'Ode on Immortality,' he declared, was the high-water mark which the intellect had reached in the nineteenth century.

Wordsworth could not return that compliment in kind. He formed no clear picture of Emerson in his mind. It is doubtful, even, if he associated the absurd writer called to his unwilling attention in 1841 with the young stranger of 1833 or the heralded American visitor reintroduced to him by Harriet Martineau in 1848. 'Do you know Miss Peabody of Boston? She has just sent me, with the highest eulogy, certain essays of Mr. Emerson. Our Carlyle and he appear to be what the French used to call *esprits forts*, though the French idols showed their spirit after a somewhat different fashion. Our two present Philosophes, who have taken a language which they suppose to be English for their vehicle, are verily "par nobile fratrum," and it is a pity that the weakness of our age has not left them exclusively to this appropriate reward — mutual admiration. Where is the thing which now passes for philosophy at Boston to stop?'

To Wordsworth, in his old age, a literature indigenous to the new world was non-existent. When he spoke of American books, he meant pirated editions of English authors — badly printed volumes which, like naughty illegitimate children, thumbed their noses at their honest parents and brought in no remuneration to the family coffers.

Young Ralph Waldo Emerson, his four visits made, left the lakes. Next day he was in Liverpool, waiting for his ship to sail on the homeward journey. The quest was over.

He had sought teachers; with one exception he had found old men. Their books brought more than they themselves could offer. Even Carlyle, shining and young as he was, held no keys to the world's riddles, though he had had the honesty frankly to admit this. But one small, golden key, infinitely precious, Carlyle did possess — that which opened the doors to friendship.

The search was, indeed, over.

CHAPTER I

RIGHT FELLOWS AND WEARISOME AMERICANS

In the summer following Emerson's visit to Craigen-puttock, Carlyle went down into the market place to sell his wares for bread. On Tuesday, the tenth of June, somnolent Cheyne Row witnessed the end of the flight from the wilderness and saw, perhaps with considerable astonishment, the first of Jane's volcanic eruptions of house cleaning, as with Scottish efficiency and thrift she made ready for domesticity the sombre four-story house which was to be henceforth her mortal habitation.

Emerson had looked on the impending change with fore-bodings, afraid that Carlyle would be filed down to the common level by the compliance and imitations of urban society. But Carlyle's well-wisher, whose brief visit had raised the inmates of Craigenputtock to such a pitch of cheer, could scarcely realize what a craving for the mur-mur of life had been induced in Jane and Thomas by too long seclusion.

Once established in the city, Carlyle plunged into the construction of his new book, building it painfully from the confused lumber of his tremendous reading. The sub-ject was the entire course of that bitter convulsion known as the French Revolution, and the book resulting therefrom was to be not a mere history, but a portrait of humanity throwing off its Promethean shackles—the spectacle of a titan at once passionate, ailing, and magnificent.

Meanwhile, what of the bread which needed to be pur-chased? 'It is now some three-and-twenty months since I have earned one penny by the craft of literature.' Wares to sell, but who would buy; or rather, who would pay,

having bought? Nothing could exceed the gravity of
Carlyle's situation. The serial publication of 'Sartor
Resartus' in *Fraser's Magazine* had been quite without profit
to its author. In fact the net result was that its eccentrici-
ties of style, in an England still accustomed to the ponder-
ous regularity of Johnson's eighteenth century, cost the
hapless publisher a heavy loss of subscribers. Yet there had
been a ray of light in the gloom: Emerson had continued to
repeat his messages of encouragement. And Carlyle, who
received only one similar comment of approval for 'Sartor,'
from an Irishman in Cork, was filled with thankfulness.

Emerson was distressed to hear how difficult was the
struggle to subsist in London. Indeed, Carlyle wrote that
he was toying with the thought of migration to America
to seek his fortunes in the West in true frontiersman fashion.
But Emerson countered with the suggestion that he reap
instead a harvest of American dollars through a course of
lectures in the New World. And he hinted that Carlyle
might presently find himself in command of a wider public
in America through the printing of 'Sartor' there as a book.

Meantime, while the household was kept together by
Jeannie's economy and foresight, Carlyle struggled on with
the story of the French Revolution. At last the first volume was done. He hurried the manuscript off to John
Stuart Mill for criticism. Mill, who had greatly aided the
start of the enterprise during the Craigenputtock exile by
sending packages of books for study, was obviously the
person from whom to seek advice, but his mind, alas, was
not entirely centred on the task. Heretofore quite unsus-
ceptible, he had suddenly become interested in a woman,
a certain Mrs. Taylor, and was in the habit of seeing her
at Kingston-on-Thames. He took Carlyle's work there
for quiet reading. One evening, in his absence, she
thumbed through the manuscript before going to bed, leav-

ing the scrawled, interlined, mauled sheaves — the throes of composition were severe as childbirth to Carlyle — scattered like trash on the desk. Next morning, all but a few pages had vanished. The servant, thinking the stuff so much waste paper, had used it to kindle the fire. When he learned of the catastrophe, Mill ran, pale as a ghost, to tell Carlyle.

Nobody in England, said Carlyle, with the bravery of a king who sees his citadel destroyed, nobody in England is to hear of the disaster save Fraser, who was to have published the ill-fated book, and Carlyle's immediate family. Then, having sought to lighten Mill's agony of remorse, he began to reconstruct a new first volume out of the ashes of the old.

Yes, at home none should know how deeply he was stricken. But to the sympathetic friend over the Atlantic, during the appalling labour of reshaping what at times seemed for ever to be gone, he poured out the pent floods of his despair.

And Emerson did not fail him. In his far away land, he was the embodiment of all that makes success of friendship. He told, in the cheerful flow of his letters, how *Sartor* was now itself a book, printed in Boston under the guidance of a certain LeBaron Russell, with a preface by Emerson himself. And when the impossible was accomplished, and the three completed volumes of *The French Revolution* were ready for the press, Emerson, having made himself wise in methods of outwitting the piratical book-makers of America who reaped the grain sown by English authors but returned to them no meal, brought out an American edition of the history and fanned the growing flame of enthusiasm in the United States till not a copy of the book remained unsold. 'I have to tell you one very wonderful thing indeed,' wrote Jane to her husband, absent on a recuperative visit to Kirkcaldy, Scotland, 'which brought a sort of tears into my eyes. The first money from F.R. is come to hand, in the shape of a bill of exchange for fifty pounds, inclosed in a short business letter from Emerson. . . So you see, dear, here is Fortune actually smiling on you over the seas, with her lap full of dollars.'

The tide was turned.

'I declare my American friends are right fellows, and have done their affairs with effect,' rejoiced Carlyle. '*Tout va bien;* neither need we now add, *le pain manque.*' Nor was there any longer necessity to think of travelling to the New World, not even for a brief lecture tour. In his inner consciousness, Thomas Carlyle sensed that he was irretrievably bound to the throbbing iron heart of London. And Scotland lay near at hand as a temporary refuge if the joy and pain and tumult of city life, though free at last from the clamour of an empty purse, grew at times too acute. While he often pretended to detest London, Carlyle loved it with all his being. Even when he reviled it and its stupid human spawn with his most scathing words, his abuse meant little. As for Jane, in spite of her chronic ill-health she throve on urban living. Her talents for nimble repartee, her droll, keen, devastating mimicry, her sprightly cruelty of tongue: all these mediums for her self-expression found release in the town, and the clever Londoners came to Cheyne Row to hear the brilliant effervescence of the lady of the house as eagerly as they did to listen to the rumbling thunder of the master's speech.

And what was this? Emerson, too, becoming an author? Surely, it was so! Carlyle saw that he had not fully recognized the capabilities of the young admirer who had dropped from the clouds on Craigenputtock: he had recognized his sincerity and his quiet benevolence, but not his talent. Emerson had, as a matter of fact, sent to him his first venture into print, a little pamphlet containing the address delivered at Concord on that town's second centennial anniversary of incorporation, but Carlyle, writhing under the Nessus shirt of the French Revolution, apparently did not notice. *Nature* began to open the Scotsman's eyes. Yet Emerson's little azure-covered book, printed in 1836, seemed to Carlyle mainly a ground plan for future building, provided that its writer could find within him the necessary materials. But in 1837 came the British friend's awakening. *The American Scholar*, Emerson's literary declaration of rights for the New World, possessed the ringing, full note of command which Carlyle could best recognize and to which his personality most readily vibrated. Other writings of Emerson, both earlier and later, rang with tones pitched to a strange key — too delicate to catch the Scotsman's ear in sympathetic response. But this oration! 'My friend! you know not what you have done for me there. It was long decades of years that I had heard nothing but the infinite jangling and jabbering, and inarticulate twittering and screeching, and my soul had sunk down sorrowful, and said there is no articulate speaking then any more, and thou art solitary among stranger creatures? and lo, out of the West comes a clear utterance, clearly recognizable as a *man's* voice, and I *have* a kinsman and brother.' 'This Emerson,' Carlyle warned Mill, who had once felt some hesitation in recommending the young traveller to the residents of Craigenputtock, 'this Emerson proves to be a very notable man.'

Next came *The Divinity School Address*, which had stirred something of a tempest in Boston's teapot and for a time had damaged Emerson's earning power as a lecturer, making burdensome the temporary debts which he had incurred in publishing Carlyle's books. *Literary Ethics* and the first book of *Essays* followed the others across the Atlantic.

Now it was the English friend's turn to render favour for favour, and in 1841 a British edition of the *Essays*, with a formidable introduction by Carlyle, was placed before the public. Just as Carlyle, ignored in London, had first caught the attention of the New World, so Emerson, through his friend's aid, was launched in Britain as an established writer.

A fair exchange. Carlyle, now secure in his fame at home as well as abroad, found the world beginning to flock to his door. Sitting in his Chelsea stronghold, he breathed the perplexing, fascinating, irritating perfume of success, and watched the ambassadors of his public stream through his portals in a tide which became almost threatening by its steady increase.

Emerson, who could never forget his experience in the Scottish hills, was eager to have his intelligent friends hear the oracle he had there waited on. The first to be sent was Henry Barnard, a young lawyer active in politics and a zealot for the adequate schooling of children in the United States. A Yankee from Hartford, Connecticut, and a graduate of Yale, he was an American of a slightly different stamp from that first Yankee who had penetrated the fastness of Carlyle's early seclusion.

Emerson had notified Chelsea of the friend's impending visit. 'See what cheer comes to me from over the water,' Carlyle wrote to his mother, with whom it was his custom to share good tidings. 'This is another Letter of the American's; introducing a Friend; whom we expect this night at tea. The good Yankees seem smit with some strange fatuity about me; which will abate in good time.' Henry Wadsworth Longfellow, Lydia Maria Child (who pled with fervour the cause of abolition of negro slavery), and Charles Sumner (American senator in the making) followed in quick succession. Yet this was only a beginning. Once Emerson and those whom he had filled with enthusiasm for Carlyle had blown their trumpets in America, the barriers were down, and the race was open to all who chose to run.

Emerson could have wished it otherwise; he still sent only his elect to Carlyle's door — 'the Divine Miss Sedgwick' (who was actually a copious fountain of sentimental fiction), Stearns Wheeler, who had been instrumental with LeBaron Russell in the American publication of *Sartor*, Russell himself, and Henry James.

In James, Emerson felt sure that the Scotsman would meet a brainy, splendid companion. And indeed Carlyle's early dismay, on finding that James was afflicted with stammering, was speedily allayed by the earnest sense of the man — sense touched even with humour. Though somewhat shy and skittish when first met, James confirmed the old proverb that a stammering man is never a worthless one.

But enough is as good as a feast is another old saying. What was started could not so easily be stopped. Five years after Barnard's visit, Carlyle broke his rule of avoiding complaint to his mother. 'I have had wearisome Americans here : they are sent by kind friends, and I study to receive them as well as I can. They claim nothing of me but a little of my company, poor fellows !'

TERRESTRIAL RED-HERRINGS AND AN UNBORN SOUL

In 1835 Amos Bronson Alcott burst into the tranquillity of Emerson's Concord life. The whirlwind force of his vast ideas puffed aside the dust of the little world, and blew the breath of a new dawn from the immensities of intellect and space. Nothing could stand against the visionary's rushing prophecies — neither logic, common sense, nor the contradicting force of fact. Emerson, the solid world swept momentarily from under his feet, soared with the wind, marvelling exultant at the tang of it. But there was little body to the blast, and Ralph Waldo, with his customary prudence, struggled to regain his footing on the ground. Once there, he proceeded to analyse the qualities of this surprising tornado.

Alas, Alcott had his limitations. The mighty fragments of his new Heaven and Earth refused to cohere, and the man himself, in spite of his torrential powers of conversation, was too inarticulate to clarify for others the formulae which should bring to pass the wished-for results. Why, he could not even write understandable prose. His intellect, fecund and stimulated by its rich diet of words, rushed heedlessly about with all the ungainliness of an enthusiastic bull calf. Furthermore, he lacked the capacity to take care either of himself or others in the actual world where a humorous destiny had placed him. Emerson despaired even that this marvellous creature could accomplish anything tangible or effective among men. Yet he felt that it was a moral duty to support Alcott; even to explain him, if that were possible, to his fellow beings. This much must be done if only for them to glimpse dimly the vision of what could be.

And now the good Alcott, after setting in motion sundry educational reforms (since children at least are plastic), was bent on travelling to England in quest of men to share his dream. Naturally he had no funds for his Odyssey, and Emerson was among those who helped to make up a purse.

'What shall we say of him to the wise Englishman?' he mused, acutely aware that Carlyle must be warned. Yet he dared not write too explicitly: besides, he cherished the wish to set Alcott without prejudice or partial justification before that sharp-eyed painter for a portrait. So he wrote

to Chelsea of his modern Diogenes : 'You may love him, or
hate him, or apathetically pass by him, as your genius shall
dictate ; only I entreat this, that you do not let him go quite
out of your reach until you are sure you have seen him and
know for certain the nature of the man.'

Carlyle was experiencing difficulties with his writing.
Though he goaded himself to the act of composition, his
right hand for the time seemed to have lost its cunning.
One can imagine the suppressed rumble of exasperation
with which he admitted Alcott, who chose this inopportune moment to knock at the door. Yet he listened
patiently while his visitor, his face radiant, expounded his
present doctrine of a simple agricultural life on a diet of
vegetables. The vegetables, be it said, presented a con-
crete problem. As it seemed impossible to get rid of Alcott, the Carlyles housed him for the night, and it became
necessary to feed the corn and cereal Quixote. The light
supper raised no serious difficulties, but Jane, with infinite
consideration, served potatoes for breakfast, and then, to
add variety to the repast, sent out for some strawberries.
When these arrived, Alcott with unshaken composure
dumped them on the plate with the potatoes, where the
two juices united in unholy wedlock. Carlyle, a sufferer
from nervous dyspepsia, was shocked to the pit of his
stomach. He could eat nothing, but rose hurriedly and
stormed up and down the room. Later, when the two
men walked together over the Magnificence of Piccadilly
Circus, he could not resist taking a justified revenge.
'Here, now, this Piccadilly has existed for ages,' he exclaimed, turning on the moist-eyed philosopher, 'and will
continue to exist long after your potato-gospel has gone
to the dogs.'

Piccadilly, centre of the world, with the clatter of its
traffic, served merely to pain and confuse Alcott. He

could not swim with the muddy torrent of London, and he had no wish to. The contemptuous light laughter of young Robert Browning, who had chanced to stray into the parlor at Cheyne Row while the humourless Alcott was in the midst of his most earnest expositions, seemed to him like the hilarity of a lost soul. Sorrowfully, with mild indignation, Alcott fastened on the conviction that Carlyle had buried all prophecy in the grave of history. Even the famous Scotsman's mirth, he felt, was sombre and had the sound of madness in it. Carlyle was a dead man, playing with the bones of the dead. Here was no longer any vision. Greatness had departed, to dwell more happily beside the streams and groves of Concord.

When Alcott had fled from Babylon, Carlyle wrote him a letter of farewell. 'You leave me . . . as an incorrigible heretic and infidel, which verily I am not, yet must be content to seem for the present! Well, I will wish you a right pleasant reunion with your native friends, with those whom you know better than you do me. To hear that your scheme of life prospers to the utmost possible extent will, you may depend upon it, be always happy news to me.' If Emerson read that letter, he must have rejoiced in his friend Carlyle. As it was, he wrote to him, thanking him for his magnanimity. He felt, nevertheless, that both Carlyle and Browning were at fault in their lack of appreciation of the visionary. As for Emerson's British friend, he did not repress the thought that the spiritual state of New England which Alcott represented was indeed a strange and wonderful business.

There was another visitor from the States in need of justification at Cheyne Row whose periodic arrival was likewise an earnest, humourless symptom of America's striving for the heights—or rather, was a thin, far shed ray from that vague intellectual nebula of America which hovered over Concord like a tinted cloud at sunrise. But this caller, dropping in unannounced yet assuming all the prerogatives of a bosom friend, was not a person, but a magazine. Its name was the *Dial*. In answering a question concerning Emerson and the journal put by Thomas Ballantyne, a reformer and publisher at Manchester, Carlyle wrote: 'It is edited, I believe, by a Miss Margaret Fuller, a disciple of his and of others, who goes into very high flights about Art, Self-sacrifice, Progress, etc., etc.' He had already warned Emerson that the *Dial* was too ethereal; too speculative. Yet his American correspondent presently wrote to say that he had taken the editorship on his own shoulders. Well!

For the sake of his friend, the rugged Scotsman perseveringly read each new issue, comforted somewhat by the knowledge that Emerson did not wholly subscribe to the ideas set forth, and planned, indeed, to doff the mantle of editorship at the first opportunity. But he found it the most wearisome of readable reading: spirit-like, shrill, and incorporeal. Yes, there might come to be too much of this mock-Emersonianism in the world. 'This New England business I rather liken to an *un*born soul, that has yet got no body; not a pleasant neighbour, either! We live in a most wondrous "New Era," do we not?'

Margaret Fuller, like Alcott, was a problem to Emerson, but a problem of a somewhat different order. Her eager intellectuality, the impetuous stream of learning which gushed from her, her soaring kite of aspiration, terrified and repulsed him. Yet there was something fascinating in the quality of that ugly, horse-like face, and in the spirit which animated it. Emerson presently succumbed, since there was nothing else to do — no escape permitted. From the hour when Harriet Martineau, that militant British female on a conquest of America in the 'Thirties, had discovered both Emerson and Margaret (her American counterpart), and had flung them together, Miss Fuller had bored persistently into Emerson's defences. Her sapping efforts inevitably brought about not only surrender but made her victim an ally, though for a time an uneasy one, glancing furtively for a back door. But after ten years of friendship, Emerson remembered only his admiration for this brilliant, exotic acquaintance, who now lived, perhaps fortunately, in New York as a member of the staff of Horace Greeley's *Tribune*, where all things cultural — new books, pictures new and old, and music — were strained through her critical sieve.

What a thoroughly qualified critic she was! One of the first readers in America of Goethe, a translator of Eckermann, an accomplished scholar in Italian, she was destined, Emerson believed, for a greater part than mere journalism had to offer. When she sailed for Europe in 1846, he wrote to Carlyle fully about her, and begged him to receive her kindly, and in some moment of special good humour and boundless leisure, when, with a free mind, he could do her justice.

Carlyle obliged. He found Margaret 'a strange lilting lean old maid,' and not nearly such a bore as he had expected. He spoke to her of Emerson with hearty kindliness, and told her a story of a poor farmer he knew, who on Sundays, when the week's labour was done, sat reading the *Essays* and looking over the sea.

But with Jane, to whom Miss Fuller had been particularly recommended, it was far otherwise. Jane did not like women who came chiefly to inspect her husband. Margaret did not share London's delighted awareness that Mrs. Carlyle had graces of conversation quite independent of her famous husband. With huge enthusiasm, sharp-voiced, energetic Miss Fuller tried to shout down Mr. Carlyle, and his wife's quiet voice was lost in the hubbub.

After Margaret's departure for France, Jane materialized her displeasure in a peppery letter to her Manchester admirer and confidante, Geraldine Endsor Jewsbury. 'My darling Jane,' and 'Carissima mia' ran the salutations of their correspondence, but the gossip which passed between them was anything but sugary. Out upon the hypocritical American, with her cant about a free and easy life for women, while at home she comported herself like a strait-laced puritan to keep up with Emerson and Company! The mask of transcendentalism which she assumed was surely just to dignify her physical inclinations! Besides, what right did an irredeemably ugly, uninteresting woman have to utter such doctrines! Jane herself enjoyed an occasional mild fling. A lively party, now and then, with a little champagne and some genteel rowdyism suited well her London mood. Surely the pleasantest company, she decided, are the *blackguards*. But it must not be hypocritically done!

Thomas Carlyle was obliged only to show himself to his visitors. But on Jane fell not only the duty of being gracious hostess, but also of being the great man's wife, porter at the gate, and housekeeper. She loved to entertain: her little parties at Cheyne Row were acquiring a fame second to that of no other house in London for the quiet skill with which she conducted them and the delight offered by her witty conversation — a deft *obbligato* to her husband's bass. Yet surely a hostess should be accorded the right to choose her guests!

And whole cargoes of Americans — celebrities and non-celebrities, properly introduced by Emerson, or not introduced at all — were landing at the Chelsea doorway. Generally the unvouched-for visitors were the most trying. On one occasion Mrs. Carlyle, returning from a morning drive, found Helen, the maid, in a great state of agitation, and 'a precious specimen of the regular Yankee,' who looked like a terrestrial red-herring, lean and tall and legged, in command of the house — seated, indeed, at Carlyle's desk littered with private correspondence.

'Oh, you are Mrs. Carlyle, are you?' remarked the unknown, surveying her from head to foot, 'I have come a great way out of my road to congratulate Mr. Carlyle on his increasing reputation, and, as I did not wish to have my walk for nothing, I am waiting till he comes in; but in case he should not come in time for me, I am just writing him a letter, here, at his own table, as you see, Mrs. Carlyle!'

Mrs. Carlyle saw well enough. Indignantly she spun on her heel and marched out of the room. But the Yankee, with all the adhesive quality of a barnacle, refused to be pried away. When after half an hour Jane returned, there he was, still enthroned on the master's chair. Erasmus Darwin, brother of Charles, and Mr. Wedgwood, of the pottery family, had dropped in, and the American, much to their covert amusement, was loquaciously doing the honours of the house. With the wife's return, the Yankee at once opened fire with a salvo of questions.

'Does Mr. Carlyle enjoy good health, Mrs. Carlyle?'

'No!'

'Oh, he doesn't! What does he complain of, Mrs. Carlyle?'

'Of everything!'

'Perhaps he studies too hard; — does he study too hard, Mrs. Carlyle?'

'Who knows?'

'How many hours a day does he study, Mrs. Carlyle?'

If Mr. Carlyle's increasing reputation bore no other fruits than congratulatory Yankees, Jane decided, she for one was prepared to vote for its abatement with all possible dispatch. These New Englanders were becoming like the locusts of Egypt. 'I counted lately fourteen of them in one fortnight, of whom Dr. Russell was the only one you did not feel tempted to take the poker to.' Jane might well withhold her poker from assault on LeBaron Russell, chief mover of the *Sartor* enterprise in the States. That venture in publishing was largely instrumental in suggesting to Emerson the idea that *The French Revolution* be converted into American cash for the hard beset strugglers in London, and Jane, in those difficult times, had remembered Emerson and his associates with gratitude and affection.

But now that security and fame had come — now that she was a London lady — it was more difficult for her, although she did approve of a few Americans, to overlook the rusticity, provincialism, and often outright boorishness of many of Emerson's countrymen. However, though they annoyed, they did afford relief from the ennuis of life. Jane delighted in a lively target for her shafts of wit. What a drawling and a yes sir-ing and no sir-ing they set up in the living room! Jane sometimes wished her absent friends could hear these flocks of magpies: it would be worth five shillings to them! And such caricatures! One was 'an American "General!"'—General Baird—the very image of Mr. Pecksniff, without the shyness. But entertaining them — playing the part of mistress of the house and consort of the great man — that was often most irksome, especially when the restive hostess was herself invited out to meet some London person of quality, like Lady Harriet Baring. Jane had gone so far as to order

the carriage at the door when it flashed through her mind
that a whole bevy of Americans, male and female, were
invited to tea at her house for the same hour. What
should be done? Jane was for giving up her social excursion till her escort, Mr. Charles Buller, made the suggestion that it was the lion whom all these strangers were
coming to stare at, not the lion's wife. Let him pour tea
for them himself in exchange for their libations at his door-
sill. Carlyle was at first quite furious at the suggestion.
But Jane, with a toss of her head, declared that *she* had no
reason to study politeness before the Americans, and left
her husband to scald his fingers with boiling water.

Yes, Mrs. Carlyle was indeed enjoying London. She
could not readily persuade her husband to share with her
the delights of society; he preferred to converse at home
with his circle of acquaintances. But to her it was exquisite relief from the provincial dullness of Scotland to
bandy a little exciting talk at metropolitan tea tables.
This stirring life was more to her mind. Emerson's pious
hope that Jane would remain free of the petty smallness
of London was founded on a certain misconception of her
nature. He had recognized her as a good wife to Carlyle.
He had failed to appreciate the demands made by her own
peculiar, gregarious, mischievous genius.

London brought her release. She took pleasure in assuming the city pose. Men, charmed by her flashing quiz-
zeries, discovered themselves on the verge of infatuation.
Her skirmishes of wit were usually conducted under cover
of a most amiable manner, and even with the passing of
youth her countenance retained an expressiveness alive
with both satire and sentiment. Her beautiful dark eyes
could not hide an inner warmth of tenderness which led
some to call her gentle and endearing, although Jane loved
to see herself in the guise of a demoniacal imp: a brimstone

of a creature behind her beautiful amiability. Her pleasure in pungent speech deflected her readily into exaggeration and caricature when a story contained possibilities of being made rounded and racy. Gifts such as hers tricked her into a habit of reckless assertion which frequently led astray her deliberate judgment. Perhaps she did not expect her cleverest hearers to be deceived, yet she often deceived herself. Jane held her husband in the palm of her hand. Trustfully he accepted her highly-flavoured opinions of people, and even repeated them as his own. That his brilliant, clever Jeannie's estimates might be untrustworthy did not for a moment cross his mind.

Carlyle she could handle with consummate skill. Even when his mood was stormiest, she could abate the tempest with her quiet voice: 'But, Mr. Carlyle, you remember he did act very nobly towards that poor man.' Once, when her husband was complaining in his direst tones of the tepidity of his coffee, and she had twice commanded fresh pots of boiling water to be brought, she mildly asked: 'My dear, what would you think of holding a red-hot cinder in your mouth, and drinking your coffee through that?' Carlyle's roars abruptly ceased.

To Jane alone belonged the privilege of deflating her husband. But in her heart she was proud of him and jealously guarded his fame. When, with the British publication of two volumes of Emerson's essays and of his book of poems, the question, 'Whether is Carlyle or Emerson the greater man?' became a favourite topic at the tea tables of the intelligent, Jane pricked up her ears and smouldered with resentment.

And what was this defection of Carlyle's young men, who had heretofore hung breathlessly on his every word? Francis Espinasse, for instance, the clever young newspaper writer from Manchester. Indignantly she told him that

Emerson had no original ideas except mad ones. And were not Emerson's saner writings just the pale shadow of Carlyle's? Surely, in their own right, not much good was to come of them. They were arrogant, and filled with short-comings. And here was young Dilberoglue, a Greek merchant whom she had met at Manchester. Jane liked him. He was most solicitous and attentive. Yet though she could write to her husband describing him as an admirer of his, she was forced to add: 'but still more, I am afraid, of Emerson's.' The North of England seemed infected with the Yankee's virus.

CHAPTER II

THE YANKEE'S VIRUS

YEARS before Jane's awareness of the peril, a drift towards Emerson had started — a movement hardly perceptible in its faint beginnings, certainly not fully discerned or understood by the cause of it, yet nevertheless the sign of a change of tide capable of floating many men on its broadening surface. Its first impulsion in Britain came in 1833 when Emerson was wandering over Europe in quest of teachers. For him it had been an amazing experience. He, the seeker, had found himself the one sought. This earliest disciple was Alexander Ireland, a youthful resident of the city of Edinburgh. He it was who became the first of the many young men in America and England who were to find in Emerson what he had been forced to discover within himself through the failure of his hunt for it in others.

Ireland was seven years Emerson's junior: modest, pleasant, and genial — a younger-brotherly man who delighted in human society. Born to hero worship, he derived as much pleasure out of furthering the affairs of others as he did from his own by no means small share of success. Decidedly optimistic, he always expected the best that could happen. He believed in fulness of life. Though brought up in business, he had a passion for literature and learning. When Emerson fell to his lot, through the fortuitous circumstance that the dignitary to whom the traveller bore a letter of introduction was too busy to show him the city, it was as though an ambassador straight from the kingdom of letters had in person delivered his credentials. Had not this stranger stood face to face with Coleridge on Highgate

Hill? He had dined with Walter Savage Landor who dwelt in the far south of Europe like an Augustan patrician, and Landor had pontificated of the heroes and men whom his teeming brain loved to juxtapose in the *Imaginary Conversations*. He was planning, before he sailed back over adventurous leagues of Ocean to a place named Boston, to seek out Wordsworth and Carlyle. Alexander Ireland begged his new-found American friend to write a letter telling what these men said to him, a favour which Emerson was glad to perform.

As the two visited Holyrood Castle, saw Canongate Tolbooth, and trod the steep streets of the rugged town, the stranger from the New World, in his low, steady voice, had talked of life and books. He spoke of Montaigne's *Essays*, which he advised should be read in the racy English of Charles Cotton — a work matchless among translations. He spoke of DeQuincey's writings, regretting that he had not met the man. Hazlitt was an admirable guide to Coleridge, and, of Walter Savage Landor's imaginings, the conversation between Plato and Diogenes was admirable and provocative. All young men, said Emerson to his companion, should write down their ideas in a commonplace book. He cited the benefits he himself derived from the practice. 'It fixes more firmly in your mind what you know, and what you have acquired, and reveals to you unerringly which of your ideas are vague, and which are solid.'

Emerson was solid enough. Alexander Ireland, putting to use this advice after the stranger had departed, found that out. What a remarkable sermon (his only appearance in a British pulpit) he had delivered with serenest self-possession in the Unitarian Chapel, Young Street! So full of calm dignity and power: spoken in so low a tone, yet with what penetrating force. Alexander Ireland could still hear the words. Edinburgh was accustomed to the brutal explosiveness of Dr. Thomas Chalmers, who bullied his auditors into hypnotic attention: this discourse, which the inattentive failed even to catch, shone like cold fire compared to a furnace blast. Ireland committed to his diary a page of enthusiasm which, when he scanned it again after the intensity of his experience had abated, read like the wildest exaggeration.

But several years later, when the little book called *Nature* came from America, when Ireland, after zealous search, found other essays in slim pamphlets or hidden away in unfamiliar magazines, he knew in his heart that he had not been guilty of overstatement. Some day, by whatever means he could devise, he must bring that voice again to Britain. He told himself, and convinced others, that here were words which should come direct from Emerson's lips.

Meanwhile Alexander Ireland had left Edinburgh for Manchester. When John Bright and his potent band of Manchester liberals, in need of a mouthpiece, founded the *Manchester Examiner* in 1845, Ireland, already known in that city for his business acumen, was presently made managing partner of the journal. Soon its influence was felt even beyond the boundaries of Lancashire.

Yet amidst all the excitement of prospering and continuing to prosper, Alexander Ireland could not forget the marvellous visitant to Edinburgh. Every pamphlet by him from America, every British reprint, he devoured with eagerness, amazed at this teacher, this heartener of mankind who for a few brief days had been personally his companion and friend.

Ireland became a man of power in the Northern shires. His newspaper was not his only key to influence. Broad humanitarianism was the distinguishing characteristic of many worthy men of the day, and Ireland, one who loved his fellow man, inevitably played his part in those enterprises which sought to check the evils that attended the rise of the new industrialism — muddily swirling tides that washed over the cities of the Midlands, choking intelligence and debasing the human spirit. What better means than adult education to combat the forces which threatened to drown the better instincts of mankind? So Manchester, in common with almost every other city in industrial England, had its Mechanics' Institute and its Athenæum (of which Ireland was a director) as centre for the diffusion of light to the darkened people through night-school classes, libraries, and lectures. Whether or not the rank and file actually craved this illumination does not now matter — suffice it to say that at least they patronized the offerings made available to them. Men and women flocked to the lectures as cattle to a salt lick, and persons whose duty it was to secure fresh speakers found themselves increasingly hard put to it to supply the demand. Alexander Ireland knew these difficulties. And the happy thought struck him that here was the opportunity again to bring Ralph Waldo Emerson to England. Margaret Fuller, on her tour of Europe, had swept through Manchester in the summer of 1846, and from her Ireland had learned of the success of his admired acquaintance as a lyceum lecturer. Before the year was out, he had invited him to visit England in the capacity of public speaker, and he presently followed his plea with more letters urging the excursion.

At first Emerson was chary of the notion. 'I have had new letters from Mr Ireland concerning Lectures in England,' he wrote to Miss Fuller, 'But I shall not be very forward. I am not young enough now to have any projects of literary propagandism there, and do not wish to collect an audience with pains, or that others should for me.' Clearly he felt the adventure to be hazardous at best, and had little realization of the elaborate preparations for an extended tour which Ireland, an energetic enthusiast, was ready to undertake. Yet he was tempted. Had not Carlyle written from London of possible lectures to be delivered there? Certainly these would furnish an excuse for a visit to the man Emerson learned to love from the time of the pilgrimage to Craigenputtock. When at last he consented to go, he regarded the engagement to lecture mainly as an excuse once more to call on old acquaintances and to see the world.

On Friday evening, 22 October 1847, he debarked at Liverpool: was cordially welcomed by Alexander Ireland: spent two days in the North: then hurried by train on Monday to visit the Carlyles in London. Thomas's cordial invitation had almost failed to reach the expected guest. During intermissions in his work, Carlyle often wandered restlessly about, visiting his old haunts in Scotland or any other place that offered asylum. For some time now he had done little scholarly labour. The second edition of *Oliver Cromwell's Letters and Speeches*, following hard on the first, had left scant opportunity for vacationing. With that work finished, and the *Latter-Day Pamphlets* — those bitter denunciations of the present — not yet begun, he had made use of the lull for a protracted absence from London. As a result, Emerson's letter, addressed to Chelsea, announcing the date of the British expedition, did not come to his friend's hands many days before the arrival of the ship bearing the American to Britain. When he at last received it (it had pursued him from one address to another), Carlyle wrote at once to

Alexander Ireland, enclosing an urgent request for Emerson's company. 'Know then, my Friend, that in verity your Home while in England is *here*; and all other places, whither work or amusement may call you, are but inns and temporary lodgings. . . Come soon; come at once. Ever yours, T. Carlyle.'

Perhaps he had been somewhat careless in informing himself concerning Emerson's plans for England. And in Manchester, shortly before Emerson himself came there, Carlyle was heard to speak of him, without much enthusiasm, as a 'flowing poetic man.' But the Scotsman had little use for poetry: even his friend Alfred Tennyson's work he regarded with some impatience, and could muster for it only reluctant and stereotyped praise. Yet there can be little doubt that he welcomed the thought of seeing Emerson. Enshrined deep within Carlyle's heart — in spite of the *Dial*, in spite of Alcott and his crew — was a brave image of his friend in Concord.

Carlyle held two conceptions of the New World. His mind wavered between a picture of an America of boundless forests — the stern but just mother, the rewarder of honest toil — and of America, land of crassest cash enslavement, a nation run rabid in the pursuit of the dollar. Into either view his idea of Emerson fitted well: Emerson independent and courageous, winning his daily bread through his own powers. He saw him boldly saying his say, fearless and alone (was not Carlyle doing the same in England? had he not coached his friend to a similar part?). Amidst all manner of shams, there he stood! And Carlyle had implored the Destinies to keep his friend free from the bottomless hubbub of philanthropic nonsense.

Darkness had settled over London when Emerson knocked at the door to which he had addressed so many intimate and affectionate letters. There was the brass name plate, the embodiment of the magic address: No. 5 Great Cheyne Row, Chelsea.

Within, the household itself had been sufficiently agitated over the traveller's expected coming. How different were Emerson's two visitations — the precipitous descent on Craigenputtock; the arrival of an honoured friend of long standing, though a friend seen through the deceptive lens of correspondence and of books. Jane, in anticipation, had set in motion the titanic forces of a housecleaning, and Jane's housecleanings had about them the turmoil of mighty earthquakes. 'I have been in a pretty mess with Emerson's bed,' she informed Thomas, still prudently on his wanderings, 'having some apprehensions he would arrive before it was up again.' A majestic four-poster was like a gothic cathedral: renovations were not lightly to be undertaken. 'The quantity of sewing that lies in a lined chintz bed is something awfully grand.' Sewing women were at a premium: one had other work on her hands for a good three months, one had a new baby which screamed when she attempted to leave it, one was 'under a course of physic.' So there was nothing for it, Jane decided, but to fall on the thing herself, which she did with the ferocity and abandon of a tiger. And the bed had been triumphantly erected by the time the visitor came.

After Emerson had established himself in the guest room — neat and trim with its partly panelled walls, its three windows facing westward, and its little fireplace — and had descended to the small parlour, Carlyle opened the floodgates of his talk, pouring out, in the broadest of Scotch accents, an oral Latter-Day Pamphlet. How mean, how despicably mean, were the contemporary politicians and the cow-like multitudes they were leading by the nose to the abyss. What contrasts to these were Cromwell, the Hero, and his Puritans! Carlyle, seated on a footstool by the hearthrug, puffed hugely, indignantly, on his long clay pipe, sending the pungent clouds of his favourite brand (Free-smoking York River mixture) deftly up the chimney, so that the room would not become redolent to the discomfort of Jane, who sat, as usual, with bent head and one hand covering the lower portion of her face, listening patiently to what she had heard so many times before. When Carlyle was aroused, only draughts at his pipe served as punctuation marks to his discourse. There were no pauses except when Jane insinuated some cool remark which had power to scatter her husband's fiery clouds of wrath and cause him to burst out in hearty laughter at his own vehemence. 'I go up and down like an ichneumon, eating crocodiles' eggs,' she said. Crocodiles' eggs, indeed! Emerson, aware of Carlyle's stock expostulation: 'SILENCE is the great thing I worship at present,' must have been not a little amused. Tonight was to be no night of silence. Emerson was amazed at the extraordinary vigour and range of his friend's speech. He perceived that the few hours' talk in Scotland had not given him sufficient knowledge of his man, and he was taken by surprise. Carlyle was no longer the student of German mysticism whom he had met in Dumfrieshire; he had become a thorough realist, but a realist who felt that the greatness of man belonged to the past tense.

Next morning the friends walked to Hyde Park; Carlyle melting all Westminster and London into his talk and laughter. That evening Thomas's brother John, whom Waldo had failed to meet when both were in Italy in 'thirty-three, helped to swell the tide of colloquy. Four long nights of talk, but talk so exciting that the hours fled by unheeded. Once Carlyle broke the chain long enough to scribble an overdue letter to his sister Jean of Dumfries.

Had Emerson been so rude as to peep over the writer's shoulder, the self-contained wanderer from Concord might well have been astonished. 'Dear Sister Jean, — . . . I have been very *busy* for the last week, and today still am ; nay further, *Emerson* the American Friend came upon us last night, and is now *here*, —nothing but talkee, talkee ; — for the rest, a very fine fellow, whom it is pleasant to talk with. He stays "till next week," I dimly apprehend ; then goes to Lancashire &c to *lecture* to all manner of Mechanics' Institutes and the like. He is at this moment rummaging among my Books in this room, beside me ; waiting till I have done writing to you !' Volumes from Carlyle's pen were as familiar as his own to Emerson. But examining them now taught him something further about their author. 'Carlyle and his wife live on beautiful terms. Nothing can be more engaging than their ways, and in her bookcase all his books are inscribed to her, as they come from year to year, each with some significant lines.'

When Carlyle finished his letter, he once more loaded his guns. Out upon literary triflers : they were an abomination to the world ! Actors and actresses were all mad Monkeys. He had once seen Rachel, star of the *Théâtre de la République,* assume an impossible, if dramatic, attitude, and learned that she accomplished it by weighting her dress with lead. Emerson was left in no doubt that to Carlyle's mind the vast majority of living persons loaded their clothes with lead. Verily, the shepherd was assuming a wolf-like aspect to his sheep.

'How can you undervalue such worthy people as I find you surrounded with, — Milnes, and Spedding, and Venables, and Darwin, and Lucas, and so forth ?'

'May the beneficent gods defend me from ever sympathising with the like of them !'

'See what a crowd of friends listen to and admire you.'

'Yes, they come to hear me, and they read what I write, but not one of them has the smallest intention of doing these things.'

In the impending years, the accomplishments of these scorned five were to be by no means despicable. Milnes, Lord Houghton, brought Keats to life in a book notable both for tolerance and perception. Spedding's edition of the works of Lord Bacon became a model for scholarly thoroughness. Charm, and an extraordinary force of character coupled with modesty, should have been sufficient to keep alive for a time the name of George Stovin Venables, an able barrister, even though his very modesty led him to cloak in anonymity his political and critical articles in the leading journals, essays which set the pace of the day for strength of style and keenness of thought on social questions. Samuel Lucas, along with his brother Frederick, was also a journalist of note: the former as editor of the *Morning Star*, the newspaper which was the organ of the Manchester School of radical politicians; the latter as champion of the Roman Catholic Church in Britain. And Erasmus Darwin was at least brother to the genius who, more than any man of the century, cut away the film from man's eyes to give a clearer vision of the Universe.

Cromwell! Cromwell the dictator, with his blood and thunder and destroying cannon, was the man. His methods alone could bring the true purification. Carlyle glowed with enthusiasm as he spoke of him, and described eagerly the marvellous thirty-five newly discovered letters of the great Puritan which he was editing and was about to give to the world.

But the American descendant of Puritans refused to bow

down in worship. He told Carlyle that the latter must not expect people as old as he to change their views and look on Cromwell as Carlyle did.

Precipitously Carlyle rose from his chair. He towered in the small, civilized room like a great Norse giant, dreadful yet admirable in his indignation and his earnestness. With his gnarled, peasant finger he made an imperative gesture across the surface of the table which lay between himself and Emerson, and said, with a terrible fierceness: 'Then, sir, there is a line of separation between you and me as wide as that, and as deep as the pit.'

Emerson left for Manchester. To his journal he confided: 'In Carlyle, a large caprice.'

THE EARNEST YOUNG MEN

No sooner had Emerson returned to the North than he found himself grist for the mill. A few days after his arrival, the *Manchester Times* remarked: 'We understand that the interest excited by the presence of Mr. Emerson in England is causing him to be presented with numerous offers of engagements from various literary societies throughout the country.' His dream of a leisurely stay in Europe speedily turned into a nightmare of hectic activity. The ordeal day after day of reading lectures came to be, in the victim's words, 'sometimes pounds of flesh.' Alexander Ireland had certainly prepared the way; prepared it, if anything, too well. 'Thomas Paine anniversaries; Roscoe Club Soirees; Infant Athenæums that hold bazaars,' Emerson wrote to his brother William, 'all beckon & solicit the attention of the new come lecturer. My Societies are to the full as droll as Pickwick's.' Nor was the demand confined to England. Scotland, even Ireland, called for their quota of edification or entertainment.

Yet amid the bustle and irritation, amid all the touring

from town to town like a strolling player, there was one compensation. Emerson cherished a weakness for young men. Ever since that day when he had sought great teachers to give him the keys to life, his sympathies had gone out to other youthful seekers. Amazingly (so his modesty taught him to think), these young men were now in pursuit of himself. Many an audience before which he lectured in England and Scotland contained, hidden among its insensate members, a leaven of young men, who turned their faces towards him as though he were a Messiah. A number of these were already familiar with his essays. Others, living too far away from the towns where he was scheduled to speak, wrote to him in a tone which made him feel like a father-confessor; like a prophet foretelling the Land of Canaan.

Yet the last-mentioned experience could not have carried in it the shock of complete novelty. Ten years before the second voyage to Britain, Emerson in Concord had first tasted the heady wine of a friendship sought through letters. The correspondent—Emerson had never met him—was a young Englishman. His name was John Sterling. A friend and fellow student of Alfred Tennyson and Arthur Hallam, he was a Cambridge man; an excellent scholar and writer of verse. At the University he had distinguished himself in debate, shining even among that brilliant constellation of young men who practised argument and all manner of spiritual fencing at the Union, for their earnest concern with theology was a major passion. Following the accepted route, he presently entered the ministry of the Church of England. But he soon grew restive in his clerical garb. He was already known to Thomas Carlyle, who saw much in him to admire in spite of his 'Church-of-Englandism' and 'Coleridgian Shovel-hattedness,' and the friendship contributed not a little to

Sterling's decision to doff his robes and ditch his Church career. The very honesty of his religious sentiment compelled the move.

As he watched his friend's spiritual wrestlings, Carlyle's interest became more lively. He showed him a copy of Emerson's book, *Nature*, and told him about that young man's descent on Craigenputtock and his subsequent career. Ill health and petty concerns delayed Sterling's intentions of writing to America, but finally, on 30 September 1839, the step was taken. Emerson replied at once. His eager heart, not infrequently reserved and shy in the presence of those whom he wished most to know, warmed to the novel relationship, and he rejoiced in the friendship of this scholar and poet he had never seen who was also Carlyle's friend.

Sterling read with care everything of Emerson's which came into his hands. Through these books and pamphlets he recognized a free spirit: one which would not mock the aspirations of man with arbitrary dogmas or hesitating negations. The glow and freshness of youthful freedom and hope lay in these writings. Sterling would not have been Sterling had he not perceived in them certain flaws. He was quite aware of Emerson's self-contradictoriness and of his fondness for paradox. He chided him for his defects, but Emerson had spoken to his sense of rightness and beauty, had stimulated his intellect, and had been a tonic to his own independence.

There were kindred loves, furthermore, which guided the two men into sacred groves where Carlyle could or would not follow. Both were aspirants to poetry: both sought to attain the mastery of that splendid dialect which to Carlyle's ears was for the most part a silly tinkling. Both looked towards a new day — towards the East. 'The problems of reform are losing their local and sectarian

character, and becoming generous, profound, and poetic,'
Emerson wrote to Sterling, and Sterling agreed. But Carlyle, with sardonic laughter, was already throwing up his
hands in despair before the walls of that kingdom of the
future, that realm of philanthropic regeneration. The
two, in their friendship, refused however to listen to the
Scotsman's pessimistic rumblings.

The love between them, these companions never seen by
each other, grew with the passing years. Emerson, in
spite of his self-dependence, in spite of his paradoxical 'un-
amiableness,' as he called it — his hesitant shrinking from
men — never lost his yearning for fellowship. The ideal
friendship was his bright star, but the ideal made him long
for the flesh and blood embodiment. He hailed Sterling
with boyish joyousness; with eagerness almost pathetic.
The peculiar circumstances of the bond offered the one
catalytic agent to blend spiritual and actual in a perfect
amalgam. 'I am a worshipper of Friendship,' Emerson
wrote to Sterling, 'and cannot find any other good equal
to it.' And Sterling replied, 'You are the only man in the
world with whom, though unseen, I feel any sort of near-
ness; all my other cordialities having grown up in the usual
way of personal intercourse.'

When Sterling published *Strafford*, a historical drama,
its title page bore this dedication to Emerson:

> 'Teacher of starry wisdom high serene,
>   Receive the gift our common ground supplies;
>   Red flowers, dark leaves, that ne'er on earth had been
>   Without the influence of sidereal skies.'

But the calamity of Sterling's own life was fused with his
writing of the tragedy of Strafford. And the spring of the
year 1844 found him dying of consumption. How strange
it was, he wrote Emerson, to see the thick crimson blood

pouring from one's mouth; to expect death every minute, yet not to die. Emerson was no novice to that desolation and horror. The gaping wounds of his own past — of Ellen's death — opened and bled anew. His friend's plight made him aghast. He hurried off beautiful letters of encouragement and comfort. He thought of taking ship to Europe: to hazard the risk of putting to the test that ethereal web of friendship which had been woven. Yet Sterling seemed to be mending. Emerson, with renewed hope, sent him an inscribed edition of the just published second volume of *Essays*. It came too late.

Four years after Sterling's death, Emerson was again in England. He thought often of John Sterling. In a lecture at Manchester he paid him a public tribute, speaking of the common love of Montaigne which had lent strength to the bonds of a unique friendship.

When letters from other Englishmen whom he had never met began again to reach him, they nevertheless caught him by surprise. These unforeseen epistles, coming from nowhere, like random feathers in the wind, stirred him deeply. In spite of the encroachments of his arduous schedule, he found time to answer. Some that he received were full of interested inquiry concerning the scope of the lecture tour. Would it include such and such a town? Most inaccessible these places sometimes were: unfamiliar names in Ireland or the North of Scotland. Other letters detailed the literary plans and aspirations of their young writers, or requested the favour of a personal interview. These correspondents were from all walks of life. They ranged from struggling artists like William Bell Scott to prosperous merchants like Joseph Neuberg of Nottingham and successful manufacturers like George Crawshay, steel master of the great foundry at Newcastle, who begged to be Emerson's host for the engagement to speak there.   Men from the Universities, journalists exiled in the British provinces, young men in government employment: they also sought to know Emerson.

William Allingham was an Irishman, a native of the little town of Ballyshannon. For a very young man, he had done well enough, according to the standards of worldly success. When he was twenty-two, he had given up his first position, that of bank clerk, to become a member of the British customs service. In the following year, which chanced to be that of Emerson's second coming to England, Allingham was stationed at remote Donegal, on the Northwest coast of Ireland.

His work and the town where it placed him, while they furnished support and lodging for his body, gave scant nourishment to his tastes in literature and to the cravings of his poetic, imaginative spirit. Twice in his life he had spent brief holidays in London, experiences rendered doubly intoxicating through his making the acquaintance of Leigh Hunt, Carlyle's neighbour in Chelsea, and the bohemian company which still blew like an irresponsible whirlwind through the disordered household of the man who had been the intimate of many poets. When he was a boy of nineteen, Allingham had hazarded a note to Leigh Hunt in London, and the man who had known and befriended Keats and Shelley was sufficiently interested in this new communicant to reply. Frequent letters began to pass between them. Hunt advised Allingham on his poetry and helpfully criticized the verses which he sent to him. So it was only natural that when William was in London on vacation, at the age of twenty-three, in the summer of 1847, he should seek out his benefactor.

He found in Leigh Hunt, then in his sixty-third year,

a tallish young old man with friendly brown eyes and plentiful iron-grey hair that fell in somewhat straggled disorder almost to his shoulders. The veteran man of letters, clad in a dark dressing gown, greeted the young poet as though they were old acquaintances who saw each other every day, and Allingham was quickly won by his easy tolerance and light earnestness of manner. When the Irishman, eager for word of the great men of London, inquired concerning some of them, he at once struck an answering spark. Carlyle? Yes, Hunt knew him well. In fact he would see to it that Dickens, Carlyle, and Browning should be made personally acquainted with the new young writer. 'Gracious Powers!!!' Allingham had exclaimed under his breath, overwhelmed by the gleaming prospect, made all the more dazzling by Hunt's remarking, 'I would do so for few.'

As Leigh Hunt had prophesied, so had it come to pass. After a few more vacations in London, Allingham had presently found himself on easy, intimate terms with several prominent Londoners, and, best of all, with the Carlyles.

And even before he attained this goal, be it remarked, he had been in correspondence with the famous Scotsman. He had opened the way through inquiries concerning a suitable course of reading to further his self-education. Carlyle, busy as he was, nevertheless always enjoyed giving advice on books. He was quite ready to aid this young Customs official stranded in a distant port, and sent him long letters filled with valuable suggestions. Allingham should study history and German. With the language, the thing to do, after mastering the grammar, was to launch directly into the mighty seas of Goethe, trying to find some navigable course through the welter, and persevering in the faith that presently the confusion would take on meaning and sense. As for histories, especially about Ireland, some general ones would prove useful but the little that had been written specifically on Ireland was mostly bad. There was need for an honest history of Ireland. Carlyle had the gift of advising with authoritative tones. These hints his young correspondent seized on eagerly and put to practice. He had been taken from school when he was fourteen. Through his entire lifetime he never ceased to regret his lack of college training. Even Carlyle's assurance that there was little to be gained from lectures did not entirely comfort him, though he sought to follow out the great man's injunction that the road to mastery lay through books. Carlyle, Leigh Hunt, and, as time passed, many other writers, became his University, and he never tired of his Alma Mater.

William Allingham resolved that the gates of the world should not close behind him. In his Irish exile he read with avidity such of the newer books as he could lay hands on — new essays, new volumes of poetry, new writings on history and politics. And when, in his diary under date of 9 November 1847, he entered the words: 'Emerson is in Manchester. I wrote to him today,' he was recording what to him must have seemed like the natural consequence of a companionship already well established.

Emerson did not fail him.

Soon after receiving Emerson's reply, Allingham wrote again — this time in the tone one adopts towards a respected counselor and sympathetic friend. He praised the American's poems, and spoke of his own ambitions in verse: how he was now at work on something which he trusted would assume the character of a modern Irish idyl — as, indeed, it did, in *Laurence Bloomfield*, published in 1864, seventeen years later. And when he sent one of his short poems for Emerson's criticism, the critic not only spoke favourably of it but also showed it to some other young men who had sought him out: Clough and Coventry Patmore, and Henry Sutton of Nottingham. He detailed his struggles with religion: his disgust with Romanism and his contempt for Protestantism, reactions evoked through his conviction that these creeds were merely 'isms,' not sincere faiths.

Confidences like these present tremendous difficulties to the oracle to whom they are addressed. Emerson knew that well enough: had not Carlyle failed him — as a prophet, of course, not in friendship — at Craigenputtock? Still, he had to accept his responsibility, and he took pains to do so. 'The more lonely and barricaded round with walls of Fate you find yourself,' he wrote to Allingham, 'the better omen for the future days.' Did not his correspondent draw the breath of youth? Emerson believed in that magic. 'I confide that we shall meet *if that be best*, as the old saints believed,' he replied in response to Allingham's lament that circumstances forbade attendance at the London lectures, 'I am preparing to leave England . . . and in today's distractions can only acknowledge your kindness by these hurried lines.' And he signed himself, 'In constant hope and regard, R. W. Emerson.'

To Arthur Hugh Clough, Oxford scholar, Fellow of Oriel College, erstwhile star pupil of Dr. Arnold of Rugby, was given the opportunity for a closer view. Clough was in his thirtieth year — a critical one — when he met Emerson. Like Allingham, he was familiar with Emerson's writings before their creator's second visit to England. The cadence of Emerson's phrases had echoed through the University common rooms, and in the hearts of certain young men there, like delphic music. In those days, the early 'forties, Oxford was in the mood for hearing voices, and Emerson, with Goethe, Newman, and Carlyle, was a compelling oracle. Matthew Arnold, whose poetry was just beginning, heard, and James Anthony Froude, and others. There were evenings of enchantment at the house of Dr. Henry Acland, who held the chair of anatomy at the University, but shared the keenness of many great medical men for things of the mind and spirit — evenings when Francis Palgrave read aloud some passage from Emerson, or recited poetry from the rich store that his sensitive critical taste was already laying by for the future *Golden Treasury*.

When Clough learned from his sister at Liverpool that the American writer was there, he wrote him a cordial invitation to come to Oxford. 'Your name is not a thing unknown to us. I do not say it would be a passport in a society fenced about by Church-Articles. But amongst the juniors there are many that have read and studied your books, and not a few that have largely learnt from them and would gladly welcome their author.' Emerson replied that there were few places in England so attractive to him. He arrived the last of March, when his lectures in the North of England were over, and spent three days.

In spite of Clough's warning, the visitor found no cause to regret his temerity in invading the stronghold of the creed. Everybody liked him, and as the orthodox mostly had never heard of him, they did not suspect him. Clough was completely won by his guest's unobtrusiveness. He was the quietest, most modest person! He talked with, not at you, and wholly declined to roar in the manner of great men. True, he was very Yankee to look at: lean and tall, and not quite without the New England twang, yet his voice possessed an ingratiating music and gave the impression of perfect intellectual cultivation. Clough found himself comparing his visitor with the foremost men of science of the time — with Faraday and Owen — and Emerson did not shrink in the comparison. Not even Wordsworth nor Carlyle could measure up so readily beside these scientists — certainly Carlyle had no such poised equanimity and sureness with which to help himself and others to receive the disconcerting impacts of life.

Froude, too, when Emerson departed, came presently to acknowledge that he had had an experience which left its permanent impression on his life. 'Your . . . visit here, short as it was, was not without its service to us; you left luminous traces of your presence in the words you scattered from you, which as yet at least the birds of the air have not devoured. One sentence spoken is worth a hundred written. . . In a few years I hope even here in Oxford you will see whole acres yellow with the corn of your sowing.'

When Emerson took a short vacation in Paris, before his London lectures, Clough was with him. And when he stood on the deck of the ship, ready to sail home to America, Clough was by his side to bid him good-bye. The young Oxford scholar dreaded to break the strong, unseen tendrils of sympathy and understanding which drew him to Emerson. Liberal in his attitude towards life, subtle and profound in thought, gifted with a searching, questioning intellect, Clough, in 1848, was the victim of his own unwillingness to accept anything which might conceivably turn from truth to formula. He fixed you with a glance that cut like steel through all defences, his eyes almost terrifying in their keen expression of investigation. Yet there was a sensitivity about him, a delicacy and tenderness, which sheathed the barb of his glance. Emerson loved Clough. He wanted to help him. As the two friends paced the deck of the vessel which was to bear them apart, Clough turned suddenly, almost beseechingly, to his companion.

'What shall we do without you? Think where we are. Carlyle has led us all out into the desert, and he has left us there.'

Emerson gazed at his burly, well-knit, robust young friend, who stood nevertheless so helplessly before him. Half whimsically, half seriously, his heart stirred to its very depths, he placed his hand on Clough's head.

'Clough,' he said, 'I consecrate you Bishop of all England. It shall be your part to go up and down through the desert to find out these wanderers and to lead them into the promised land.'

Soon Emerson's ship was steaming down the Mersey from Liverpool, to lose itself to the eye of the beholder in the huge welter of the Atlantic.

Many young men had spoken thus to Emerson of Carlyle as the American traversed the length and breadth of England. Carlyle! Carlyle seemed to feel it his function to mourn, denounce, and tear to pieces, most content apparently when he could make others as dissatisfied as himself. Emerson recognized that the Scotsman's guiding genius was his perception of the ultimate sole importance of truth and justice. Yet how could these young men discern that principle, obscured as it was by the acrid smoke and flame of criticism and contempt with which he was choking and searing the world where, perforce, they had to make their living? His style of writing alone was ruination to many of them.

Emerson did not hesitate to warn young Francis Espinasse of the danger. He would have warned anyone against imitating his own manner or of the peril of an unquestioning acceptance of his own ideas, so firmly did he believe in the integrity of every individual mind. Yet whether he bade them beware either of others or of himself, nothing he could do could prevent these earnest young men from seeking to fill their cups at his well.

Carlyle had assumed the rôle of Emerson's John the Baptist to them, and was still crying in the wilderness. And the American pointed with confidence to the future from which the Scotsman had turned fretfully away. In his writings, and under the spell of his personal serenity and self-conquest, they thought that they perceived the cloudy symbols of a dawning era. They came to believe that a new order of man was arising. Sorely they felt the need of utopia. They were experiencing the effects of a financial depression not of their own making. They lived in an atmosphere of political and religious stuffiness which they had not the means effectively to ventilate. The expanse of Europe, dark under storm clouds, heaved like a restless sea before their eyes. The crushing force of industrialism, with its dirt, squalor, and excesses of poverty and riches, bore down their spirits from the high places naturally assumed by youth. Then they read and heard Emerson, and his words aroused ideas and emotions so compelling as to hinder them from sleep. They were profoundly moved by the beauty and the power of his words and of his modes of expression. He seemed in some marvellous way to clarify their own inmost thoughts and feelings. He assured them of the greatness of the human soul, teaching that around each individual spirit moved all external nature — science, history, religion, and the creative wisdom of man. He gave them the strength to believe in themselves. Worshipfully they followed him, repeating his phrases as though they were revelations sent from the skies. He had shown them the door to life; he had armed them, they sensed, with a philosophy which would conquer the world. And conservative British magazines, like *The*

English Review, began to speak reprovingly and fearfully of an Emerson cult.

These journals need not have so concerned themselves. Emerson had not given anything so specific to the young men as they themselves supposed. He had not presented them with the one true formula; with the philosopher's stone that could turn a world of lead to gold. They did not know it, but there was nothing so solid which they could draw from his soaring thoughts. What he had given them was an attitude towards life — a hopefulness and a trust in themselves which served many of them to the end of their days. Those who preserved this perishable essence were for the most part men not greatly given to analysis or self-questioning. But the majority of these earnest young Englishmen of 1847-1848 were too intellectual, too well educated and inquiring, perhaps, for their own happiness. As they grew older, they were shouted down from the heights by their prudent Anglo-Saxon temperaments. They analysed the crystal talisman that had held them aloft, and lo, it evaporated under their steady gaze. They felt like men coming out of ether: dazed at first, then — some of them — even slightly angry. Most no longer needed Emerson, for time had brought them their pittance of success.

CHAPTER III

INVARIABLY it is the lot of the visiting man of letters to be wined and dined, provided that Fame's unpredictable fingers have placed on his brow a crown of laurel large enough to be visible to the unlettered multitude. Although he followed with quiet persistence his usual course of self-effacement, Emerson became the recipient of much hospitality of the gastronomic sort. He breakfasted with old Samuel Rogers in select company, and Henry Crabb Robinson, most fastidious of hosts among the diners-in of London, entertained him at table. In the metropolis and in the Provinces, he had to learn to fill a chair as principal guest. And he was often invited to dinners for other men. On one notable occasion he saw John Bright and the M. P.'s of the Manchester Liberal group fêted by their constituency at a great banquet to celebrate the triumph of Corn Law repeal. These were of the average run of revels. But two festivals in particular stand out from the common sort: one a nineteenth-century Belshazzar's feast; the other, a banquet of the Half-Gods.

On 18 November 1847, Emerson found himself utilized by the Manchester Athenæum as one of the show pieces at its Grand Soirée — elephantine celebration staged for the glory of the society, the diversion of its members, and, most important of all, for the replenishment of its coffers.

The movement which brought into being Mechanics' Institutions and kindred organizations in England and Scotland began in 1823, initiated largely through the efforts of manufacturers and philanthropists. The manufacturers believed that some education for the working man, particu-

larly in the field of science, would render him more worthy
of his hire, and they also shared to some extent the view
of the humanitarians that learning for old as well as young
was the most powerful lever with which to elevate mankind to a higher plane of existence and a greater degree of
happiness. By the middle of the century, the spawn thus
cast over Britain had mushroomed into a tremendous
growth of about four hundred local organizations with an
aggregate membership of a hundred thousand persons, and
hardly a town worthy to be so named failed to have its
Philosophical and Scientific Institution, its Athenæum, or its
Mechanics' Institute — the names were almost inter-
changeable.

Such rapid growth might seem to indicate a flourishing
condition, but alas for the hopes of the founders, this did
not necessarily follow. The organizations had not been
the product of spontaneous enthusiasm among the working
classes; instead, they had been brought into being largely
through the efforts of the wealthy. When they were
turned over to the mechanics — who were often apathetic
to the cause, if not actually hostile to it — the institutions
suffered in consequence. Membership itself became hybrid
— clerks, shopkeepers, professional men, merchants, and
schoolboys gradually supplanting the factory hands.
Sometimes this tendency worked benefits — placing in
charge a group of intelligent and interested men with vision
to direct the enterprise. More often, the change led to a
confusion of cross-purposes and to financial dissolution.
To remedy such an unfortunate state of affairs, and to revive
attention, the directors of an individual institution often
had recourse to the expedient of changing the original
policy of the movement. They would adopt the practice
of giving popular lectures rather than educational ones,
and in addition would furnish such diversion for the mem-

bers as concerts, theatrical entertainments, and dances. Most lucrative invention of all till its repetition made it tiresome and unproductive was the annual soirée, a great splurge of oratory and dancing, of food and bromidic wisdom which brought paying guests in large flocks to the grand banquet halls.

Previous to 1847, the Manchester Athenæum had held four monster annual celebrations, that of 1845 having attracted a crowd of 3800 persons, with Thomas Noon Talford, versatile jurist and author, and the friend of Charles Lamb, acting as master of ceremonies. Charles Dickens, Benjamin Disraeli, and Viscount Morpeth had distinguished themselves as chairmen on the other occasions. But the year 1847 presented a more sour face to the hard-pressed directors than they had previously encountered. England, particularly the North of England, was in the stormy seas of commercial depression and panic, and the temper of the people was such that the wisdom of even attempting a soirée to bolster the finances of the Athenæum was open to grave question. But the British are a hardy race, notoriously so. After some heated debate among its Directors, the Athenæum announced, with fanfare of the trumpets of journalism, that the great soirée of 1847 would veritably be. Since financial success was dependent largely on attracting crowds through the elaborateness of the affair, every effort was bent to the task of puffing up the occasion to an appearance of splendour and display.

From day to day, as the time for the momentous occasion drew near, the *Manchester Guardian, The Times, The Examiner* — all the choir of papers, indeed — swelled the rising chorus of acclaim. The public was subjected to a mass attack of advertisement and ballyhoo — dignified but insistent. Names of distinguished guests, as these sent in their acceptances to attend (not, of course, as paying diners, but to shine at the Speakers' Table as bait to attract payers!), began to be announced in the press, with crescendo effect, fully a month before the event. *The Guardian*, in a manner suggesting a hushed, excited whisper, breathed the hint that Mr. Ralph Waldo Emerson, among other notables, would be present. And *The Examiner* hazarded the opinion that the names of Dickens, Cobden, and Emerson would alone be 'a sufficient guarantee for the attractiveness of the entertainment.' Emerson's great success as a lecturer at the Athenæum, remarked another journal, would render him a guest welcome to the members, and added, hopefully, that his presence would be sure to attract many Americans to the soirée for the purpose of doing honour to their fellow-countryman. Presently the *Athenæum Gazette*, official organ of the Society, gave out a completed list of the distinguished guests, prefacing it with the statement that 'in no instance has the name been announced of any gentleman who has not promised to be present' — a precautionary remark indicative that in the past less honest directorates had sometimes permitted their zeal for glamour somewhat to outrun their veracity.

A concern of major importance, of course, was the choice of a suitable ringmaster. In this year, the difficulty of making a selection was increased by an approaching general election, for it was a wise rule of the institution that its affairs be kept free of all suspicion of partisanship. Surely a scholar could best be trusted not to break the thin ice of neutrality! The Directors proclaimed, with justifiable pride, that the toastmaster's chair would be filled by no less a person than 'Archibald Alison, Esq., F.R.S.E., the elegant historian of Europe during the French Revolution,' who could be relied on 'most eloquently to sustain the fame which the Soirées had now attained.'

The huge Free Trade Hall, capable of holding eight

thousand persons, was to house the expected multitude.
Price of admission was set at five shillings a couple, and
gentlemen could bring extra ladies at three shillings each.
Only members of the Athenæum and their invited guests
might attend, the management warned, because so many
applications were pouring in that it seemed obligatory to
keep down the crowd. But the *Manchester Guardian*,
grown suddenly cautious, and with that puncturing effect
on inflated enthusiasm peculiar to the press, remarked that
in the present day of commercial gloom overcrowding was
scarcely to be apprehended, and pointed out, with what
might have been a slight touch of malice, that the price of
tickets had come down one shilling from former years.

What, the affair was not to be as resplendent as ever?
No such calamity should come to pass, provided that the
committees in charge of refreshments and music knew anything about their duties! *They* had manfully toiled to
arrange a tempting programme. For dancing, the Double
Quadrille Band was to blare forth its mightiest. To titillate
the palates of gourmets there were such dainties as jellies
and ice-creams (raspberry, and orange, and lemon!),
seed and plum cakes, figs and almonds. For more hearty
feeders, mountains of roast rounds of beef had been commanded, to be supported by boiled hams, tongue, turkey,
fowl, and veal pies. An American touch was added to the
bill of fare by the inclusion of New York soda biscuits,
hardy pioneers among a more effete, aristocratic gathering
of cheese cakes, buns, and a great variety of light confec-
tionery. As Manchester was a centre of the temperance
movement, objections had been raised to the sale of wines
and spirits; so the Directors compromised somewhat by
deciding against the more vigorous intoxicants. But wines
escaped the ban and were lavishly supplied — champagne
and claret, hock, sherry, and port. And to refresh the

dancers during intermissions, large punch bowls of port and sherry negus flowed like Ponce de Léon's fountain. Teetotallers were given every opportunity to console themselves with ginger beer and soda ; and, to provide hot water for the tea and coffee, the ingenious caterer had caused to be hauled to the banquet a locomotive boiler, capable of holding over two hundred gallons of steaming fluid at a time.

So much for the gastronomic aspects of the affair. To regale the eyes and ears of the feasters, the Directors had rounded up an imposing array of honorary guests at the High Table. There were Richard Cobden, Viscount Brackley, John Bright, and John Bowring : all distinguished members of Parliament. From London came George Cruikshank, the popular comic illustrator, who assuredly could have found there ample material for his skilled pen, and William Harrison Ainsworth, the novelist. Beside them sat Robert Blackwood, well-known among publishers. The Dean of Manchester lent the dignity of the cloth to the festival. The author of *Pickwick Papers*, alas, could not appear, to the partial disappointment no doubt of the gentleman who was reported to have travelled from beyond Edinburgh expressly to see and hear him, Cobden, and Emerson. Yet the stranger had enough to engross his attention. The platform of honour held seating accommodations for two hundred and eighty persons, and in the front row of the speakers' table, in full view of the crowd, were forty-two chairs reserved for the great men of the day. As they filed to their places, they were greeted by hearty applause. When Richard Cobden, famous native son, came into the hall, wild cheering broke out from the assemblage. The banquet was officially opened by the appearance of Archibald Alison, who entered to assume the chair, with dignified precision, at exactly quarter past seven.

After the feast, the flow of wit and reason. One sympathizes with the speakers — Cobden, Emerson, Dr. Bowring, George Cruikshank, and the chairman — in the gigantic task they faced as they rose to ignite some answering spark in the sated diners who lolled, like bundles of wet faggots, before them. Archibald Alison took the safe course. He began with reminiscences of his early Shropshire home, touching, by way of grace notes, on the innocence of childhood and the beauties of the English countryside. Warming to his work, he praised the gods of gold, of silver, of brass, of iron, of wood, of stone, and of cotton, and paid his compliments to the great city of Manchester which upheld the spirit of culture in the midst of industry. Then he proceeded to a review of the history of commerce, discovery, and learning from the earliest times to the present, throwing formal wreaths, in the way of quotations from Lord Bacon, Dr. Johnson, and Gibbon, among the flowers of his own rhetoric. Contented with his efforts, and at ease in the pleasant feeling that his task was done, he gave way for the next speaker.

Some moments elapsed before Cobden, as favourite hero of Corn Law repeal, could make himself heard above the din of applause. Next came Emerson, then Dr. Bowring, and after him, George Cruikshank, who told of an orator, speaking after Burke at an election meeting, who remarked merely: 'To what Mr. Burke has said, I say ditto.' Yet Cruikshank, bitter yet sentimental caricaturist of mankind, was a man of infinite resource. Mentioning his recent group of eight pictures on the results of drink, he told the women of his audience that if his craft had produced anything worthy of consideration, it was because of his desire to save them from brutality and intemperance.

When Emerson faced his hearers, it was to him as though the garishly lighted hall, the smell of cooking, the triviality of entertainment that pandered chiefly to the eye, to pride, and to the stomach, with but a passing gesture of recognition for the mind, had suddenly vanished away. Instead, he saw England, the age-old fortress of his race, a people which had faced the vagaries of history with courage, fortitude, and humour. Here were the hills of England; her primrose valleys and her streams. Here were her citizenry and the spirit which could and would endure. When he began to speak — at first haltingly and in a low tone, then with increasing strength and earnestness — there was a quality in his voice which caused some who knew him there to look up in wonder. Not till the days of Emerson's antislavery speeches immediately preceding the American civil war was a feeling similar to the emotion released by the stimulus of this England again to take command of the quiet scholar. Possibly he was in error to let his mind be swayed by the stir in his heart. Today his words, spoken in a manner so remote from his usual vein, have in them, perhaps, the quality of race-worshiping fanaticism. But in that day and hour, addressed as they were to inhabitants of a town in a state of mind bordering on demoralization — for when has Manchester not felt most keenly the pinch of bad times? — Emerson's words extolling the greatness of the English race, even in adversity, gave encouragement and life.

Has the speech, with the passing of a century, lost all savour? Or does recurrent human experience permit those existing in this present to understand the specific emotions of a day long since forgotten? If the life has gone out of them, one has but to stop one's ears to the echoes of these old phrases. The *Manchester Guardian* reported Emerson's words, the morning after they were spoken, as follows:

'Mr. Chairman and Gentlemen, — I feel myself a little

in the position of some countrymen of mine whom I remember, when a deputation of Sauks and Foxes came to
the capital of Massachusetts and were received there at the
Senate House by Governor Everett. Impressed a little
by the greatness of the population about them, and certainly with the new splendour and wealth of such cities
as they had passed through and entered, the red men said,
after hearing the congratulations of the governor, "We
have no land to put our words on, sir, and yet our words
are true." I have no land here to put my words on, and
yet I hope they are true. It gives me great pleasure to see
this anniversary of the Athenæum; it gives me great pleasure to sit near the distinguished gentlemen who have addressed you; and yet it has seemed to me whilst they spoke,
that for many years I have never not been near to them. —
(Hear).' Emerson turned towards Cobden, and continued : 'Sir, the argument of the league, and its leaders,
are known and respected in every quarter of the globe, and
certainly by all the friends of free-trade in America. And,
sir,' said Emerson, bowing to the chairman, 'when I came
to sea, in the ship which brought me here, on the table in
the cabin lay your History of Europe; the property, I
suppose, of the ship, or the captain, as a sort of programme
or play-bill to instruct the seafaring New Englander, who
was coming to Europe, in the events and institutions which
awaited him here. I have seen other gentlemen here this
evening whose gaiety and genius is certainly almost as
familiarly known to my own friends and countrymen as it
is here. Why, sir,' and Emerson nodded to Cruikshank,
'the drawings, caricatures, and the wit of *Punch*, go duly
every fortnight to every bookshop and to every book club,
and to every boy and girl in Boston, New York and Philadelphia. So I find it with all the names with which your
institution and your present meeting presents me. But,

sir, these compliments, though true, would come better from those who better understood and felt these matters than I can hope to do ; and I pass from that to what I know will interest those gentlemen very much more than their own praises, — namely, that which really draws me to the shores of England — that which is good on holidays and working days — that which is good in one country and in another country — that which draws the solitary American to wish to see England, sir, is the moral peculiarity of the Saxon race. It is that commanding sense of right and wrong ; it is that honesty of performance ; it is that which is the imperial trait which has given to this race the sceptre of the globe. I see it equally as the foundation of the aristocratic character of the people, which though it may perhaps sometimes lose sight of its origin, and wander into strange vagaries, if it lose that moral quality, will be paralysed, and cease to be ; and I see it no less in the honesty of performance in trade and manufactures, in that solidity and thoroughness of work which is the national badge. This conscience is one element ; and the other, sir, is that habit of friendship, if I may so call it, that fidelity of friendship, which I see here running through all classes, that elects all worthy individuals to a fraternity of kind offices, filling them with a warm, staunch fellowship and support from year to year, from youth to age ; and which stands in very strong contrast with the short-lived connexion, with the excess of courtesy, and the very superficial attachments which exist in other races, — an affection, an attachment, a permanence of regard, which is alike lovely and honourable to those who render and those who receive it. (Applause.) Mr. Chairman, in looking at these traits in the English character, it has given me great pleasure to observe that in this time of commercial disaster, in this time of gloom, of bankruptcy, of affliction, and of beggary in the neighbouring districts, the Athenæum has chosen to hold, with its usual spirit, this its anniversary. It seemed to me, because of these peculiarities which belong to the English character, a certain duty well becoming the managers of the institution; they seemed to me to say, "For all that has come and gone, yet we shall not abate the spirit or the splendour of our annual feast; no, not by an oak leaf; no, not by a chaplet." And I wish, sir, to say, that I was brought up from my childhood in the belief that this British island from which my forefathers came was not a lotus garden, was not a paradise of serene skies and roses, a masque and merriment all the year round; no! but a cold, foggy, mournful country, bearing no fruit well in the open air, but robust men and virtuous women, and these, too, of a certain wonderful fibre and endurance — a certain people whose very good qualities were not very swift to shew themselves, — whose virtues, as I was told, never came out until they quarrelled. (Laughter and applause.) I was told, to use a country phrase of ours, that they did not strike twelve the first time — (laughter); good lovers they were, and good haters they were; that you could not know much of them till you had seen them long, and could not know anything good of them till you had seen them in action; in their prosperity, it was said, they were apt to be a little moody, a little nervous and dumpish, but that in adversity they were grand. — (Laughter.) And I ask you, sir, if the wise ancient did not hold in less esteem that bark which was parting from its native port with all colours flying, than that ship which was a proved sailer, which was coming back with battered sides, and torn canvas, and stripped of all her banners, yet having ridden out the storm? And so, sir, I felt towards this aged England. When I see her now, that the possessions, the trophies, the honours, and also the infirmities of a thousand years are gathered

around her, connected irretrievably as she is to so many
ancient customs not suddenly to be changed; oppressed as
she is by the transitions of trade, by the new and all-incal-
culable modes, and fabrics, and arts, and machines and
competing populations; yet with all this pressing upon her,
that she is not dispirited, not weak, but strong, very well
remembering that she has seen many dark days before,
knowing with a kind of instinct, that she can see, with her
old eyes, a little better in a cloudy day; and in the battle,
in the storm, and in calamity, feeling a stout vigour and a
pulse like a cannon. — (Applause.)   When I see this, sir,
— when I see that in her old age she is not decrepit, but
is still daring to believe in her power of endurance, of expansion, then I say, "Hail, mother of nations, mother of
heroes, all hail; still equal to the time, with a strength still
equal to the hour, with a spirit wise to entertain and swift
to execute, a policy that the heart and mind of mankind
at this moment requires, and thereby hospitable to the for-
eigner, and a true home to her own generous and thoughtful children."   So be it, sir; long, long be it so from age to
age!   If it is not so, sir, if her courage is to go down with
the momentary calamities of her commerce and her trade,
I will go back to the capes of Massachusetts and to my
little Indian stream, and say to my countrymen, "the old
race is all gone, and if the hope and elasticity of mankind
exist, they must be found on the ranges of the Alleghanies,
or nowhere." — (Loud applause.)'

Not till almost ten o'clock were the speeches over.
James Crossley, president of the Athenæum, made a brief
address of thanks to the orators, then commanded the
tables to be removed, and the guests, mindful, some of them,
perhaps, of Emerson's words of optimism, forgot the burden of their affairs, and danced to the tunes of the double
quadrille band.   As for the Directors, when they emerged

from consultation over their accounts, they announced with gratification that the fifth annual soirée, after all expenses had been defrayed, had netted a profit of £53. 10s. 5d. The lions had paid their keep.

THE BANQUET OF THE HALF-GODS

The second banquet was entirely of Emerson's devising. There is no record which reveals the quantity or quality of the food provided. But there do survive certain testimonials, some of them cynical in tone and realistic, some of them sentimental, some amazingly bizarre, which bear witness to that extraordinary feast of the Half-Gods.

It was held in Emerson's temporary home in England, his Manchester headquarters, for he had taken lodgings in the house of a Mrs. Massey, at No. 2 Fenny Street, Higher Broughton. The district where he had essayed domesticity is not in Manchester itself; indeed, from the heart of the city, a half hour's walk is necessary to reach the place. At the time when Emerson lived there for a brief space, Fenny Street was in a pleasant though unpretentious residental district of modest houses, each fronted by its little garden. With the deterioration so often characteristic of such regions, it was already entering into decline, and here and there lodging houses were insinuating themselves. But certainly one of the most pleasant of these was that in which Emerson had settled himself. This was a two-story dwelling, situated on a corner and set well back from the street. His quarters consisted of a pleasant bedroom and parlour, with large windows open to the sun and moon, bright and airy because the land below fell away unobstructed towards the River Irwell. Beyond the loops of the stream and the undulation of long-backed hills rising from the margins of the slow current stretched the far expanse of the Lancashire countryside.

Into the house thus situated, Emerson, on the twenty-ninth of January 1848, welcomed a peculiar assortment of guests for his leave-taking.   He was about to desert Manchester for a time, and the cities which lay near it, for Scotland.   His retiring disposition usually caused him to shun the more formal amenities of society.   Yet his keen, sympathetic interest in human beings urged him, especially when he was travelling, to risk the hazards of more stereotyped sociability.   Because he loved men, he rejoiced most in those rare occasions when he could face, not their formal masks, but the men themselves.   In his jaunts from town to town he had encountered a scattering of persons, chiefly young men or men young in spirit, whom he wished better to know.   A few had sought to keep themselves aloof from his thought, like his stiff-necked young friend of Concord, Massachusetts — Henry David Thoreau — and he loved them the better for it.   Many of them had entertained him, and some — he marvelled — had hung on his every word as though he were a prophet.   Such a one was Joseph Neuberg, well-to-do merchant of Nottingham, a German with the inherent gift of hospitality, who had welcomed the lecturer with the utmost cordiality and kindliness in his pleasant house overlooking the silver Trent and its green meadows.   There Emerson had met Henry Sutton, a shy young poet, and Philip James Bailey, author of the much discussed *Festus*.   In return, the American was able, later in the year, to introduce his Nottingham host to Carlyle, a person whom Neuberg had long admired from afar, not daring to thrust himself on his hero without what he deemed a sufficient excuse.   Yet in effecting this meeting, Emerson perhaps rendered to Carlyle the greater favour, since Neuberg presently made himself indispensable to the harassed historian of *Frederick the Great*, never flinching before the mustiest tasks of research to which

Carlyle set him, and, in Germany, performing the mightier feat of keeping Carlyle contented, in spite of his lamentations over the vexations of travel, on a tour of Frederick's battlefields.

Another such was W. B. Hodgson, a doctor of law, but for the time being principal of a Manchester Boarding-School. He was a close friend of Alexander Ireland, and an admirer of Emerson's *Essays* from their earliest appearance. A great classical scholar, and a man full of anecdotes and jokes. There was something almost whimsical in his appearance. Clad in complete black, and bushy with a quantity of whiskers and dark hair, he was always skipping and grinning about Emerson during the period of the lectures at Manchester.

These, and many more, came to Fenny Street on Emerson's invitation, to bid him farewell. One was so poor that to be present he had travelled all the way from Huddersfield to Manchester on foot across the moors of Yorkshire, a distance of more than twenty-five miles, then returned the same way. This pedestrian was George Searle Phillips, a man of erratic genius, a cynic, but one who had searched the heavens and still held the glittering light of star-dust in his eyes. Along with Francis Espinasse and Alexander Ireland, he has left behind a full account of what transpired that evening at Emerson's lodgings. Each speaks for himself, bringing to life, each in his own way and through the lens of his peculiar ego, the actuality of the past as he saw it — Ireland, the kindly sentimentalist; Espinasse, the icy young realist; George Searle Phillips, the idealist turned cynic. To Ireland, the guests appeared principally as young enthusiasts — ardent, hopeful, eager moral and religious reformers and independent thinkers. Espinasse felt them to be a strange collection of mystics, poets, prose-rhapsodists, editors, schoolmasters, ex-Uni-

tarian ministers, and cultivated manufacturers — the only
bond of union among them being their common regard for
Emerson.   Phillips, when he knocked at the door of Emerson's house and entered the hall crowded with hats, coats,
sticks, and pedantical umbrellas (it rained that night),
found himself of the opinion that a more motley, dissimilar,
ill-assorted mass of humanity had never before, perhaps,
met together at the table of a philosopher.   Here were all
kinds of odd and unrelated people : playwrights, and mu-
sicians, and artists; Christians; infidels; pantheists; and
mere book-worms.   They all talked their small talk and
literary gossip — Phillips observed, deciding that few had
any real relationship to Emerson — and left Emerson to
draw round him the small number there present who really
loved and reverenced him.

Phillips has cloaked his account in anonymity, writing
under the pen name of 'January Searle.'   But among the
many volumes of Alexander Ireland's library is a slim,
battered one which contains January Searle's description of
the dinner.   On the flyleaf Ireland has written, 'I paid
5/ for this, it being quite out of print and unobtainable.'
Opposite the characterization of each of the main figures
that gathered round the table, the owner of this copy has
written a name, revealing as actual human creatures these
strange beings who might otherwise seem to be mere figures
in a dream.

To Phillips should go the privilege of carrying the burden of the story, with such modifications from Espinasse
and Ireland as are needed.   Let him take off his rain-soaked
coat and enter the lamp-lit room.

When the host perceived Phillips, he rose with a warm
smile to welcome him, rendered all the more cordial because he had hardly expected his young guest, though
invited, to make the long journey.   He was most happy,

he said, to see so many people round him who had interested themselves so kindly and in such various ways in
his mission to England. 'There are some men here,' he
remarked, 'to whom I should like more particularly to introduce you, as persons of mark and genius.' With that,
'a tall, thin, ungainly man, about thirty years of age, speaking in squeaks at the top of his voice, making all kinds
of grimaces and strange gesticulations, with a small Puritan head, which was more than half *forehead*, approached
to our side of the room, desirous, as he said, of pointing
out a fine passage in Plato, to Emerson, which he had just
been reading.' This was Thomas Hornblower Gill, poet
and writer of hymns, an ardent admirer and follower of
Emerson, who had, indeed, arrived in Manchester from
Birmingham the previous night for an evening with him
undisturbed by later-coming guests. But to return to
Phillips and his description of the expounder of Plato :
'Without more ado he put the volume within half-an-inch
of his eyes, and read the passage. After which he com-
menced a long dissertation upon it — twisting his body into
all conceivable and inconceivable forms, rolling up the
whites of his eyes, and moving his head from shoulder to
shoulder with extraordinary activity. Learned and eloquent, he poured forth a stream of talk — not presumptuously, but with a diffident confidence . . . whilst Emerson sat
silent and listening, with that calm pale face of his, the eye
thoughtful but not excited, and the mouth occasionally
lighted up with a faint moonlight smile. He was evidently
pleased, and so were all who listened to that wonderful six
feet of brain and nerves. Nor was much exception taken
to what he said. An occasional objection made the speaker
stop — roll up his small, twinkling, swinish eyes ; turn his
head, which seemed to be hung on a swivel, — and then,
with rapid recognition, and rapid speech, start off again

in eager, genuine earnestness, and overwhelming energy of lungs, throat, and tongue. After this display, and when the speaker had grown calm, and sat reposing at the bottom of his now empty and exploded volcano, Emerson rose and presented us to him in form, and never was there such an extraordinary scene. He shot bolt-upright from his chair, and stood for a moment long and lank before us; and then his body fell — not in a curve but at right angles, dividing itself, as if on inscrutable hinges, midway down the spinal marrow, and his face came in contact with his outstretched hands. In a moment he recovered his perpendicular, and wheeling round on the pivot of his right heel, and bowing at *us* with his nether parts and at the *opposite window* with his head, he returned to the place from whence he came.' Emerson smiled, and the guests who had witnessed the amazing eruption of this queer, fantastic, eloquent man, whose body seemed made of Birmingham stubtwist, repressed the gales of laughter which threatened to burst from their constricted throats.

'That man,' said Emerson, 'is a fine scholar, has a fine mind, and much real culture. He is well read in literature, in philosophy, in history; and has written rhymes, which, like my friend Ellery Channing's, are very nearly poetry.'

This led to talk of Emerson's friends at home.

'I will give you,' he said, 'a copy of Channing's Poems. Thoreau,' he added, 'you will hear of by and by. He is now writing a book, most of which I have heard, called "*A Week on the Concord and Merrimack Rivers*."'

Presently Henry Sutton joined the cluster surrounding the giver of the feast. Since the days of Nottingham he was already well known to the host. The title page of his recently published book, *The Evangel of Love*, bore the inscription, from Emerson: 'That which befits us, embosomed in beauty and wonder as we are, is cheerfulness and courage, and the endeavour to realize our aspirations.' Emerson had praised his work, and was most hopeful of Sutton's future career. It is a little characteristic of the difference between the Sage of Concord and the Sage of Chelsea, remarked Espinasse, tempted to the comparison, that Carlyle's only comment on this and another mystical book by the same writer, was a contemptuous expression of wonder that a lad in a provincial town should have presumed to handle such themes as he dealt with. In anticipation of the coming of his guest, who was a vegetarian, Emerson had ordered prepared for him a special dinner in conformity with his beliefs. Through the eyes of Phillips, Sutton appeared 'a thin, timorous, young man; not more than twenty years old — with strange, mystic eyes, and a head and face like George Herbert's. A very singular young man, loving God and man too much to be a priest, and yet not quite happy out of the pale of the church. A devout follower of Emerson, at this time; and tinged with his thought. A genuine spiritualist; not in name merely, but in life and endeavour. He lived on roots and water — that nature and God's thought and inspiration might flow through him without impediment. A beautiful gentle-natured young man — a poet also, as well as a preacher and an apostle. He sat at the right hand of Emerson, . . . and was the St. John of the company.'

In one talkative group Phillips observed four Scotsmen — a Doctor of Laws, an ex-Unitarian minister, the editor of a celebrated Manchester paper, and the proprietor of that journal. The Doctor of Laws was W. B. Hodgson. The ex-Unitarian minister Phillips found 'brilliant as a Vauxhall exhibition — full of metaphysics and poetry, which last he was constantly repeating, or rather singing in a half musical, half savage Scotch drawl — a man of talent, genius, and many capabilities; but acrid, fierce, egotistical, and intolerant of interruption.' This was William Maccall, well known in Manchester and the Northern provinces. Thomas Ballantyne was the editor of the Manchester paper, a man who rose to his place from the ranks of the harddriven Lancashire weavers, and himself a 'hard, iron man, learned in Adam Smith, and possessed by the glitter of Carlyle.' The newspaper proprietor, of course, was Alexander Ireland, who saw himself described, in Phillips's pages, as a 'dark, bilious man, with black hair, kind intelligent black eyes, a friendly, genial face, and a most true and affectionate nature. He had been brought up to business, and was the business man of his firm; and it was mainly through him that the paper had so solid and influential a position. He was fond of books and of the fine arts; and had one of the finest and rarest private libraries in the city. He loved Emerson, and was beloved by Emerson, and managed all his business transactions for him.'

So did one witness of the feast appear to another, and Phillips also drew the third, Espinasse, for his gallery. Espinasse had taken his place near the centre of conversation, 'digesting all that passed, and sneering in his Mephistopheles moods at much that was worthy of reverence.' He was a 'dark, Shakespear-browed young man, with the general *physique* of a Spaniard. He wore eye glasses, and seemed to belong to nobody but himself. Now and then he uttered some cold remark, which fell upon the company like ice; he enjoyed the confusion and silence which he had caused. Or he would utter some witty sayings, which made everybody laugh, and him smile sardonically. He was a great reader; and had been some time connected with the British Museum, and was a perfect catalogue of the names of many thousands of volumes in the library of that wonderful emporium. A very clever, and when he liked, a very fascinating man — and an admirable writer of English prose.'

With one description by Phillips, Alexander Ireland would by no means agree. 'There was one man there — about whom we shall say no more than that he reminded us of Judas at the Last Supper.' George Dawson was thus characterized — a demagogue of the lecture platform, who had the gift of swaying audiences to his mood like meadow grass whipped by the east wind. 'A most unjust remark!' Ireland scribbled in protest on the margins of his copy.

When the guests filed in to take their places at dinner, Emerson sat at the head of the table. On his right hand was Sutton, the favourite Apostle. At his left, 'that odd compound of stuff from Birmingham,' Thomas Hornblower Gill. By the side of Gill, George Searle Phillips, not without some apprehension, took a chair, nor were his fears without cause. Gill was so short-sighted that he could not be held responsible for the management of his tableware. As he was in the act of addressing Emerson, his hands, starting with spasmodic motion, knocked violently against his plate, dashing it and its contents into his lap. 'There was a slight buzz and titter round the table, then silence, then a rapid dashing talk, and then a round volley of laughter (caused by some witticism, of course), and in the midst of it our friend recovered his plate and the fragments thereon. . . Then the wine was passed — and then came another scene. Emerson invited him of Birmingham to drink with him. The glasses were filled, but when our friend was in the act of raising the glass to his lips, he let it fall upon the table, and the wine gushed like blood in all its rich indignant stains over our unfortunate shirt front.'

After the feast, and the post-prandial babblement, Emerson, on urgent request, read his newly composed paper on Plato, bringing to a serene close an evening which, Espinasse felt, would otherwise have been a failure. Unlike Ireland, both Espinasse and Phillips believed that the meeting, because of the heterogeneity of the participants, furnished little opportunity for high discourse or a genuine exchange of thought and feeling. Emerson, as was his habit in a large company, said little, but contented himself with ministering to the wants of his guests. Ireland, in disagreement with the other two, recorded his opinion that the banqueters all appeared to be delighted by this opportunity of coming into closer contact with Emerson. With fine graciousness and delicate courtesy, he observed, the host listened to everything his guests had to say, 'and made them feel, as was his wont, that *he* was the favoured one of the party, and that *he* especially was imbibing much wisdom and benefit from their discourse.'

But for Phillips, after the magic of Emerson's lecture on Plato, the evening fell flat and dead. Leaving the chattering guests, he wandered out of doors into the rain, to seek refreshment and consolation, beneath his dripping umbrella, in a cigar. When after some hours he returned, most of the crowd had left. Sutton alone, and the man from Birmingham, remained. The four sat through the long night. Only then, only with an intimate group, with the busy world asleep under the gentle mesmerism of the falling rain, Phillips knew, would Emerson light up his discourse with the lamps of the wise and the good throughout all ages, and grow large and eloquent.

Next morning, the sky dim and frozen, the three breakfasted with their host, then each took his homeward journey, bidding adieu. Thus passed into the limbo of forgotten feasts that bizarre and fantastic banquet of the Half-Gods.

CHAPTER IV

It must not be thought that Emerson's march through the British Isles had been an unimpeded triumph. His lectures, which not infrequently seemed outrageous to minds accustomed to nineteenth-century conventions, were quite capable of breeding prejudice if the critic could not know the man himself. Indeed, personal acquaintance might not in all cases turn away wrath. Someone writing to the *Manchester Courier*, injured in his sense of religiosity, protested that the American's 'bold enunciations' would contaminate the minds of the young men who heard them, while a writer to the *Nottinghamshire Guardian* moved heaven and earth to seek the cancellation of the lecturer's engagements in that city on the grounds that he struck at 'the foundation of those principles of Christian faith and practice which are founded on eternal truth, and which we have been accustomed to hold so dear as truth itself.'

With such warnings ringing in his ears, Emerson may well have faced his engagements to lecture in Scotland with hesitation. Does the land of Calvin ever permit liberties with her godly beliefs, or fail to punish triflers? Firm, established as her grey hills, drab as they, her ways of holiness resist the assaults of those who presumptuously dare to question. North of the Tweed, certainly, the nineteenth century furnished no arena for theological give and take. The Church *held*, and there was an end on't.

If Emerson's eye chanced to fall on the pages of *Tait's Edinburgh Magazine* for January 1848, such doubts as he had may well have given place to trepidation. The leading article of the issue bore the title, 'Ralph Waldo Emer-

son; or, the "Coming Man."' Its author, creator of the
pun, was George Gilfillan, minister of Dundee, and Dundee,
after the fulfilment of engagements at Edinburgh and Glasgow, was to be the scene of Emerson's next appearance.
Obviously Gilfillan did not wish the speaker to reach town
uninstructed or uninformed. 'Some of his expressions
have been imprudent, and even outrageous. What, for
example, did he mean by this: " . . . Man on the *gallows*,
or in the *brothel*, is always on his way *upwards*." (There
can be little doubt as to the *gallows*, that he is!) Such es-
capades as these are certain to be misunderstood by one class,
and to disgust another; and we can assure Mr. Emerson
that they are unworthy of his genius — that they tend to
injure his object — that in Scotland they will not be endured — and that these are the things which have made, to
our knowledge, some of his best and oldest friends tremble
lest his visit should be productive of more evil than good.'
It ought hastily to be added that among these best and oldest friends Gilfillan included himself, and had a right to
make the claim.

George Gilfillan prided himself on his position as literary
critic and as the advocate of misunderstood genius. And
has not a champion, where correction is deserved, the right
to chide those who come under his protection? Thus,
while free in discussing their faults, he was the staunch de-
fender of Percy Bysshe Shelley, that misunderstood revolutionary, and even supported Edgar Allan Poe, devil's
disciple in the mind of many an upright critic of the day.
Gilfillan employed a far weightier battering ram against
the walls of public opinion than the ephemeral periodical.
He believed in the might of books to present his views, and
his first *Gallery of Literary Portraits* came from the press
in 1845. 'The men he has selected,' the critic-author announced in his preface, 'are, in his judgment, the leading

lights — the *decora et tutamina* — of their age.' Prominent
among his luminaries was Ralph Waldo Emerson. And
in the article in *Tait's*, Gilfillan reaffirmed his belief, first
uttered in the 'Portrait,' that Emerson was, ' — let Americans say what they please — . . . their truest and strongest
spirit.' Like Carlyle, like many literary midwives, Gilfillan felt that there was a tenuous spiritual alliance between himself and the man from Concord. This opinion
he had reached through reading his works; soon he could
test the man himself.

Personally, mentally, physically, it would be difficult to
find two men more remote from each other than Ralph
Waldo Emerson and George Gilfillan. But there were
points in common which could deceive the casual observer.
Both were fighters for freedom — yet in how different
ways! Gilfillan must needs lash out, strike with mailed
fist, and hurt to cure. In reproving Emerson for preach-
ing nature as 'a healing influence of universal efficacy,' the
rugged Scotsman cries: 'Surely the beauties of nature are
an appliance too refined for the present coarse complaints
of degraded humanity, which a fiercer caustic must cure.'
In brief, he was a child of Calvin, and though in many respects broad and liberal, could not escape his heritage. He
had, as might be expected with such a full spirit as his,
passed through the flames of a youthful period of struggle,
and had made 'a fluctuating progress through doubts and
darkness to a modified form of orthodoxy.' It was while
he was tracing this path, even drawn towards Pantheism —
mumbo jumbo of the century — that the writings of Emerson and Carlyle most intimately journeyed with him.
But although Gilfillan designated his way as fluctuating,
yet the progress of such as he is under an irresistible com-
pulsion. By 1836, he was ordained to the office of the

ministry as pastor of George's Chapel, Dundee. And by 1848, he was one of the notable men of Scotland.

His very energy put him in a commanding position. He preached with vehemence and force, tears streaming from his eyes, or bellowings of wrath straining his throat, according to the demand of the emotions — always genuine — of the moment. In vigorous, bombastic, colourful style — verging not seldom on the magenta — he penned his articles for journals and wrote his opinionated books. He lectured with authority and assurance. He was a fervent advocate of the cause of the Abolitionist. As for the education-of-the-people movement, he interested himself hugely in it, with all his robust energies. And his breadth, his genuine sympathies, his courage, are perhaps best shown by the part he played in bringing to Dundee lecturers whose heterodoxy was as conspicuous as their ability. Gilfillan never feared the consequences of such action, and more than once found himself in the tangles and vehemences of church reproof. He welcomed excitement. He was a zestful man.

Inevitably he made the Watt Institute of Dundee (the equivalent of the Mechanics' Institutions and Athenæums of other towns) his special charge. In behalf of the men who came to lecture, he acted in the capacities of reception committee, general sponsor, and host, welcoming them to his home with naïve spontaneity. He was a man of elemental, direct personality, absolutely incapable of calculation — acting on the impulse — big, noisy, frank, and trusting; one who took the whole world into his confidence. In description of him and his home, an admirer could write: 'Paradise Manse was as well known as the famous house in Cheyne Row, and dispensed a freer hospitality. Gilfillan trod with full right "the plainstanes" of Dundee

High Street, and everyone knew him. He went with all
the air of a chief newly come down from the glens, but
any child could thrust a little hand upon him and claim the
attention of the minister: there was always something simple in the broad port and thrown-back head.'

And now the American philosopher was coming, whom
he had so highly praised; with whom there would be fine
talk, and the confidence of man to man!

On Monday, 21 February, Emerson arrived. That day
he made his bow to the members of the Watt Institute and
others who cared to attend. The audience was assembled
in George's Chapel and the lecturer spoke from Gilfillan's
pulpit itself. The topic originally advertised was 'Shakespeare,' but at the instance of the lecturer, it was changed
at the last moment to 'The Spirit of the Times.' One
wonders what possessed Emerson to abandon the harmless
subject first announced for the more perilous and inflam-
matory one. Had he learned of his host and sponsor's reputed liberal opinions? At any rate, Emerson as he spoke
that evening boldly declared his conviction that this was
an analytical age, a period of individualism; that many of
the prevailing institutions of the past, if now found want-
ing, must, in spite of defence by those holding fast to the
conservative and the traditional, be swept aside. As the
audience filed out of the building dedicated to the service
of Calvin's God, some shook their heads in disapproval, and
ominous mutterings were heard.

Family worship after supper was a fixed custom in the
Gilfillan household. That evening, shortly before the
time for assembly, Gilfillan showed Emerson to his room.
But as the family prepared to bow their heads in prayer,
Mrs. Gilfillan noticed the absence of the guest.

'Where is Mr. Emerson?' she inquired.

'He has gone to his bedroom,' said her husband.

'Have you asked him to come to worship?'

'No, I don't think he would like it. His views are very different from ours. It might embarrass him.'

'Never mind that, George. Go and ask him. Let the refusal come from him.'

Obediently Gilfillan climbed the stairs. There sat the attacker of formulas, coat off, on the bed.

'The goodwife, Mr. Emerson, wants you down to worship. Will you come?'

'Of course I will,' said Emerson.

Next day the traveller went to Perth to lecture; then, after a night in the sister city on the Tay, returned to Dundee for his second engagement. In Dundee, during the philosopher's absence, there had been rumblings. Verily, George Gilfillan had risked not a little as the prophet's keeper. The officers of the congregation, alarmed by criticism which had drifted to their ears, were eager, in anticipation of the dreaded second lecture, to rescind the privilege of the use of the church. But Gilfillan, with his usual courage, refused to hear of this, although he did compromise with his deacons to the extent of closing the pulpit, so that Emerson spoke instead from the preceptor's desk. In the words of a witty commentator on the episode : 'The Celestial powers, let us hope, recognized the distinction, and were appeased.'

Gilfillan, stout in defence of his guest, was moved to declare of the lectures which he had heard that not one contained 'a single objectionable sentence.' Indeed, he was full of praise for the second discourse, on 'Eloquence,' and lauded in particular Emerson's rendering of a passage from the *Odyssey* descriptive of the oratory of Odysseus. 'It was translated into prose — the prose of his better essays — by himself, and was read with a calm classical power and dignity, which made a thousand hearts still as the grave. For five minutes there seemed but two things in the world — the silence, and the voice which was passing through it.'

That evening Gilfillan again sought Emerson in his bedroom. He was fascinated by his guest, and, as his early discoverer in Scotland, the powerful medium for the spread of his reputation, as the author of the *Literary Portraits*, he felt that he had every right to examine the man whom he regarded almost as a protégé. There was so much to be talked about; questions to be asked and answered; problems to be further elucidated, agreed on, or refuted. The minister of Dundee was a positive man. Loose ends were things not lawful in his philosophy. His frank, transparent nature could not tolerate afterglow; there must be utter white light, or blackest midnight. Emerson was a phenomenon to be carefully investigated and plumbed. In one point, if not in more, Gilfillan felt that the seer from Concord had failed him. Where was that radiance which, he heard, sometimes shone like a divine light on his countenance? 'We watched Emerson's face very narrowly, but could not, for our life, perceive any glow mounting up its pale and pensive lines.' 'I was discoursing with him somewhat confidentially,' he records of his talk with his guest, 'the gas-light between us, when I became suddenly aware of two eyes looking into my very soul. It seemed as if the body had vanished, and those strange serpent glittering eyes alone remained!' Gilfillan was shaken out of his innocent unawareness of himself. He felt uncomfortable; checked. Emerson's glance, 'searching and soundless,' had broken the back of his eager probing. 'He was very pleasant and amiable-seeming,' Gilfillan continues in reporting the encounter, 'but there was a deep in his character as well as in his thought.'

Emerson's glance, indeed, had peculiar qualities, noticed

by several and, like his thoughts, interpreted differently by each observer. Another minister, describing the philosopher's gaze, found in it an unforgettable 'singular and surprising lustre . . . not a surface glitter, but a soft unfathomable transparency, which made his looks . . . like an embodied supplication.'

Emerson, of course, had not satiated Gilfillan's hungry questioning. It was his constant practice to decline all temptations to controversy, and the eager clergyman was forced to retire, his cup unfilled.

The day after the lecturer's departure found Gilfillan writing, in his breathless epistolary style, a letter to William Allingham almost vocal in its praises: 'I have been, as I expected, highly delighted with him.' The recent host singled out particularly for recommendation his late guest's 'simplicity, *bonhommie*, ease of manner, quiet depth of talk when the subject pleased him, gentleness, and gentle *humour* in private — in public his masses of essential thought, his strong intellectual faculties, the calm cherubic power he wields over his audience, the severe graces of his delivery, his high, but not stern abstraction, his indifference to praise or blame, his gleams of real insight, and the truly classical and not affected polish which glitters around the whole style and manner of the man — constitute a unique and noble whole such as I have never in the same measure met before. And then how modest he is withal!' One can fancy Allingham drawing a deep breath before dipping into the swirling waters of the letter's closing lines! 'And yet our bigots here and elsewhere are assailing him with every species of coarse abuse, as if he were a circulating Satan. Nothing so tends to rouse me to a mood in which I would crave a rain of Hell-fire from above upon this miserable age of humbug, as when I think of such conduct. Such treatment to a harmless stranger-son of Genius, invited by Britain to come over and help it, and without the remotest thought of proselytizing a babe, *is* damnable and casts a fearful light upon the state of our times. What a want of confidence such persons discover in their own faith !'

Is there perhaps too great assurance in the last sentence of this letter? Gilfillan would not admit that he was shaken. Besides, his was a loyal heart. Not instantly could he leap to safety. But his disturbed senses must have told him that he was treading uncertain ground. His preconceived vision of the man had failed to meet his seeing eye. He had not found the 'rapt, simple, dreaming enthusiast,' the anticipated rosy being of his conjecture. He had knocked, where he believed he had every right to be admitted, and the door had not been opened to him. 'Emerson of America is always on his guard — is cold in seeming, and has at times an expression of eye which is profound rather than pleasing, subtle rather than clear.' Gilfillan's positiveness had been befuddled by his meeting with Emerson, and the experience was painful. Clearly he must assume some position, but what?

The *Second Gallery of Literary Portraits* was published in 1850, two years after the American's departure. It contained the largely commendatory sketch which had appeared in *Tait's* in the month prior to Emerson's Dundee visit. But there are a few additions, and these are enlightening. Gilfillan now took the American severely to task for his independence; his relinquishment of all authority other than the promptings of his own soul. 'When we think of such a mind owning a faith seemingly so cold, and vague, and shadowy; and when, in his lectures, we find moral and spiritual truths of such importance robbed of their awful sanctions, separated like rays cut off from the sun — from their parent system and source — swung from

off their moorings upon the Rock of ages — the Infinite and
the Eternal — and supported upon his own authority alone
— when, in short, the Moon of genius comes between us
and the Sun of God, we feel a dreariness and desolation of
spirit inexpressible ; and, much as we admire the author and
love the man, we are tempted to regret the hour when he
first landed upon our shores.'

Four years later, in 1854, the third *Gallery of Literary
Portraits* revealed that Gilfillan had leapt for firm rock,
and the rock was not Emerson's. Gilfillan had evolved
out of the rebuff to his exuberant personality a chimera of
hideous proportions, and every line of the newest portrait
reveals that the 'circulating Satan' had arrived.

Back in 1844, Thomas Carlyle, writing to his American
friend in Concord, Massachusetts, chanced to mention
George Gilfillan. He spoke of him as 'a person of great
talent, ingenuousness, enthusiasm, and other virtues ; whose
position as a Preacher of bare old Calvinism under penalty
of death sometimes makes me tremble for him.' Carlyle
was not infrequently a shrewd prophet. The trend of
Gilfillan's religious experiences ran its due course until at
last he became a believer in the pre-millennial advent of
Christ. In fact the poignancy of his hopes impelled him,
as usual, to write a book. But curiously blended with his
convictions of faith were his injured sensibilities regarding
Emerson, and now the American was numbered among the
chief enemies of God. The final chapter of *Christianity and
Our Era* bears the title : 'The Deepening Crisis — Signs of
the Second Advent of Christ — the Coming.' It is at once
a beseeching prayer to the 'God-Man' in whom he trusted
in his darkest hours, and a frenzied exhortation for Christ's
return. 'Come down ; the tumult of thine adversaries
groweth continually . . . Come down ; for the time — the
set time — is nearly come.' And Emerson is transmogrified

into an evil, devouring beast, a monster such as assailed
Bunyan's Christian in the Valley of the Shadow. He 'is
one of the *few sceptics* who has *personally*, and by *name*,
insulted the Lord Jesus Christ, and through him, that Humanity of which Jesus is the Hope, the Glory, the Ideal,
and the Crown . . . Emerson, with Julian the Apostate,
Voltaire, Paine, and Francis Newman, must bear the brand
of using language to Christ which no man of culture would
now apply to a Cæsar, a Danton, or a Napoleon. . . .

'We have heard a dog baying at the moon — we have
heard of a maniac spitting foam at the stars — we have
watched the writhings of crushed mediocrity as it gazed
on the bright pages of genius — and we have understood,
excused, pitied, and forgiven all such in their morbid or
mistaken feelings. But how one calling himself a man, and
reputed really a man of genius, could, in his most unhappy
hour, have uttered a word against our Brother — God — the
Eternal Child — the Babe in the Manger — the Boy in the
Temple — the Carpenter in the Shed — the Weeper at the
Grave — the Sufferer on the Cross — the Risen from the
Tomb — the Exalted to the Heavens — the Friend by eminence of our fallen Family — the Expected from the Clouds
— the Type and Test of whatever is holy, and charitable,
and lovely, and lofty in the race of man — passes our conceptions, and has strained to its utmost *our* power of forgiveness.'

At long last, Gilfillan had got free of Emerson. ' "Trust
thyself ?" No ! Christianity says "Mistrust thyself —
trust God — do thy humble duty, and call the while on the
lofty help that is above thee." ' But storms subside
through their own violence. In reminiscent mood, in his
diary, he jotted down under date of 13 April 1863 : 'I have
been looking into Emerson's "Conduct of Life." He
shines in fractions, like bits of broken glass.' Remarking

that he had not heard from Emerson since the visit to Dundee, Gilfillan added, 'He has heard from me, and somewhat too fiercely, I admit, though, at the time, most sincerely.'

What a deal of pother a two days' meeting had aroused! How end the history of this event? Would it be an unkindness to quote Gilfillan's remark, made in 1848, that 'the great lessons of a practical kind which Emerson teaches, or tries to teach, are faith, hope, charity, and self-reliance,' and recall that he it was who said, in the same year, of Emerson's detractors: 'What a want of confidence such persons discover in their own faith?' Or should one be more charitable? The long fight had weakened the stout warrior. On 9 April 1864, he wrote in his diary: 'This is a beautiful day, bright, and with that fine spring softness of feeling, and warmth of breeze, which used to be so delightful. How enthusiastically I used to quote the words of Emerson about spring bringing

> "Life's sunshine and desire;
> And from mount and meadow
> Breathes aromatic fire."

But now much of this is gone, perhaps never to return.'

The impact, in this universe, of minutest finite particle on particle; even the influence, without direct contact of matter on matter: what energies are liberated, what forces created, what movement begun, what endings, births, and deaths determined by one such conjunction! How much less predictable the results where life touches life, and spirit, spirit! No two unicellular organisms, blindly colliding in a stagnant pool, retain their first identity or quite reassume their previous individuality after the encounter: change, superficial or profound, for one protozoan or the other, or for both, is the consequence. And what two human creatures

that dip momentarily into each other's being may part un-
altered? Twenty-four hours of Ralph Waldo Emerson's
presence expand like an eternity in the subsequent record
of George Gilfillan's struggle with existence.

There were many meetings in the period of Emerson's
journeyings in the British Isles. Several have left behind
the traces, devious or simple, of their course. In addition
to Gilfillan's, four such encounters, at different times and
places, and concerning two women and two men, have in
them sufficient interest, or absurdity, to warrant resurrection.

MISS GOOSEBERRY OF MANCHESTER

In every town there is to be found some woman whose
house is the radial centre of the life of the intellectual
set. And Manchester, in the middle of the nineteenth
century — bustling, ugly, business-like Manchester; known
throughout England as Cottonopolis — was no exception to
the rule. In that city reigned Geraldine Endsor Jewsbury, Jane Carlyle's friend and an author of some reputation. Possibly this last characterization should be changed
to lack of reputation, since her recent novel, *Zoe*, had
stirred up a fuss on the grounds of its immorality, giving
Geraldine, in Jane's opinion, quite a new sort of distinction
for a young English gentlewoman. Yet there was little
of the manner of the successful authoress discernible in
Miss Jewsbury's technique in managing her salon. She
had nothing about her of the blue-stocking, nor was she
given to talking of her own books. Her gifts as hostess
lay in her ability to keep her little parties light and in-
formal. Even Carlyle, who generally railed with vigorous picturesqueness at all manner of symposia, accepted
Geraldine's with remarkable equanimity and stayed con-
tentedly at her house during one of his longer visits to

Manchester, made in the course of a solitary pilgrimage
about the land to recover from the birth throes of a book.
Like Jane, Geraldine had become an unconventional, brilliant talker, who nevertheless could guide her own and her
guests' conversation into tranquil channels, a knack which
made her house neutral ground where persons of very
different opinions — political, social, or religious — could
gather for a pleasant evening free of argumentation or
formality. Her sister Maria had married long ago, left
home, and died; and Geraldine, in lengthening spinster-
hood, lived on in Manchester, keeping house for her gre-
gariously inclined brother Frank, who was a business man
in the city.

Jane Carlyle, of course, is not to be trusted. In her own
manner, she was fond of Geraldine, but she was also
amused by her ways, and sometimes annoyed. In the last
mood, she was quite capable of uttering funny, sly remarks
about Miss Gooseberry of Manchester, to a chorus of delighted guffaws from her admiring husband. Geraldine,
she said, had one besetting weakness. She was never
happy unless she had on hand some *grande passion*. The
difficulty was that, since bachelors took alarm at her im-
pulsive, demonstrative ways, she was compelled to expend
all her fervour on married men.

The Jewsburys, Geraldine and Frank, lived outside the
limits of the town, at Number 30, Carlton Terrace, in the
suburb of Greenhays. Before their house stretched meadows not yet defaced by the invasion of brick and mortar
which Manchester, with the power of an irresistible volcano, was already thrusting forward like a horrid lava flow
along the path of the city's expansion. To this pleasant
retreat, following in the steps of most other celebrated visitors to Manchester, the lecturer from America had in due
course made his way.

Miss Jewsbury had known all about him long before he came on his second visit to England. Alexander Ireland and the Carlyles had seen to that. Geraldine, who worshipped Jane with unquestioning admiration and usually echoed her opinions, had read the *Essays*, and she told Jane that Emerson owed himself entirely to her husband — at least, what was good in him he derived from Carlyle. For the rest, Miss Jewsbury decided, his writings revealed him as a dry, cold, sententious Yankee, who spiritualized profit and loss, and lived soberly and honestly because he saw that it paid well. Such a man, felt Geraldine, held no appeal for her; she could not take to the likes of him!

Yet when Emerson began his speaking engagements in Manchester, Miss Jewsbury was first in the vanguard of the faithful who never missed a lecture. Her name was always prominent in the lists of celebrities in attendance as announced by the press, and she was not behindhand among those who sought to do him honour at their homes. Perfectly silent, perfectly gentlemanly, and perfectly reserved, Emerson moved about his hostess's drawing room. For her, this was an enigmatic experience indeed. Geraldine was puzzled and eager; she felt strangely thwarted. Although she greatly wanted his approval, she fancied he did not take to her. Was she too tumultuous for him? A gossip had told her that Emerson considered her too satirical. Was that the trouble? 'I had far rather the Quaker liked me,' she confessed to Jane. But at least he had written her a very pleasant note in acknowledgment of her hospitality. And when he quitted England for America, all unknowing he left Geraldine still wrestling with her problem. In a letter to Mrs. Carlyle, quite unmindful of the amused conjectures her confidences were sure to arouse, Geraldine wrote: 'I have a great affection for Emerson, in spite of the provokingly serene ether he always seems to breathe. He has such a fine spirit in him, and so much humanity, too.'

A POINT OF SYMPATHY

During the first days of his extended tour of Britain, Emerson held to his policy to refuse all invitations to spend nights in the homes of the citizenry. But presently he found himself glad to seek relief in private homes from the clatter and routine of his public life. People, he felt with gratitude, were very kind to him. He began thoroughly to enjoy the opportunities they gave to share with them their domesticity. Why, he delightedly wrote to his mother, their solicitude for his comfort included even such thoughtfulness as warming pans between cold sheets!

From Rose Hill, Coventry, an invitation had come from Charles Bray, author of a book called *The Philosophy of Necessity*. In the course of his British crusade, Bronson Alcott had met Bray, and had liked him. Even though he had no other reason to go to Coventry — no engagement to lecture there — Emerson decided to accept. At midnight, on Tuesday, 11 July he got off the train at Coventry and found his host waiting for him on the station platform.

In addition to being an author, Charles Bray was a business man, a well-to-do ribbon manufacturer of the district. He was a person of quick discernment and natural liberality. His pleasant house on the outskirts of the town was surrounded with lawns and gardens, and flanked by tall trees where nightingales often sang in the evening. And his family and their circle of friends were as pleasant as his house. Emerson, always sensitive to his environment, whether of people or of places, expanded in this atmosphere. He wrote in the guest book which Mrs. Bray handed to him: 'If the law of love and justice have once entered our hearts, why need we seek any other?' To these words Mrs. Bray added the line, 'Emerson (as he sat in the drawing room window, July 12, 1848).'

In the morning, the host and hostess took their guest into the garden, where the little group conversed for a while under a beautiful acacia tree which was one of the treasures of the place. Emerson spoke of Concord, and of his wife and family whom he hoped soon to see. He told how he had bought a rocking horse for his two little girls, and a crossbow for his son, and his eyes sparkled at the thought of how his children must have grown during the nine months he had been away from them. The gathering was presently joined by some friends, among whom was a young girl of twenty-nine who was introduced as Mary Ann Evans. She was not very prepossessing to look at, with her prominent, masculine nose and her poorly formed, loose, broad mouth. But her bronze-coloured hair, arranged in great coils over her ears, made up for the first impression and her eyes had a way of looking one through and through that commanded one's startled attention. No, she seemed no ordinary person. Emerson found himself greatly drawn to her.

'What one book do you like best?' he suddenly asked, when they had conversed a few minutes.

'Rousseau's Confessions.'

That reply he had hardly expected. But his intuitive sense presently acknowledged its fitness.

'So do I,' he said. 'There is a point of sympathy between us.'

He spoke of her with admiration to Charles Bray. Surely, he remarked, she was possessed of a serious, calm soul. She had in her the qualities of a Sibyl.

The rest of the day was filled by a pleasant excursion to Stratford to see Shakespeare's grave. Then Emerson left his new friends at Coventry for a brief visit to George

Stephenson, whom he had met at Chesterfield during the period of lecturing in the provinces.

But Mary Ann Evans did not put out of her thoughts the memory of the departed guest. She knew that for the moment their minds had touched and blended, by whatever alchemy governs such fusings. In her diary she wrote: 'I have seen Emerson — the first *man* I have ever seen.'

Years later the woman who as a girl had written thus — now known to the world as George Eliot — sat reading in a volume of Emerson. How fresh with beauty and meaning the words still seemed! For the second time she recorded her thoughts: 'My heart goes out with venerating gratitude to that mild face, which I dare say is smiling on some one as beneficially as it one day did on me years and years ago.'

THE HALE AND COMELY ENGLISHMAN

At Chesterfield, the spire of St. Mary's mounts crookedly toward the skies, for all the world like a gigantic replica of the crumpled horn of that afflicted cow that lived in the house that Jack built. Its wooden frame was made, according to a legend told locally, of unseasoned timber, during a not unusual period of clouds and mist. Then at last the sun shone forth on the completed work, and the spire, like a garden sunflower in worship of its God, followed the glorious beacon in its course, and thus in the passage of a single day the miracle was wrought.

So said the myth. Yet in the middle of the century a real miracle worker had come to end his days in the pleasant town of Chesterfield. This was George Stephenson, designer and builder of the first practical railway locomotive, who through his wizardry had revolutionized transportation and spun a vast spider's web of steel over the length and breadth of England. The now famous engineer had sprung from the humblest beginnings. He was the son of a mine worker who, at twelve shillings a week, stoked a pumping engine to keep down the water seepage in the coal pits of Wylam colliery near Newcastle. On his slim pay, his father supported wife and a family of six children. The first habitation George could remember was a crudely built affair near the pits, the home of three other families of workers besides the Stephensons. A single room in this place, with clay floor, unplastered walls, and rough ceiling through which the beams showed, served all the functions of home for George, his parents, and his brothers and sisters.

Patient industry and a knack for useful contrivances launched George Stephenson on his way, though he was eighteen before he knew even how to write his own name. When as a very young man he was made engineer of a pumping engine, on a twelve-hour shift, he devoted much of the time not on duty to taking his machine apart, cleaning it, and studying it. Thus did he give himself a thorough knowledge of the principles of combustion engines. He loved machines as he loved animals — they were personalities to him. Presently the bony, large-framed youth, who had already won some local notoriety through the performance of feats of strength in weight lifting and putting the hammer, became even better known as an inventor : a naturally ingenious craftsman who had discovered, among other things, how to make a lamp which would not ignite the deadly gases that caused such terrific explosions in the mines in the days when miners carried open flames to guide their steps.

But steam and the fascinating possibilities of its power remained Stephenson's chief interest. And in 1836, the

revolutionizing year when the Manchester-Liverpool railway was opened for service, it was Stephenson who was
chiefly responsible for that wonder.

By 1848 he had reached the sixtieth year of his eventful,
adventurous life : a hale, splendid old man with handsome
ruddy face and dark blue eyes. Any artist would have
been eager to use him as a model fit to personify the dignity, strength, and heartiness of a fortunate race of men.
Although he had retired from active work, and lived like
an old conqueror in a stately mansion named Tapton
House, built on a height overlooking the town, he still retained a tremendous interest in all the fascinating puzzles
of the natural world. And along with his passionate curiosity about science in all its branches he had a great fondness
for people and enjoyed entertaining and being entertained. Another engineer, Frederick Swanwick, once a
pupil of his, was his closest friend in Chesterfield, and the
two were often in each other's company. When Emerson had come to town to lecture, Swanwick, as his host,
had the happy thought of asking Stephenson to dine with
them. And the old inventor came that evening to Swanwick's house.

Through some oversight, Stephenson, when he arrived,
was not immediately brought into conversation with Emerson. But he presently took the matter into his own hands.
He strode vigorously across the room, seized the stranger
by the shoulders, gave him a friendly shake of welcome,
and demanded in his big, full-bodied voice : 'What is it
about you Americans that we can always tell you by ?'

Shades of Boston and Beacon Hill, where frigid restraint
keeps her solitary vigil and the powers of reserve control
the rigid householder ! Had some of Emerson's Boston
acquaintances (he had such, now that his light was begin-

ning to shine beyond the limits of Concord) — had they witnessed this scene, they would fully have expected a deadly chill to pervade the room and ice to fall from the ceiling. Even Oliver Wendell Holmes, least inhibited of the lot, could observe of his friend Emerson: 'What man was he who would lay his hand familiarly upon his shoulder and call him Waldo?' But did the Brahmins really know him? Emerson was delighted with Stephenson. He regarded that hearty shake as an accolade. He rejoiced in the mold of the man. Here was the fibrous, full-blooded stuff of which the best Englishmen were made! Here was one who could build, could create with his hands, putting to shame the puny wielders of pens! He told Stephenson that he had everywhere been struck by the haleness and comeliness of English men and women. At once the two launched into a discussion of anthropological questions: did or did not the air, climate, moisture, soil, and other conditions exercise an influence on the physical and moral development of races? In such talk, on all manner of topics, the dinner hours passed all too quickly. And when Stephenson fell into a reminiscent mood, speaking of the earliest efforts of men towards steam locomotion and of his own first experiments, Emerson and Swanwick listened with breathless attention.

After the meal, when the group returned to the drawing room, the inventor launched forth enthusiastically on a new subject — electricity. But mere explication would not suffice. He commandeered the dining room poker to serve as impromptu equipment for experiments, and when it proved insufficient for the need, ordered another poker to be brought from the kitchen. Verily, the elemental powers that move the Universe crackled and leaped within the room at the beck and call of the magician. Emerson treasured each moment of that evening. Why, it had been worth crossing the Atlantic if only to have seen Stephenson!

FULL OF A GREAT DESIRE

When David Scott was one year old, his four brothers, within the space of a few weeks, died, one after the other. From this shock the surviving child's parents never fully recovered. Other children came, but Robert Scott and his wife lived on in an atmosphere of brooding melancholy, deepening at times into the tenebrous nightmares of religious gloom. Mrs. Scott, when she spoke to her later born, often addressed them by the names of those who were dead, then corrected herself, with a look of vague puzzlement and sorrow.

David's father, a prematurely old man, harassed by constant illness and the fear of poverty, was an engraver. He planned to bring David up in the craft which he himself had practised for so many patient years. When he was young, Robert Scott had dreamed of becoming a painter of landscapes. He had a knack for catching the delicate tracery of ferns, grasses, and leaves — sublimating the aptness he inherited from yeoman forbears who had worked in leather. But the hard face of necessity frightened away that hope. Yet in his son David, the gift lost in the father seemed destined to assert itself with a more imperative urge. David's skill came not alone from his father's side; his maternal grandfather had been a sculptor, though a very mediocre one. Thus the accidents of marriage and begetting had conspired, apparently to some purpose.

When David was sixteen, he was already busy with a multitude of original designs. At twenty-one, he abandoned his father's trade as a thing not to be endured. It is the duty of the engraver to show no personality. That must be left entirely to the artist whose creation is being reproduced. Engraving is the most laborious and painful of tasks. Every line, every dot, must be cut with infinite precision — the same gestures over and over again — to insure the metallic smoothness and characterless finish demanded by publishers in obedience to the dictates of taste in nineteenth-century book illustrating. Just before he renounced his father's craft, the young rebel drew a little sketch, labelled 'Character of David Scott, 1826.' It showed him seated at the engraving table, his hands clenched, an expression of despair on his face.

David began at once to work in oils. 'Thou Power,' he prayed, 'by whose aid man raises the imperishable name, wrap around me thy tongued flames, and of the present make immortal days. May I live not without a consecrated purpose in my life; may I reach and grasp all means for this ultimate consummation. Grant that I may hold on with undeviating step. Strengthen the will — endow with the power — break the arm that would retard.'

He had an enormous faculty for introspection — and he did not know how to play. His diary received all his confidences, and through it he studied himself. 'This day has passed away very worthlessly,' he wrote, when on a visit to the seashore with some quite pleasant and kind people. 'General society great loss of time; those leviathan-mouthed affairs, dinners and tea-parties, walks with ladies, &c, are to me continual regret and ennui.'

By now he had developed into a youth of remarkable appearance. His hands, in their approach to sculpturesque perfection, were startlingly beautiful. In figure he was of medium size: slender, with a frame suggesting at once the ascetic and the high-strung athlete prepared to strip for the contest. A cloudy mass of brown-black hair fell about his temples. From time to time he would toss it from his pale forehead with a proud gesture possibly not quite unstudied in its effect. Perhaps the most arresting feature of his appearance, when one scrutinized it, was the colour of his eyes. They were blue, but blue with the shade of a night sky — eyes abnormally large, set deep in his delicately modelled face which was saved from a suggestion of effeminancy by its high cheek bones, slightly sunken cheeks, and the strong, thin, patrician nose. Yet equally striking, perhaps, were his exquisitely chiselled lips: the lower full and round, the upper arched as in a Greek statue. This was their appearance when relaxed; often they were pressed together in a firm line of determination, and sometimes the upper one seemed to curl with something not unlike the shadow of disdain.

His earliest paintings were historical in subject. The first which he attempted was a canvas showing Lot and his daughters fleeing the cities of the plain, and he began drawing the figures to the scale of life. A fellow artist advised him: 'Shoot a lower aim, you speak a dead language.' At this, Scott wrote in his diary, 'What am I to do?' But he continued his work as before.

When he was twenty-two, he first exhibited a painting. It was called 'The Hopes of Early Genius dispelled by Death.' He wrote of his efforts: 'Think I have gained more distinctness in my ideas regarding art. . . The overwhelming and perplexing have now resolved themselves into different parts and separate difficulties, and I think I can now discover with clearness the mighty structure that before was wrapped in mist.'

He found himself irresistibly drawn towards allegory. The outer world he saw merely as the projection of the inner. All history, he perceived, taught this lesson. But it was another matter to convince the public of this. The public wished to be pleased, and Scott, unlike many of his fellow artists, sought not to please, but to awe and educate, even, if need be, to terrify and disgust. Fear, discord, and death were the mightiest symbols, and he never hesitated to paint them in all their forms. Yet he painted less frightening and terrible subjects, too. He was twenty-five when he wrote in his diary : 'Sold "The Cloud" to Francis Grant — the first of my pictures that has been sold.' But he was unable soon to make a similar entry.

His own objectives became again like shadows in the night. 'Some time ago I thought I saw clearly what ought to be essayed in art; now I think differently from these. Do I see any firm ground at all? Is there any reason in nature or in society, that a man aspiring to the highest forms of art, should be treated as a visionary?' His big canvas, 'Lot,' had been rejected by the British Institution. To spare the artist's feelings — the painting was a poor one — the committee tried to explain by saying that the picture was too large. 'Reject a work of art for its size!' Scott exclaimed, 'You might as well reject a man for being tall.' Other pictures, sent to the local exhibition of the year in Edinburgh, were also being returned, although some of his work had been accepted in previous seasons.

David found himself at the end of a road. A little book of his allegorical fancies, published for him by Constable's, had proved to be a complete failure as far as money was concerned, though it had received favourable notice even in the metropolitan press of London. His financial resources were diminished to the vanishing point. And while his confidence in his genius still held fast, he was filled with doubts over his medium of expression.

So he made a will (he was twenty-six), packed his clothes, and left Edinburgh for the Continent. Paris, Geneva, Milan, Laggo Maggiore, Venice, Parma, Florence, Siena, Rome. At Rome he halted, procured fresh paints,

and set up a studio. In his travels he had seen man's greatness in art but the Italian frescoes were themselves a sign of
the scathe of time — the general design of the artist still
visible; but the colour faded, the spirit gone. 'So is it with
all the frescoes I have met — the claws of destruction are in
them.'

In his studio he began a picture showing Love seeking
to escape from Time. But his progress was hampered by
illness. He had never been sick before; now illness was
his constant companion: for months he had not been free
of it. He felt crushed. But though he was never to be
well again, he could still paint. Next to him, a Spanish
artist had a studio. Through the damp partitions, David
could hear him sneeze and cough, blessing himself at the
end of each attack.

He had started another large canvas. It was to portray
Discord. In it, a gigantic, powerful figure of a man wrestling brutally to be free of its encumbrances, flinging about
wife and child, and smashing the household gods. The artist had resolved to paint henceforth only what was real and
strong to him — the configurations of the truth which lay
behind the appearances of things. He was disgusted at his
own prettiness in several canvases he had done, although
critics told him they had real merit. 'This picture of Discord is for all countries; I must work for the world, as all
should do, or for my own country, Scotland.'

When the big painting was finished, a tide of vacationing British scribblers and of artists expatriated at Rome
flowed through the studio to inspect the work: Severn
and Macaulay, Jeffrey and Darnley and Rothwell. Each
connoisseur praised a feature of the canvas to which his
immediate predecessor had taken exception. Yes, the
composition was powerful, and the outlines of the figures
surely drawn. Most did agree to that. Whereupon Scott

had to explain over and over that the thing was an abstraction. When they had all filed past, he sat alone in the
studio, despairing. A year in Rome was gone. He
packed his canvases.

Once more in Edinburgh, and in his twenty-ninth year.
His fortunes now seemed somewhat to improve. He was
a member of the hanging committee for the Annual Exhibition, and a few commissions, on which he was already
engaged, had come his way. But five years had passed
since he had received any remuneration for his work.

He was one of the few painters in England who understood the technique of fresco, and when a competition was
opened to select the artist who was to decorate the new
Houses of Parliament at London, David's friends believed
his moment had arrived. But Scott, with stiff-necked independence, refused to conform to the criteria which were
to determine the award. He would not submit drawings
which manifested the desired qualities of precision, correct-
ness, and technical mastery of design. These he knew he
possessed, but he believed the artist should make a cloudy
beginning, gradually shaping his work to the urgings of
his genius. In consequence, his rapidly, carelessly exe-
cuted designs were passed over, and the commission was
lost to him.

When one of his paintings was skyed by the committee
of the Royal Academy at London, which two years before had turned down his picture of Achilles addressing the
Manes of Patroclus, Scott refused to send more canvases,
although some members of the Academy later acknowledged that the rejected work was excellent.

'Discord' had been exhibited before the Royal Scottish
Academy in 1841, and filled most of the visiting public
with astonishment and bewilderment, although several
critics saw in it a windy, tremendous power of blackness

and storm. David was now on the point of beginning another great subject: it was to show Vasco da Gama and his crew encountering the Spirit of the Cape. For his work, he set up his studio in a house he had recently acquired in Easter Dalry, not far removed from the busy world of Edinburgh. But to the casual visitor the quiet spot might well have seemed a thousand miles away. Old trees hemmed it about, and their shadows made earth and sky sombre. A morose old watch-dog dozed in his kennel at a corner of the drab building. The hedges were busy with finches and robins, and these alone gave a semblance of life to the neighbourhood. Within the building, in the wide, high studio, damp and cold even in summer, Scott laboured on his vision of the demon of the cape — a huge, dim, fearful colossus, his streaming white beard a part of the storm, the shafts of lightning from his clenched hand threatening the Portuguese navigator, who stands resolute on his ship while his terrified, half mutinous crew, sensing the presence of the awesome spirit they cannot see, cower on the deck of the tossing vessel. Thus was it to be — the forces of the universe, and, opposed to them, a steadfast, self-reliant hero, a match for his fate! Scott toiled at his conception for two years till the mighty canvas, filling a whole side of the studio with tempest and confusion, stood momentarily at rest. The only brightness in it came from the shafts of electric fire darting from the shadowy god of the lonely sea, flashes raising the dim figures on the ship's deck into fitful relief. But the picture suggested, not that revealed moment of light, but blackness and a rushing wind, and the uncurbable will of titanic forces.

At the instigation of one of David's admirers, a hall was rented in Edinburgh for the display of the huge canvas. But the public were apathetic. They read the title of the picture, and decided that Vasco da Gama, a Portuguese explorer, meant little to them. The artist had not even made him plainly visible! Though the doors stood open for two months, few people passed through them, and Scott was forced to meet the expenses of the exhibit. Rarely had he been overwhelmed with a greater sense of depression. The pages of his diary were filled, in these years, with the combat of hope and despair that used him for battleground.

'Desolate, and very weary of suspense.'

'Morning a bright Sunday — calm within and without. Of late, more than in all my previous life, I have been conscious of repose and consolidation of thought. At first there was a struggle in darkness; then a growing out into dimness; and now into the light, but with the same purposes as ever.'

'The meaning attached to art is differently understood now from what it was some very short time ago. There are now frequent indications of this extending itself in proper directions. My papers were the first of their kind in the periodicals. Since then, art in its intellectual relations is a frequent subject.'

'A joy visited me one day, and in the next unaccountable darkness. When is this perplexing net to resolve itself into a strengthening mantle?'

'Read lately the essays of Emerson — a worthy thinker.'

'In Emerson I find many things that meet conclusions formed, and feelings expressed by myself. He is a less sectarian and more unfettered doctrinist than I have yet met. As yet, however, I have not arrived at the basis (if he has indeed defined such) of the superstructure of his mind.'

Time brought Emerson himself to Scott's studio to face that question. When David learned that he was in Edinburgh, he insisted that Emerson should sit for a portrait. Emerson loathed to be photographed or painted, and Scott

himself had little use for portraits, but here there were
compelling inward circumstances which caused both men
to waive their prejudices.   Through Margaret Fuller, the
traveller had heard of Scott.   'What he does is bad,' she
had told him, with perhaps too hasty a judgment, 'but full
of a great desire.'

But when he saw the author of the *Essays*, David Scott
was deeply troubled.   He did not at all measure up to ex-
pectations.   Emerson at first appeared guarded, and Scott
felt him to be severe, and dry, and hard.   How could one
symbolize the person who seemed thus to contradict the
image in the painter's inward eye?

The two men first met at an intimate dinner given for
the American lecturer by an Edinburgh hostess, Mrs.
Crowe, who delighted to bring together visiting celebrities
and the luminaries of her city.   Besides David Scott,
Thomas DeQuincey was there, and Dr. Samuel Brown,
from whom the Athens of the North expected great accomplishments in science.   The guests talked their literary
talk, David, as was his custom, scarcely participating.
Philip James Bailey and his poem 'Festus' came up for discussion, and Emerson remarked that he did not esteem him
a true poet: there was not a single line of his which bore
the stamp of genius.   At that, Scott broke his silence.
His words fell like doom on the company.   In the peculiar
cadence, melancholy and slow, which had become his
habitual mode of expression, he chanted the words from
the poem: 'Friendship hath passed me like a ship at sea,'
then he sank again into his silence, refusing to take further
part.

But as he worked in his studio on the portrait, Emerson
sitting there before him, he saw at last what to do.   In the
dim light of the great room his subject grew, somehow,
luminous.   Emerson should stand in the gloom, as David

had seen him stand facing his stiff-lipped Scottish audiences, but behind him, arching the threatening skies, he
would paint a rainbow.

When he quitted Edinburgh, Emerson wrote a letter to
Scott. How vividly he recalled him and the studio, hung
with its smoky, tenebrous paintings: Vasco da Gama star-
ing into darkness and tempest, Wallace defending Scotland,
Adam and Eve singing their morning hymn, Cain, and
Sarpedon carried by Sleep and Death! And that strange
portrait of himself, with its rainbow allegory! 'I carry
with me a bright image of your house and studio, and all
your immortal companions therein, and I wish to keep the
ways open between us, natural and supernatural. If the
Good Power had allowed me the opportunity of seeing you
at more leisure, and of comparing notes of past years a
little! And it may yet be allowed in time; but where and
when?' A year later, David Scott was dead.

CHAPTER V

A SPRAY OF WILD CURRANT

ON 26 February 1848 Emerson saw the last of Scotland — bleak, wintry Scotland with its iron-grey look. He left with considerable relief. He had shivered in Glasgow, a grim city stretching its soiled fingers in the corrupted air of its industrialism. A heavy snowstorm had nearly blocked his passage between Dundee and Perth. He had met interesting, friendly people in Scotland, but also people less friendly, less interesting. Many Scotsmen, he decided, looked drunk even though they were sober. They were great talkers, and they loved to argue. He longed for spring, and the benediction of tranquil landscapes. He was looking forward to a visit to Harriet Martineau, an old acquaintance whom he had entertained, twelve years ago, at Concord. She lived at Ambleside, in the English Lake District.

He entered the region by way of Kendal. To the north, winter fought stubbornly for possession of the earth. South of the Lakes glared the smelting furnaces of England : the hot, iron lungs of England. When Emerson, the previous autumn, was travelling in the black belt, he had noticed that even the sheep on the moorlands assumed the characteristic sootiness of Leeds and Bradford. Begrimed by the smoke, their matted wool dangled untidily from their backs. But now, behind the defences of the hills, winter was rebuffed to the north, and, to the south, the contaminating breath of the factories could not smirch the sheep that grazed on the uplands, their fleece silver as the vapours which rose at dawn from a thousand becks and rills.

In the Lake District, if one knows where to seek, the

outposts of spring are early visible. In spite of the northern latitudes, the miracle of the resurrection — promise that the world has not wholly died under swirls of snow — is almost companion to the frozen, killing breath of winter. Even before the old year has died and lies buried under a shroud of brown and whirling leaves, reckless snowdrops hang their green-tinged bells of porcelain, to be blended presently and hidden with a sifting mantle of white. In late February, beguiled by the promise of random hours of sunshine, the throstle and merle essay tentative bursts of music, and when evening draws veils of mist over the shadowed valleys of Cumberland, swarms of fragile-winged insects dance briefly in fantastic sarabands. Before spring's more obvious heralds, her spies are abroad, and Emerson's was an eye trained to perceive them.

His way took him along the upper reaches of the irregular crescent of Windermere — narrow Windermere, with the appearance of a majestic river. At the head of the lake is the valley of the Rothay, flanked to right and left, where the brown waters of the stream enter, by Todd Crag and Wansfell. A mile up the course of the torrent lies the village of Ambleside. Harriet Martineau had placed her house, The Knoll, just to the north of the little town in the direction of Wordsworth's lake, Rydal Water. Here she planned to establish the focal centre for her busy, restless life. In her dynamic soul there was one quiet chamber which craved peace and domesticity, and she longed to fill its need.

At the Lakes she knew that she could gratify this tranquil element of her nature yet at the same time give expression to those driving impulses of her genius which had already resulted in such amazing productivity. When the British and Foreign Unitarian Association had offered prizes for three essays, one to persuade Catholics to embrace

Unitarianism, one to accomplish a similar miracle with
Mohammedans, and one to convert the Jews, Harriet, a
young woman on the threshold of her career, sending in
her anonymous contributions, had captured all three
awards. Having thus exhausted her fund of arguments on
this faith, she herself characteristically quitted the fold.
Her fluent pen next rushed through thirteen volumes of
tales, each story to illustrate some principle of political
economy designed to bring wiser government to the world.
Then came a volume called *Life in the Sick-Room*. Harriet for a time had enjoyed ill health with tremendous intensity, keeping her friends in suspense on the brink of
her impending dissolution. But when the time came for
her to die and she had recorded her experiences of death's
pains, she grew well and hastened to resume her ways of
vigorous life. She wrote a novel, *Deerbrook*, and an historical romance. She made herself conversant with the
world's innumerable problems.

Even Thomas Carlyle noticed favourably this dynamo
among women, although in his more irritable moments,
after the novelty of her had worn off, he declared her to be
blown up with self-conceit and the most wearisome of
females. But this was but a temporary mood with him,
during a period when she was pestering him with her latest
fancies — animal-magnetism and mesmerism. When these
abated, he was ready to accept her again. Wordsworth
himself remained undismayed when he learned that she was
to become his near neighbour, and showed his interest by
writing to his crusty, jolly old friend, Henry Crabb Robinson, of the doings of the good Harriet, as he called her.
She was taking great pride in planning her house, he observed, using her versatile ingenuity in the working out
of each detail. Yet once the slow process of construction
began, she fled away. Instead of watching passively the

agglomeration of brick and stone, she rushed off on a tour
of Egypt, the desert, and Palestine, intent on her mission
of revealing those regions to her British public as, a few
years before, she had opened their eyes to the United States
through her two books, *Society in America* and *A Retrospect of Western Travel*.   Miss Martineau was moved by
a perpetual urge to botanize humanity.   She recorded her
observations with an almost appalling confidence and sureness.   Her affliction of deafness seemed but to sharpen her
faculties.   Even her ear trumpet, as Emerson noticed when
he first met her, acted as chain as well as medium, making
Siamese twins of the two interlocutors.   Emerson himself
had not escaped.   He too had been poured from her cornu-
copia and speared on her pen point.   In her books on the
New World Miss Martineau did not hesitate to declare her
opinion that Americans were narrowly conventional and
were guided by herd philosophy.   Literature in America
she found practically non-existent.   The reading of English reprints and a servile adulation of English thought, she
contended, were smothering the young plant.   Therefore
when she discovered in Emerson a person of genuine origi-
nality, she signified her delight by several pages of pane-
gyric which must have convinced many a British reader
that this American was one of the few great men of the
New World.

This Emerson, she told her public, was a remarkable
person: the exact opposite in intellect and character from
what was commonly regarded as typical of the States.   In
a land bent on selfish material gain, he was a thinker and
scholar, yet without bookishness or narrowness, nor dulled
with the dust of other men's thoughts.   In the hectic life
of the nation, he was a man withdrawn from the fevered
activity of the crowd, yet no hermit useless to society.
He neglected no political duty, nor was he careless of the

march of events that affected the well-being of mankind. She affirmed that while he would enter no controversy, yet he fearlessly took his stand and abode by his principles. This she knew, indeed, from personal experience, for he had befriended her and supported her right to free speech when conservative Boston was in a state of outraged shock over her bold, unfeminine public denunciations of negro slavery. Her account of him ended with a brief comment on his personal charm. Though he was earnest in spirit, his manner, she said, was lighted by an exquisite humour and a quiet gaiety. The world lay all before him, she believed, and nothing short of triumph was his destiny.

Emerson, when he read those pages, was filled with shame, and some indignation. What did Miss Martineau mean by taking away his privacy and thrusting him before his time (if ever that time was to come!) into the arena of the gladiators to be stared at?

But he had forgiven her, and he was happy to be coming to her door. She, in turn, now regarded her early praise of him as fulfilled prophecy. Ever since his landing at Liverpool she had showered him with invitations to visit her in her new house. As she was inordinately proud of it, she wished for Emerson's presence to put the seal of approval on its domesticity. And the establishment, as the guest presently discovered for himself, ran with the smoothness of oil and was filled with the peace of the mountain tops. Considering the almost explosive energies of the woman, this was amazing. But Harriet was ever a bundle of contradictions to her acquaintances : living when they expected her to die, and finally dying when they least foresaw it.

The house of her creation, which she had occupied for only six months prior to Emerson's visit, was delightfully situated. Its front windows faced southwest, looking out on the meandering Rothay and its meadows. Beyond could be seen the rocky slopes of Brow Head and Lough-rigg Fell. In the garden below the terrace stood the sun-dial lettered with the words: 'Come light! visit me!' a motto of which the old poet Wordsworth heartily approved.

Once settled in her home, Miss Martineau lost no time in swinging into a strenuous course of life which, according to the diverse natures of these observers, struck with admiration or terror the hearts of her new neighbours. Even on winter mornings she would rise before daylight and set off at once on a brisk walk. Often she would startle the household of some farmer, miles away from Ambleside, by pausing at the door for a cheery good-day in the pale dawn, before the cows had been turned out to pasture. The village postmistress became accustomed to her appearance, with a friendly greeting, at the Ambleside post office with a large bundle of correspondence under her arm in time to catch the earliest mail for the south. She loved to climb the hill behind her house, following the Kirkstone road till she reached a height which offered a panorama from the end of Windermere to Rydal. How delicious was the world when the morning star hung over Wansfell and a little shred of moon shimmered like gossamer among the amber clouds of the opening sunrise! Even rain could not deter her pedestrianism. But if it stormed, she generally contented herself with a brisk walk to Pelter Bridge and back. Yet every morning found her at the house in time for an early breakfast, fresh to begin her writing day at eight. Henry Crabb Robinson, whose ideal centred round dining in bed, was visiting the Wordsworths that Christmas, and saw much of Harriet. Certainly she manifested an enviable strength of will! 'She rises at six, walks out by moon light, bathes and has finished breakfast at half past seven. And then works at her books till 2 —!!!'

But Harriet knew better than to inflict her ways of life on her guests. She respected her privacy, and theirs also. Her mornings were sacred to her writing, whether there were guests in the house or not. They could divert themselves as they saw fit. On her return from her early morning walk, she brought Emerson the first green spray of the wild currant, which she had found growing in a sheltered nook. The elfin hand of Spring had touched the hillsides.

Emerson had planned to stop at Ambleside for only a day, but what with the blandishments of the season, what with Miss Martineau's urging that he should remain for a long ride on horseback to see the country, he decided to linger. The excursion, from Harriet's point of view, was a disappointment. The sky grew overcast, and the fells and meadows, she regretted, assumed, instead of green, their dunnest bay-colour. Yet even the sere bracken, before it begins to rot away under the rains of April, holds the warm brown of its dying autumn splendour. In the moist, more sheltered valleys the larches are touched with life, and Emerson surely could not have regarded the day as of no value.

There was one custom of Harriet's which must have met with his unspoken approval. Every evening, before retiring to bed, she would go out on the porch or the terrace for a moment of silence under the arching night. Then is peace indeed, quietude wedded to one sound, that of the Rothay whispering between its banks. February turns to April in the semi-opaque atmosphere, heavy with moisture that yet does not feel moist, and the garden, barren by daylight, becomes a shadowy enchantment, a realized dream of unreality. The little rabbits, frisky after their winter's hibernation, twinkle over the dew-spangled grass, and the dim outlines of the trees spread their nets upward toward the stars.

On Sunday afternoon, Emerson and his hostess set out afoot to pay their respects to William Wordsworth. Steel-grey days and blue are the order of February, and today the sky was again dull. Yet the roadsides of the Lake District are never wholly without colour. No sprightly dance of daffodils was to be seen for a month yet, but clumps of blue-green leaves showed where the yellow flowers would soon be nodding in the March air. Festoons of dark ivy hung from the bare trees as if in promise of the later leaves. In protected corners, the glistening blades of the cuckoo-pint formed little patches of pallid emerald. And everywhere, close to the warmed earth, lay rosettes of bluebell leaves, like fairy spear shafts, bright and gleaming. And the air was fragrant with the smell of earth.

At Rydal Chapel the two pedestrians turned upwards, leaving the post-road for the short ascent of Rydal Mount: a diminutive hill, though steep and breath-catching. Wordsworth's house stands near the top, on the left-hand side. Emerson and Miss Martineau passed through the familiar little gate and walked along the path over which broods a cluster of dark evergreens. To the southeast lies the tranquil valley of the Rothay, and far beyond may be seen the shifting surface of Windermere, dark now under February skies. Wordsworth liked best to see it on a fine winter's day, when it shone like a light thrown into the picture. Westward was Rydal Pass and the small lake like a jewel in a rugged setting — an outlook towards the sunset for Wordsworth's last years.

Emerson found little change in him. He seemed much as he had appeared fourteen years ago: an old man then, old now. Emerson's feeling was natural enough. The

American, recalling the journey of his youth, remembered only a meeting with one who had himself stopped moving while the world spun on. In reality, Wordsworth, as his intimate friends well knew, had aged greatly in recent years. Not long before Emerson's second visit the poet's daughter, Dora, whom he loved dearly, had died. It is hard for a person who has centred his affections during life on three or four chosen ones to survive the shock which comes with the breaking of the circle. In the silence of his room the lonely old man suffered long weeping spells which would not subside. For a time after Dora's death, there were fears that his sanity was affected.

But Emerson, meeting him again, found him full of talk. Wordsworth spoke with praise of Longfellow, a mutual friend, but regretted that the American possessed so infelicitous a name. The three conversed for a good hour and a half, then Emerson and Miss Martineau took their leave. Wordsworth wanted to accompany them on their way towards Ambleside, but rain had begun to fall, and Emerson would not suffer his host to brave it. So they left the old man at the door, gazing after them.

OLD CRABB

Emerson did not much wish to lecture in London. He was surfeited with lecturing. But when an imposing testimonial was handed to him, signed by Charles Dickens, Thomas Carlyle, Barry Cornwall, Bulwer Lytton, and John Forster, he capitulated. His first course was before the Literary and Philosophical Institution in the West End. It was attended largely by the fashionable and literary people of the city, who paid the munificent sum of a guinea for the privilege. The series was presently followed, again on request, by another at more plebeian Exeter Hall.

An exciting though abortive French uprising in February

had commandeered British attention shortly before Emerson's London appearances.   Some of the British aristocracy,
in fact, were still suffering from a resultant attack of nerves.
Moreover, far closer home, fears of a Chartist uprising were
agitating the city.   The appointed day, however, a dreary
cold one, had passed harmlessly by.   Yet although there
was no open violence, confusion and excitement remained
the characteristic moods of the year.   Small wonder that
when people, a twelvemonth or so later, tried to recall what
Emerson had said, they found it difficult.   The circumstances of the time (a revolution happening, as it were,
daily) did not furnish a transmissive atmosphere for somewhat ethereal discourses.   But the scene itself — Emerson
and his group of hearers — was vivid enough to memory.
Even when they are threatened with doom, citizens of a
great town must divert themselves.   Established life holds
a special relish when its very existence is in jeopardy.
Great folks, consequently, attended Emerson's lectures as
they would have attended an opera or a ball.   Lord Morpeth showed his good-natured face and the Duke of Argyle
his red head.   The Duchess of Sutherland sometimes sailed
in with a fair daughter, and was privileged to sit up forward, within the division which separated the speaker from
the audience.   And, it must be confessed, she seemed even
to pay some attention.   The fragile figure of Lady Byron,
her face muffled in a blue veil, was visible to beholders, and
the beaming countenance of the literary ringmaster of Lon-
lon, Mr. Monkton Milnes (not yet created Lord Houghton) was also to be seen.   Thomas Carlyle generally posted
himself right in front of the lecturer, and when anything
brave was said, expressed his joy audibly by vigorous hand-
clappings or loud Scottish Covenanter gruntings of approval — or at least of meditation — greatly to the edification
of the audience and to the secret discomfiture of the un-

happy performer. Young James Anthony Froude, up from Oxford, was there, and there saw Carlyle for the first time when Clough, also in attendance, pointed the Scotsman out to his fellow collegian, a fateful gesture which gave Carlyle, as many later thought, his Judas Iscariot. Every man you rubbed shoulders with either bore a title or had written a book. Henry Crabb Robinson, the chronicler, in his voluminous diary, of fifty years of London and of Europe, was of course present, generally fast asleep.

Harriet Martineau had laboured valiantly to bring Crabb Robinson to a due appreciation of her friend Emerson. Had not Mr. Robinson observed the *vague nobleness*, she enquired, and thorough sweetness of the man, which moved people to their very depths without their being able to explain why? But no, Mr. Robinson had not cared particularly to notice, and quite provoked Harriet by his obstinacy. Was not the good woman succumbing to the vice of exaggeration? How could she declare that she never read a page of Emerson's books or talked with him for half an hour without finding herself raised to her highest point?

Crabb Robinson, though a man of careless and liberal kindliness, did not like Americans. They had slippery ways of finance and their bonds too frequently proved worthless. In his shrewd adult sagacity, he believed that a young nation should be humble before its elders — seen, because that now could hardly be remedied, but most certainly not heard.

Crabb had read the *Essays* when they first appeared, edited by that madman Carlyle. He had been shocked by them, especially by *Self-Reliance*. *Self-Reliance*, he held, was mischievous, likely to foster that conceit which was already the ruling vice of Americans, and to extinguish in

their minds any glow of veneration which might still remain.   No more deplorable habit of feeling, Mr. Robinson
decided, could be found than that of looking up to nothing.

When the second volume of essays was published, Robinson, who did not like to be unprepared on any topic of
London chatter, tried again.   The day, though in mid-
summer, was unpleasant — wet and cold — so old Crabb read
steadily on, not bothering to get into his shoes to take his
usual saunter in the garden.   Hour after hour he sat within
doors, warming his slippered feet before the fireplace as
evening made the dampness grow chillier.   Well, here
was one interesting thing about Emerson : Crabb hastened
to embalm his discovery in the turgid amber of his diary.
'This is remarkable — his essays decrease in value as the
volume advances & I read backwards so I have left off
with a very favourable impression.   The Essay on The
Poet has really something valuable in it.'   One recalls the
remark of an auditor of the London lectures : 'Do you
think, if we should stand on our heads, we should understand better ?'   When he laid aside the book, old Crabb's
first, unfavourable attitude still dominated his views, and
persisted to the time of Emerson's visit to London.

On 7 April 1848, Crabb sat down to write his
brother Thomas a customary gossiping letter.   The season had begun.   There had been a pleasant little dinner at
Thomas Taggart's, and Mr. Robinson enumerated with
approval the select and agreeable company — the convivial
Charles Dickens among the number.   Then, in the evening,
after the repast, more guests had arrived.   For one thing,
the Martineaus, just before the party broke up, had brought
in the American, Emerson.   Had he mentioned Emerson
in an earlier letter ?   If not, a full report should follow
presently ; Emerson was a character who ought not to be
pushed down to the bottom of the eighth page.   Soon,

from his brother's letter of April 22, Thomas Robinson
learned more about the American celebrity. Crabb had
examined him again at a dinner given by Edwin Field, who
could generally be counted on to arrange highly agreeable
parties. Thomas Wilkinson had also been there: a very
remarkable man, an opinionated person – a mystic and follower of Swedenborg and a great admirer of William
Blake. For some reason or other, Emerson would not talk
much, and had said nothing worth noticing. Not till after
a further encounter did Robinson feel ready to size up the
wanderer from the States. 'Unless you already know
something about him I shall not be able to make you care
about him now,' he wrote, warming to the task. And then
old Crabb hastened to supply the deficiency by pumping
up the necessary information from the deep well within
himself which served as catch-basin for the world's chatter.
'*Emerson* is a Yankee writer who has been puffed by
Carlisle into English notoriety.' Crabb was somewhat
shaky on the spelling of Carlyle's name, for whom he
shared Wordsworth's detestation. 'As a writer, I have
taken a great dislike to him. He is a bad imitator of
Carlyle who himself imitates Coleridge ill, who is a general
imitator of the Germans.' Mr. Robinson felt that he could
not accept a copier in the third degree. 'His style is ultra
in affectation & I thought his sentiments calculated to
inflate the youthful Yankee-mind into precocious conceit.'
It was therefore with a feeling of predetermined dislike,
Crabb declared, that he had had the curiosity first to look
Emerson over at a soirée of Lord Northampton's. Then
and there, Miss Martineau had won her vindication: in an
instant Crabb's more violent prejudices had melted away
and his personal dislike had vanished. 'He has one of the
most interesting countenances I ever beheld, a combination
of intelligence and sweetness that quite disarmed me.'

When Crabb had spoken to the foreign visitor, he had been a little disappointed to hear the pronounced Yankee twang which did detract somewhat from the charm of Emerson's face. But further meetings served to intensify the spell of Emerson's personal manner, and he spoke so rarely that his voice had little opportunity to grate on the ear of the well-bred Englishman. It was a pity, indeed, that Emerson refused to talk. 'He said nothing to keep up his reputation, & did not play first fiddle as was agreed — Perhaps, in part, my fault — I say in part — for I did not usurp that post, but divided it with others.'

Mr. Robinson, ever judicious in his human intimacies, gave Emerson his card, an act which signified permission to call at Number 30, Russell Square, where, in his big corner house, Crabb Robinson maintained his bachelor kingdom : the rooms a confusion of objets d'art of various degrees of merit, with busts of his famous acquaintances gazing stonily down from their posts of eminence.

But Emerson had not at once availed himself of the privilege. Doubtless, Mr. Robinson thought, the American had mentioned him to Carlyle, with fatal consequences, since with Carlyle old Crabb was at swords' points. Or he may have heard of his anti-Yankee sentiments. But here the knowing amateur of life did Emerson an injustice. The visitor from the States merely was busy. And presently he did drop in to leave his card.

The diplomatic amenities had been satisfactorily consummated.

Crabb Robinson was to dine at the annual feast of the Antiquarian society, and the thought occurred to him that here was a chance further to cultivate Emerson and to aid in his presentation to London. So he took him to dinner, and was gratified to find him known by name to the

aristocratic company.   Crabb presented him to Sir Robert
Inglis, and to Lord Mahon, the chairman.   Emerson was
seated next to Collier, the Shakesperian scholar, who presently took the chair when Lord Mahon retired.   Much
good-natured conversational sparring took place among
the banqueters, Mr. Robinson himself participating heartily.   'We were merry,' he wrote in his diary, 'Emerson
retired early, after responding to his health briefly and well.
I had drunk freely for me.'

When the lectures began in June, Crabb was ready to
do his social duty by them.   'Tuesday 6th.   I heard Emerson's first lecture on the Laws of Thought.   I could not
keep awake as I never can over sermons.   The lecture was
full of sparkling thoughts and naivetes, but I brought away
with me only this one thought — that the laws of thought
were the same as the laws of the natural world — there being a system of analogues as I should say in *rerum natura*.
A good audience there & a number of acquaintance.'
Crabb, as he gave his wandering attention to the discourse,
was reminded of the rhapsodical exercises of mind of his
friend Coleridge (during those lectures, incidentally, Crabb
Robinson had more than once been observed to drift into
slumber).   These addresses by Emerson, he decided, left
a dreamy sense of pleasure, not easy to analyse or render
an account of.   Yet this may hardly be called Robinson's
own diagnosis — Harriet Martineau had furnished him with
that clue in her letter in defence of the American.   Yet
whether or not his opinion was first or second hand, Mr.
Robinson, loyal to the demands of the London season, attended all but one of the lectures of the first series, all the
while continuing to make his observations on them.

'They have offered amusement to many — while those
who have a "passion for clear ideas" [another formula fur-

nished by Miss Martineau!] shake their heads at what they
cannot reduce to propositions as clear and indisputable as
a sum in arithmetic.'

'I went to Emerson's 3rd lecture which pleased me far
better than the first — yet my memory is so bad that I can
report nothing of what I heard. The most remarkable
point he urged was the high dignity of *Instinct* — His manner was very impressive occasionally, but in general feeble.
Here was Miss Carter who requested me to stay with her
at the Lecture Room until a cab [came] for her.'

Not only did he lend his presence to the lectures; he
also fêted the lecturer. 'Tomorrow he is to breakfast with
me — I shall have a party of eight at my table, unluckily a
jumble of individuals ill assorted, and I anticipate no pleasure from the meeting.' Yet the repast was more successful than Mr. Robinson's gloomy apprehensions had led him
to expect. There proved to be no dissonance, and the host
himself took great pleasure in the company assembled to
meet the guest of honour. This time Emerson was not too
sparing of talk, and Crabb himself, as he acknowledged to
his diary, was in fine spirits. Thrusting out his long chin,
which had portentous powers of extension, to emphasize
the climaxes of his remarks, then slowly drawing it in again
— an odd habit he employed at conversational crises — he
was full of amusing anecdotes, his peculiar gestures serving
to intensify the humour of his stories. He loved convivi-
ality, and, in spite of his seventy-three years, was capable
of displaying surprising youth and levity.

After entertaining the speaker, Crabb persisted in his
faithful attendance at the lectures. 'I heard Emerson's 4th
lecture which was full of brilliant thoughts, but I was unable to connect them. He praised Owen & called Fourier
a great man; yet he seemed to speak of all their efforts as

hitherto unsuccessful. Wilkinson whispered to me "All lies" but my attention was at the moment flagging. I hurried away to dine in the Hall.' The Hall was that of London University, of which Henry Crabb Robinson was a trustee. 'Heard Emerson lecture on Eloquence, less original but more intelligible.' 'Heard Emerson's last lecture which everyone seemed. . .' Seemed what? At this point, alas, the diarist's pen momentarily faltered while its master sought for those brilliant words which, at last, might have phrased old Crabb's one genuine contribution to critical thought — old Crabb who had seen and read so much, who knew Wordsworth with such intimacy, who had talked with Goethe, yet, through all his years, had never achieved one noteworthy passage of literary opinion. But the pen left blank the space, then jogged on at its customary amble. 'It was on Aristocracy and contained nothing to offend the highborn' [Lord Morpeth, who had paid closer attention, requested Emerson to omit those sections which through their criticism of an idle nobility might arouse the common people to a revolt]. 'He expatiated on the influence of the *Individual*. Perhaps many think his lectures uninstructive but everyone likes the man.'

Robinson even went to one of the second series given at more popular prices and intended for more plebeian audiences. And for once Crabb found himself moved to admiring attention and praise. 'I heard a lecture from Emerson on *Domestic Life*. His picture of childhood was one of his most successful sketches. I enjoyed the lecture, the most liberal ever heard in Exeter Hall I daresay.' Society had pursued Emerson even to the auditorium more usually devoted to Chartist agitations and other upheavals of the mass mind. 'I sat by Cookson,' Mr. Robinson wrote in his diary, 'and also by Mrs. Jos. Parkes. She had ordered

her carriage at 10 and the lecture was over soon after nine.'
But old Crabb gallantly waited to see the lady to her conveyance.

When John Chapman, Emerson's British publisher, arranged a farewell party of two or three hundred guests for
the night of July 1 to speed Emerson on his homeward
journey, Robinson, even though he entertained misgivings
as to Chapman's social status, had every intention of grac-
ing the affair with his presence.   But the destinies, as the
unfortunate man was returning home late from his club,
interfered.   'In Dean St. stumbled against a step & fell
on my left knee which broke my pantaloons, but I also
sprained the muscles of my right buttock.'   Such are the
consequences of being a diarist in London.   Henry Crabb
Robinson dined alone at home, and never saw Ralph Waldo
Emerson again.

'POOR EMERSON!'

After his October visit to the house in Cheyne Row,
Emerson, as he traversed the British Provinces, was gradually reducing the consternation and astonishment which had
possessed him on seeing Carlyle's dreams and transcendental
visions changed to realities.   He was now prepared to behold his friend with serene and sceptical calmness.

Since their autumn meeting, they had exchanged a few
letters — for the most part brief ones.   And Carlyle, though
he had a contemptuous opinion of platform speaking and
was convinced that his American friend was wasting time
in exposing himself to the provincial stupidities of a sort of
intellectual canaille, had wished Emerson god-speed in the
lecturing business.   Carlyle's own short experience with
it, when he had spoken of 'Heroes and Hero Worship,' had
convinced him that the effort produced a mere detestable
mixture of prophecy and play-actorism.   Yet if Emerson

wished to try it — apparently he saw good reason to — why let him go ahead. And Carlyle assured him that the guest room at Cheyne Row remained vacant to receive him, when the tour was over; was, in fact, to be henceforth regarded as his room — his London sanctuary.

'Thanks that you keep the door so wide open for me still,' wrote Emerson in appreciation. He would always come in — but not, he silently resolved, as a staying guest! Too many precious things would be risked thereby. So when in the spring of 1848 he returned to London, he established himself, not in Chelsea, but in the Strand, at the house of John Chapman, his British publisher.

Shortly after his arrival in the city he did invite himself to dine with the Carlyles and they had accepted this assumption of his prerogative as an intimate acquaintance. But after this reunion, the friends of Craigenputtock days saw comparatively little of one another. Though the Universe of London held them, it was so vast that, without real effort from them, the human particles within it were not often brought in confluence. And Emerson was busy with the wonders of the city; Carlyle with the troubles of the times. Carlyle was entering the valley of his sternest mood. Visitors, always likely to plague him with schemes for mending the world, were generally unwelcome. As he thought about such callers, he felt that the marvel lay not in his surliness to such people, but in his magnanimous resistance of the impulse to shoot them on sight. 'Nobody comes to the house now, but a few followers of mine,' remarked Mrs. Carlyle with her ready wit, but not at all complacently.

Carlyle's respect for silence, his distrust of speech, had grown within him till they were on the point of bursting forth in a torrent of abuse to overwhelm these leaderless, feckless years of the world. The violent *Latter-Day*

Pamphlets, full of bitter declarations of doom and denunciation, were breeding within him. He could see only the poor present and its immediate consequences. In damning contrast lay the strong, glorious past. To the more distant future he would not look. Emerson could scarcely refrain from smiling at the vocal and visible manifestations of his friend's gospel of silence. It was droll to hear this talker talking against talkers and this writer writing against writers. Yet Carlyle took so to heart these degenerate days, it was an unkindness to be amused at him. What a sad contrast between the magnificence of his genius and the poverty of his aims! Nothing much would come of Carlyle's rantings, Emerson felt. He did not see his way very clearly or very far, and all his volcanic rumblings presaged no definite earth-moving course. Emerson decided that he himself preferred to continue to live by the limitless promise and the infinite possibilities of the future.

Carlyle's immediate woes were multiplied because of a cold which had attacked him in February and lingered with annoying persistence throughout the spring. First he had been racked by coughs, yet would not stay in bed in spite of the admonitions of his wife and of his brother, Dr. John. Next he was plagued by an inflamed sore throat, and Emerson, happening to call at the time, discovered that for once he could obtain a fair share of the conversation. And the affliction left Carlyle's nerves in a tangle.

Jane, too, found her usual portion of winter sickness, and, as the season waned, her ill health lingered in the form of splitting headaches. The household in Cheyne Row was in no mood to turn a pleasant face to a degenerate world.

One March Saturday, after a fatiguing ride by omnibus, Jane chanced to find herself in the Strand opposite a bookshop which carried the name of Chapman on its shutters.

She bethought herself of a small errand she had with the concern. So she stepped to the door to ask Chapman the single question which would resolve the matter. But the proprietor was not in the shop; he was in his dwelling above it. Strange! instead of descending to receive the lady, he sent for her to come up, a command which filled her with no little indignation. But she complied, following an employee who conducted her along two flights of stairs. There the clerk handed her over to a maid with whom she continued the arduous ascent up a third stairway which seemed to have nothing less than heaven as its goal. But instead of Saint Peter's gateway, Mrs. Carlyle discovered merely a wooden door. When it opened to the maid's knocking, Jane found herself deposited in the arms of Emerson! There were two Chapmans on the Strand, and she had inadvertently let herself into the wrong establishment. Useless to explain that she positively had *not* called to see him. He welcomed her in, called her a noble child, and insisted on showing her his apartments. There was nothing for it but to pay him a regular half hour's visit.

Later, Jane told Joseph Neuberg, who, true to the promise made at Nottingham, had been introduced to the Cheyne Row household, that she positively could not get up the least interest in Emerson, or affection for him, amiable though he was. Indeed, people who were at ease in Zion, she declared, surpassed her powers of comprehension, and she fled from them as much as the forms of society would allow.

On an evening when the Carlyles were sitting quietly at home, the door bell sounded. Up sprang the inmates in answer to the summons. And when the caller was admitted, he was somewhat mystified by the effusiveness with which the master and mistress of the house welcomed him in. But his puzzlement was dispelled as he was taking his departure. 'When the bell rang,' remarked Jane, 'both Carlyle and I said, "It's Emerson," and when you were shown in instead we couldn't help expressing our feeling of relief.'

The apocryphal story has been told of the silent night at Craigenputtock, the two men sitting together without a word, puffing their pipes in mutual satisfaction and accord. Another legend has attached itself to the history of this friendship, but it carries in it at least the germ of truth. This tale deals with the streets of London. Carlyle, so the story goes, was angry with Emerson for his optimism. He was determined to show him human pettiness and sin, and to make him believe in the devil. So the Scotsman took the American the rounds of all the horrors and abominations of the city — the gin shops and evil stews of the great Babylon. Finally, as a grand climax, Carlyle terminated the walk by bringing his tranquil friend to the House of Parliament, resounding with the din of idle debate. At each exhibition, his guide, speaking with the accents of the raven prophet who cried, 'Woe to Jerusalem!' demanded of Emerson, in broad Scots, 'Well, do ye believe in a devil noo?' But Emerson's faith in mankind remained unshaken.

Thomas Carlyle could not resist teasing his friend a little on the score of the lectures and their manner of delivery. Certainly, he remarked, it was easy enough to stand on a platform and read from a paper. Was that what one called lecturing? The Scotsman shuddered every time he recollected his own self-torture before a London audience some years ago, when, with a mere bundle of notes to guide him through the smoke and sparks of his inspiration, he had declaimed with fire and fury concerning the heroic in human affairs. But Emerson would make no reply to Carlyle's bantering, good-humoured though it was.

This contrast in manner was apparent to several who watched the two side by side as Emerson spoke in Exeter Hall. There stood Emerson — calm, unmoved, a being on whom the outward world apparently could make no mark. Carlyle, beside him, looked like a wild Saint John of the wilderness, with the flames and murk of genius within him. His thick dark hair lay confused on his forehead, and his fierce glance seemed to demand of the audience the question: 'Do any recognize me here?'

Francis Espinasse, down from Manchester, had a long talk with Carlyle about those lectures. He spoke especially of the high ethical ideal which the speaker held up to his auditors. But Carlyle, somewhat perversely, maintained that Emerson's ethics consisted chiefly of prohibitions. Espinasse tried to recall a figure of speech which the lecturer had used: how man's life on earth could be compared to a bird alighting on a rock, resting for a while, then winging onward into infinite space. Carlyle's sole rejoinder was to remark cryptically: 'Merchant! you figure well.' When Espinasse pressed for an explanation, he was told the following story. Once an impecunious Dumfrieshire man entered a shop where he had in the past made purchases, but not paid. The shopkeeper tendered him the account. After studying carefully its calligraphy and arithmetic, the recipient murmured, in a tone of mournful admiration: 'Merchant! you figure well.' Espinasse was left to puzzle out the bearing of this anecdote on the lecturer's words.

As Emerson himself had half foreseen, when he heard that his friend was quitting Craigenputtock for the town, London had worked a change on Carlyle. There were barriers of prejudice in the city, and some were towering between the friends, raising obstructions more difficult to conquer than three thousand miles of ocean had ever been.

Yet even in London, or near it, there was possible some avoidance of these.

Thomas Carlyle had long wished to visit the great silences of Stonehenge, that strange monument the origins of which lie obscured from men's knowing beyond the farthest reaches of memory. In the first days of July 1848, he found himself journeying towards the place, and the companion of the way was Emerson, whose duties as lecturer were at last ended. Amiable ghosts of the earliest days of their acquaintanceship hovered over the pair. Strange, too, that eight years before to a day, Carlyle had written to his friend John Sterling — whom both of the present travellers had loved — a letter suggesting a restful, relaxing expedition with Stonehenge as its objective. Then, as he had told Sterling, Carlyle had found himself dyspeptical, melancholic, half mad in the London summer. He craved solitude — solitude with one understanding companion. Now, in much the same mood, Carlyle had Emerson as fellow wayfarer.

They left London by train for Salisbury. The weather smiled benignly on them, and continued clear during the ride by carriage to Amesbury. True, Emerson made one tactical error of conversation which threatened to becloud tranquil skies, yet it brought only a passing shadow of disapproval over Carlyle's mobile face. The New Englander had been praising the English — they were as good as they were handsome. But nevertheless, he added, America played the game with an immense advantage. Her prodigious natural resources and her youth were sure to make her, in time, the stronghold of the British race. England was an old, exhausted island which must one day be content, like other parents, to be strong only in her children. No one can bear to be told that he rides a jaded horse, especially if he holds a share of ownership in the steed.

Carlyle was privileged to attack Britain, but he scolded his country as an old loving wife scolds her husband. Naturally he would not entertain the American's proposition, even though Emerson had as his ally the hopeful, expansive spirit of a new world, and was himself a symbol of it. The America of the first half of the nineteenth century — vulgar as she was, ignorant as she was, afflicted as she was with sores of commercial and political corruption — drew vigour from her pioneering will. She was on her path onwards. In the responsive quickening of her blood she gave proof of her awareness of her motion. To see purpose in life, to be hopeful, a nation must be going on a journey. The ultimate destination, or even a clear perception that there is one, do not matter. Vain enough, perhaps, in the end, are all such voyages. What thrills, what inspires, what lends a semblance of success, is purposeful movement. Something of all this, as the two followed the path to the Druids, Emerson sought to convey to his friend.

The wayfarers reached the George Inn, at Amesbury, in time for their evening meal, then set out on foot for Stonehenge, two miles distant over the plains. The weather had changed. With a dim, cold, windy evening closing round them, they were like men going to meet eternity. Not a house was visible on the broad downs, under the grey sky — no witness to fix the exact moment of the present. There was nothing but Stonehenge, its monoliths like a group of brown dwarfs in the vast expanse. The angry clouds heaped themselves like chaos in the winds, and all earth seemed filled with an unspeakable sadness. Yet overhead, too, larks were soaring. The grey blocks of stone brought to mind the flight of ages and the march of vanishing religions. They leveled to earth the petty obstructions which separated the two pilgrims — differences of nationality and of temperament. Carlyle was subdued and gentle. He talked of happiness, and of sadness, too. 'I plant cypresses wherever I go, and if I am in search of pain, I cannot go wrong.' The two friends clambered among the trilithons to find a nook sheltered from the wind. There Carlyle smoked in silence. Too soon, too fast, fly those moments when, obscurely, gropingly, men feel timelessness about them, and the present, heavy with its burden of human vexations, has ceased to be.

At dusk, Carlyle and Emerson left the ancient monuments. Craigenputtock was their first; this their second place of meeting.

Showers wet them as they hurried towards their Inn. Late as it was, men and women were out attempting to protect their spread windrows.

At the George, which now seemed dismal enough, the wearied pedestrians had tea, but to Carlyle's disgust there was not even milk with it. The old town of Amesbury, sunk quite silent now, lay torpid under the clouds.

Within the next few days the two companions visited Wilton, Bishopstoke, and Winchester. They saw Winchester Cathedral, grim with the dust of kings, and there the Scottish historian laid his hand with an affectionate caress on the stone effigy of William of Wykeham. At Salisbury they heard the cathedral organ, which Carlyle found not quite religious in its music, but somewhat as if a monk were panting to some fine Queen of Heaven. Then the train returned them to the city, and Carlyle was once more swallowed up by London.

A week afterwards, he wrote a letter.

Chelsea, 19 July, 1848

DEAR SISTER JEAN,

 . . . Emerson, as perhaps you know, is gone to America again; left Liverpool by the Steamer of Saturday last. He was very kindly treated here by the people he got among; and is a man who praises everything, and in a languid kind of way is *content* with everything. I think he goes home, very happy with his journey hither. I found him very amiable, gentle-minded, sincere of heart ; but withal rather *moonshiny*, *un*practical in his speculations, and it must be confessed a little weari-some from time to time ! The things and persons he took interest in, were things generally quite of the *past tense* with me ; and the best I could do generally was to listen to such psalmody-ings as those of his *without* audibly wishing them at the Devil ! He got among a poor washy set of people chiefly, 'friends of humanity' &c — to keep wide *away* from whom is my most necessary struggle here,— so in fact I have not had very much relation to him at all ; and as he sedulously keeps the peace with all mortals, and really loves me very well, I managed without difficulty to keep the peace to him ; and our parting was altogether friendly. Poor Emerson,— I shall not see him again ; and, alas, what good could the sight of him do me, or of me do him ? That is the sad lot of mortals in this world. He zealously assured me of many deep (silent) friends in America ; but I answered that for that very reason, I ought to continue silent to them, and never behold them in the body : if they once found what a 'fiery ettercap' I was, and how many of their delightful philanthropies I trampled under my feet, it would be a great vexation to both parties of us ! — I attended all Emerson's lectures here,— pleasant *moonshiny* discourses, delivered to a rather vapid miscellany of persons (friends of humanity, chiefly), and was not much grieved at the ending of them : after which, near ten days ago, I accompanied him into Wiltshire . . . to visit a strange old Druid Monument called *Stonehenge*, . . . and so, after gifts given and kind wishes expressed or understood, we parted in peace. . .

Adieu, dear Sister : be diligent, faithful, cheerful where you are : that is all one can conquer from the world anywhere, and few so much as that. Kind remembrances to James.

Your affectionate
T. CARLYLE.

Probably Jean, well versed in Scottish idiom, had no need to inform herself what an ettercap was : a large spider, fierce and belligerent of nature.

CHAPTER VI

INCREDIBLE RECOIL

ONE day, late in December, Emerson chanced to pause before the counters of a Boston bookstore. Idly he fingered the leaves of this volume and of that. Here was a curious title: *The Bothie of Toper na Fuosich!* Bothie; what did that mean — a little bower, a cottage, was it? With increasing attention he skimmed through the pages. The book dealt, he perceived, with Oxford Undergraduates — a party of them, reading with a tutor, during the long summer vacation, in preparation for the examinations that ended the final term. Such was their custom, he knew: to choose some pleasant region (as these had chosen the Scottish Highlands), and there, with books and vigorous physical life, make ready for the college doomsday. His all too brief stay among them had whetted his eager curiosity over these Oxford gownsmen. He rejoiced to find this narrative poem which would bring them in person before him. But chiefly he rejoiced in a second discovery, totally unexpected: the poem was by his staid and reticent friend, his good Oxonian host, Arthur Hugh Clough.

At home that evening, Emerson read the *Bothie* through. How one of the collegians, Philip, weary of books, left the group to wander among the hills; how he met and courted first a lively, shallow Scottish lassie, next a high-born lady (these two rather idly); lastly the maiden who lived in the bothie of Toper na Fuosich, and in her found both the love and the symbol of democratic ideals which he had been searching for — that was the simple enough thread of the plot from which Clough had woven so rich a texture.

It was a marvel how Clough had concealed from him this

genius, this sensitive gift for imagery, this broad, humorous, and kindly understanding of human nature and the problems of adolescence. Emerson felt almost vexed that during his brief acquaintanceship with Clough he had been so fooled into mistaking for the whole man what he now perceived could have been but a fraction. Certain things in the poem were quite to be expected : its republicanism, for instance. In England he had found the young Oxonian's brave pamphlet on the Irish distresses which resulted from the terrible famine of 1847. He was aware of the vehement indignations that brooded under Clough's calm and gentle nature : the outraged sense of justice which compelled the Fellow of rich, proud Oriel College to denounce from the very seat of privilege the carelessness and selfishness of the thoughtless or indifferent possessors of wealth, and to urge on them self-sacrifice for the poor. What took Emerson quite by surprise was the frolicsomeness of the poem ; its freshness, its richness in the wine of youth. It was full of exuberant animal spirits. This quality at first seemed not at all consistent with the grave young man whom he had met at Oxford, who carried, as his special responsibility, the weight of the world on his shoulders, and knew no remedies with which to lighten the burden.

Emerson had of course recognized his young friend's learning. And the verses gleamed throughout with the intellectual light of Oxford. But they veritably glowed with the well-muscled healthiness of boys, and with their delight in living. Gradually Emerson's more obscure memories recalled to him Clough's flashes of vivacity during their excursions together through the intricate and varied maze of Paris. Why yes, now that he thought of it, he had really come to discover Paris, the kindly, fascinating, livable town, through Clough's guidance, shaking off the Puritan aversion which had spoiled the city for him in 1833, the year of his first visit. Clough, in those pauses of relaxation from serious living, his friend remembered, had enjoyed life with gusto. How gaily he spent his money in Parisian cafés! What a delightful companion he had been when he released the brakes that held him in check! A singular person, Emerson now felt him to be. Indeed, a complete reappraisal was imperative. Poem and man assumed special charms by the study of the one through the other. Clough did not separate his genius from himself. His poem was a mirror that reflected an endearing image.

At Oxford, Emerson had seen the tutors and students hampered by the restraints of term time. With the aid of the *Bothie*, he was learning to see Clough and the undergraduates in the joys of their freer life. They climbed the heathery mountains; they ran races; they plunged with daring skill into the green depths of a pool, dropping like swallows from the granite ledges over which poured the amber flood of the waterfall. Competent, brave, lovable youths they were; varied in type, yet each stamped by Oxford with the mark of her natural aristocracy. The dandy, resplendent in blue waistcoat gorgeously ornamented with buttons of coral. The tutor: grave and old in learning, skilled in ethics and logic, yet wise also in knowledge of the minds and hearts of his young men. The carelessly well-dressed young man of the world: lively, cheerful, cigar-loving; a witty dialectician in the game of coining words, who invented for the group's amusement a whole new language — a word to label every occasion. These and others, characters which he had sensed yet not fully known in the University town, lived and breathed and faced the world squarely and gaily in this saga of a vacation in the Highlands.

When Emerson bade Clough a reluctant farewell at

Liverpool, the older man had sensed that Clough was in danger of sloughing off all beliefs. No man, even for the sake of truth, can go intellectually naked through the world. While Emerson had faith in his friend's star, nevertheless he felt some fear for its dimming. Clough seemed so puzzled; so uncertain of the road.

The *Bothie* was a mighty reassurance. It was the work of a man secure in his attitude toward life; it was spoken with the voice of a conqueror. Philip, the young collegian who was the central figure of the poem, was guided skilfully through the treacherous waters of adolescence to the sure land of a forward-looking career. When he and Elspie Mackaye, the Highland girl, married in violation of the musty social conventions of old England, they left behind them the outworn land, which offered so little promise, for a pioneering life in New Zealand, to plant there, along with corn and flax, the seeds of a new democracy. Tilling the earth, teaching it to produce, forcing it to his will, Philip also instructed his own soul to be obedient to the laws of the Universe. His youthful radicalism, his chartism, his hatred of Lords and Ladies were to lose their scornfulness and other juvenilities; the fundamental urge for the rebuilding of the world was to remain. Surely Clough was now master of himself, and certain of the way. How else could he handle with such deftness, such humour, such penetrating discernment, the cruel puzzlements of youth, and its joys as well as its hells?

Tennyson would have to look to his laurels! Furthermore, this was a kind of fresh and better Carlyle — Emerson reflected, rejoicing in his new friend. Here was the tone Carlyle had lost when he turned his back on the future to look toward the past. Here was modern treatment of a truly modern question, done with a vigorous abundance of experience. Emerson clearly perceived that the poem and its author constituted the most real benefits which he had drawn from his British visit.   Might Clough himself, in the fields of action and intellect, follow the pioneering career which he had set before Philip!   Such was Emerson's devout wish.   He loved to quote verses from the *Bothie* as he walked to Walden Pond — they harmonized so well with the exhilarating music that breathed through the tall pines.

Emerson fully expected the news when a letter came announcing that Clough had severed his connexions with Oxford.   Through his association abroad with Clough, he had been made aware of the impending step.   He quite realized that his young friend, in giving up his distinguished position, was leaving a career of brilliant prospects.   Yet was not the world a broad field for Clough's tilling?   Was he not fashioned of the stuff that works success?   And surely, the man who had written so brave, so hearty, so humorous a poem as the *Bothie* had acted with wisdom in leaving Oriel College.   Walls of dogma should not be permitted to confine so free and promising a spirit.   Oxford had blundered into the incredible folly of describing the poem as indecent and profane, immoral and communistic.

University Hall, an adjunct of non-sectarian London University, was henceforth to be Clough's address.   He had been awarded the headship there.

With the summer of 1852 came a letter from Clough which delighted Emerson, filled him with a fresh amazement, and also with a kind of sorrow for England. England, it seemed, was not furnishing the proper environment for Clough's expected success: he was harbouring the thought of crossing the Atlantic to fashion a career for himself in America.   University Hall had not prospered, and a professorship at London University, Clough's sole position, carried an honorarium of only £30 a year.   Like his hero Philip, Clough wished to marry, and for bread there was need to grow such wheat as he could.

Of course there was a tremendous injustice, a sort of malicious humour, in the thought of Clough's safest means of support. That an Oxford top-sawyer should be forced to tutor the dunderheaded sons of the rich in order to win a living seemed an assault on the fitness of things. Yet such employment could be found as readily on one side of the ocean as on the other. And Emerson was sure that America was a land of many opportunities for a man of Clough's abilities, prestige, and titles. The British were perishable merchandise to bring over the Atlantic. They did not transplant well in the thin soil of New England. Yet for Clough, Emerson held no fears. He urged him to come by the first boat to survey the prospects.

How good it was to see his friend again! Emerson was somewhat puzzled by the sense of weariness which Clough occasionally displayed; it seemed hardly in keeping with the resilient spirit that had created the *Bothie*. But the older man put aside his misgivings. Clough was a stout, solid, reliable man. He appeared to fit in so well. He had none of the insular narrowness, the hereditary prejudices, which so often rendered British visitors intolerant and intolerable. Clough's liberal turn of mind harmonized admirably with the temper of American life. He was destined, like the hero of the *Bothie*, to be a colonizer, though as a sower of seed for the mind, in a free and welcoming land, on a soil truly republican. The Englishman was taking so generous an interest in the activities of his new friends, and was himself contributing wise articles to American periodicals — *Putnam's* and *The North American Review*. He was working on a revision of Dryden's translation of *Plutarch's Lives*, and would publish under American imprint volumes worthy of Oxford scholarship. Why, he had even acquired a taste for American soda water!

Here, at last, was an English oak which would prosper in the replanting. Here was a tree pushing down new roots; shooting out fresh, vigorous growth; giving promise of becoming a landmark for the delight of beholders. Emerson promised himself future joys in seeking its grateful shade.

Meanwhile Clough, trustful of greater things, gathered about him a little flock of students, and Emerson went happily about his own business. The active lecturer, secure in his hopes for his friend, was away much of the time on extensive tours, and in the interim there were week-ends of sociability at Concord.

Clough may have found some lack of scholars to teach in Boston and Cambridge; certainly he found no neglect on the part of his new world in respect to hospitality and entertainment. He was welcomed with every sign of good fellowship. The Americans liked him. They liked his combination of earnest thinking and genial humour. They liked to hear his wise speech, and to watch the play of his poetic fancy. Before some — the more pompous and established, perhaps,— he became silent as an oyster. But for the most part he was fortunate in his New England friendships. With Emerson there were long hours of animated talk and argumentation. Emerson generally loathed debate, but with Clough he found it a stimulating and joyous business: his young friend was always gentle and good tempered. As for Clough his conviction grew daily firmer that Emerson was the best man in New England. But he found also other kindred spirits; persons nearer his own age. There was Charles Eliot Norton, son of a wealthy family. Clough frequently visited him at Shady Hill, dazzling the young Bostonian's eyes with the

textures of his gorgeous dressing gowns (Norton, though
of ascetic temperament, possessed nevertheless a faint trace
of the orchidaceous, a tendency held for the most part in
check by the rigorous northern climate). Although
Clough lived much of the time with the severity of a
monk, something of the Oxford delight in dress was in
his blood, and his occasional manifestations of it in Cambridge, Boston, and Concord, when he clothed himself in
a superb and radiant manner, piqued the interest of the less
gaudily plumaged natives. The Nortons were as brothers
and sisters to him; for Emerson he had a more filial regard.
In a word, though he frequently amazed them, he was a
success among these New Englanders. Emerson gave him
a banquet at the Tremont Hotel, and the best men attended: Longfellow and Hawthorne, Ellery Channing and
Lowell, Greenough the sculptor, and Charles Sumner and
Theodore Parker. It was very swell,. a grand party,
Clough, who was not backward in acquiring the idiom,
informed his fiancée in England.

He walked frequently with Emerson. The two would
follow the path to Walden, or seek the higher blueberry
patches. Clough sent to his future wife a piece of bark
from the canoe birch, a token gathered on one of these
strolls. It reminded him of his childhood. For a brief
time his family had lived in America, at Charleston, South
Carolina, and he recalled dimly an early excursion to New
England, where he had first received a vision of white
birches.

Surely the auguries justified Emerson's hopes for his
friend's American career.

Then, with startling suddenness, Clough sailed for England. A letter from Emerson had brought him to Concord; a letter from Carlyle fetched him back to London.
Carlyle might seem to have forgotten all about his young

men; his face may have been turned from them. Yet from the corner of his eye he still watched those few whom he held dear. Clough he valued more than any of the youths he had learned to know since the death of John Sterling. Clough was another Sterling to him, and also to Emerson. The Scotsman honoured his young friend for having relinquished a soft, compromising bed at Oxford to pick up a difficult living in London. He was endeared to Carlyle because, like Carlyle, he was ever on the watch for the elusive jewel, Truth, in the rubbish heap of the intellectual lumber of the day. So when an opportunity came to bring Clough back to London, Carlyle grasped it. Lady Ashburton, the Scotsman's charming friend and admirer, had secured through her connexions a post for the young scholar in the British Council Office. It was only a clerkship in the Education Department, yet it promised a steady income of £300 a year in exchange for six hours of work a day.

Clough needed a morning and afternoon to make his decision. He could now marry with some assurance of security. He left so precipitously that many of his American friends were for some days unaware that he had gone. They sent him a box of wedding presents, but there were so many contributions it was difficult to accommodate them all in a single crate. Emerson's gift was a silver candlestick.

For years Emerson could not recover from the grief of this astonishing desertion. It was a lasting regret to him that Clough should have fled without giving America half a trial. He had felt so certain of his friend's permanence in America; so sure of his success. He would not kill the hope that Clough might yet come back, bringing with him his wife to establish his castle. He locked in a cupboard some articles of clothing which Arthur had failed to gather before his hasty departure. These should serve as hostages for his return.

He knew his friend had liked America. He was aware that Clough had enjoyed the greater freedom which he had there found. He believed that Arthur was more than unwilling to be re-Englished. How could he return so readily to the Old World, leaving behind the young, the hopeful, the humane Republic?

A clerkship in the Education Office ought not to be the final reward which England had to bestow on one of her most promising sons. The thought flitted through Emerson's mind that perhaps Britain harboured too many fine young men: their lives were stunted because places for them were made all too slowly. The weary note seemed to be creeping again into Arthur's not frequent letters. He was planning nothing. His non-competitive routine labour appeared to be lulling him into a mood of lethargic drifting. He wrote that the British ship was really so big that one could not see that it moved. Ah, that was the pity of it, Emerson mused. Why should such a person as Clough be merely a stoker in the hold? Was he going to write nothing more; do nothing more? One anonymous poem had come out of England which many in America seized on as Clough's. But Emerson was not deceived, and it turned out, indeed, to be by Coventry Patmore.

But when a fledgling among American periodicals, *The Atlantic Monthly*, was established through the efforts of a little group of enthusiastic men, Clough promised to write for it. *The Atlantic Monthly* was worth the founding if only for that one result, Emerson felt. Eagerly he awaited his friend's words in the pages of the magazine. Clough's poem, *Amours de Voyage*, a narrative in the manner of the *Bothie*, was to appear in instalments beginning with the issue of February 1858.

How good it was to find again the true, the brilliant, the sensitive Clough! Yes, this new poem was durable with the sincerity of British culture, yet subtle, delicate, and perceptive in its use of the right word, and in its intricate shadowings of characterization. The new hero, Claude, bore much resemblance to Philip of the *Bothie*, who in turn had suggested Clough, as Emerson had perceived, years ago, on reading the first poem. Only Claude seemed more indecisive than Philip; he looked with more puzzlement into the confusions of his own mind, and was at a loss to choose his path. So had it been, however, with Philip, yet he had triumphantly found his way.

With each succeeding issue of the *Atlantic*, Emerson read avidly the fortunes of this new lover, who manifested, in his love, the outward coolness and carelessness, the inward passion and earnestness, of a man from the frozen latitudes. With what keenness of understanding, what deftness of minute observation, Clough traced the ravelled threads of conflicting thought and feeling which hindered the lover from making a direct and bold attack on the heart of his mistress!

'Hang this thinking, at last! What good is it? oh, and what
  evil!
Oh, what mischief and pain! Like a clock in a sick man's
  chamber,
Ticking and ticking, and still through each covert of slumber
  pursuing.'

As he read the instalment preceding the final one, Emerson thrilled at the conquest of youth over infinite doubts.

The Canto was glorious in its promise of an awakening which would carry the lover to the rewards of active life. The poetry soared to the mountain tops, and triumph was in the rushing wind of its exaltations.

Bitter disappointment welled in Emerson's heart when he ended the final Canto. As he read, his eyes saw further than the printed page. He had a vision of the Arthur Hugh Clough that was Philip — Philip who succeeded, spurning an outworn country, a region bound about with the iron hoops of custom: Philip going instead to plough fresh soil in a new-born land. He saw also the Arthur who was Claude — the indecisive, questioning non-participant, the victim of an extraordinary recoil, who stood irresolute between offered actions, and then passed, defeated, through the portals of his own dissolution.

How did the lines go? 'I have slunk from the perilous field in whose wild struggle of forces the prizes of life are contested?' Why should that be? This was such a cruel surprise, such a bruising tumble from the peaks into the shadows of a broken dream in the valley below.

What was this Arthur Hugh Clough? Did Emerson really know him? What a maze of contradictions he had shown himself to be! So able, so conscientious, yet so unaccountably failing. Where had Arthur written the lines:

> 'All at cross purpose ever with myself
> Unknowing whence, or whither?'

They were early in his career, were they not? Had Emerson, after all, been right in his first pained sympathies when he stood with Clough on the deck of the ship at Liverpool? Was he indeed a man whose brilliant intellect played the game of checks and balances with the impulses of his eager spirit, blocking its flight?

'There is a tide, at least, in the *love* affairs of mortals,
    Leads to the marriage-morn and the orange flowers
        and the altar. . . .
Ah, it has ebbed with me !   Ye gods, and when it was
        flowing,
Pitiful fool that I was, to stand fiddle-faddling in that
        way !'

The poet who wrote thus had stood on shores of other
seas, and watched other tides ebb away over the dreary
sand flats.

Clough was always surprising and amazing his friend.
Emerson was astonished when Clough died, in the forty-
second year of his age.   He had always seemed so robust !
Was it not he who was the swimmer breasting the mountain torrents of the Highlands, as described in the *Bothie* ?
How could he die so young ?   Emerson had brushed aside
rumours of Arthur's failing health : they seemed too preposterous.   His friend was so typical of the burly, long-
lived British race.   He had relied on Clough's life mainly,
he supposed, because Clough's genius promised a large and
long career.

Emerson surrendered before the astounding contradictions in his friend.   There was no use trying to resolve
them.   If only he had lived longer, these diverse qualities
might have blended for accomplishment.   But he was gone,
and could be written down only as a failure.   His pitying
friends could say : poor Clough, he accomplished nothing.
Yet how tantalizing to remember that, a sympathetic
spectator, he had followed the cause of liberty when Italy
was the prey of all her invaders, and, as the Austrians
stormed the walls of the city which the men of Brescia
sought vainly to hold, had written the glorious 'Peschiera,'
that expresses, perhaps better than any other poem in the
language, the hope of victory amid the smoke of defeat.

The amazing aspiration, the amazing retreat: they were both present in the conclusion to Arthur's last completed poem, *Amours de Voyage*. Useless to reconcile them now.

'Go, little book! thy tale, is it not evil and good?
Go, and if strangers revile, pass quietly by without answer.
  Go, and if curious friends ask of thy rearing and age,
Say, "I am flitting about many years from brain unto brain of
  Feeble and restless youths born to inglorious days:
But," so finish the word, "I was writ in a Roman chamber,
  When from Janiculan heights thundered the cannon of
    France." '

It was Emerson's custom to choose the better part. He read the *Bothie* again. How grievous that the good Clough, the generous and susceptible scholar, should die! The wine of youth was still in the poem.

CHAPTER VII

'FROM OLD YEARS, A HUMAN FRIEND TO ME'

WITH Emerson, after 1848, in Concord, Carlyle in London, and stormy leagues of water between, something had to be done to satisfy the urge of old custom and to ease the pain — imperceptible perhaps, but surely there — of old wants. But when the far spun contact was resumed, when letters again began to pass from house to house in old and new England, there could be no denial that an accident had occurred. Those latest messages seemed the same — almost the same. Yet there was an indefinable something at fault. It was as though a single light had been turned off in a well lighted room; as if a subtle change of air had killed the promise of a perfect summer day, although leaving behind a day fair enough as it was. That was the two men's problem. Each, whether he knew it at the time or not, was to play the part of alchemist. Each needed to sense what had been amiss in a past experiment, what needed to be done for the realization of the next. And what of friendship itself — the philosopher's stone?

Although Carlyle dearly loved Emerson's independence, he had nevertheless expected to find him somewhat more of a spiritual son of his. Discovery that Emerson failed him there left Carlyle plunged in an abyss of solitude. Had he not warned his friend to beware of philanthropic 'foolishness'— thus he termed it — and had not Emerson ignored the advice? So the Scotsman had made up his mind that the American was of smaller dimension than he had anticipated. Here was Emerson, a gymnosophist sitting idle on a flowery bank, apparently unconscious of the struggle with the world which left Carlyle a bruised

and weary wrestler! Of course this view of Emerson
hardly dovetailed with Carlyle's pained awareness that
some of his own best young men, wincing before the undiscriminating lash with which he belaboured the times,
had deserted his leadership to follow the American. But
Carlyle was in no mood to reconcile paradoxes: he was
fit only to be annoyed at them. And if Carlyle was aware,
and he must have been, that Emerson was speaking of him
as a danger to the mind of youth, he had real cause for
chagrin. Certainly he was piqued to learn that Emerson
had warned Espinasse not to let his style be ruined by the
infection of *Sartor Resartus* and *The French Revolution.*

But the American also had been disappointed and annoyed. Espinasse, whose keen eye missed nothing, observed that the only time when Carlyle's friend had lost
his calm self-possession was at mention of Carlyle's name.
The Scotsman's heart was as large as the world, he had
said on that occasion, but he was growing morbid. And
when he was again in Concord, and some friends inquired
of him how it fared with Carlyle, he replied, 'Oh, he sits
in his four-story house and *sneers.*'

One disagreement rankled especially in Carlyle's mind:
he could not forget some amazing ideas of Emerson concerning the future course which thinking Americans
hoped to shape for the United States. Though not necessarily speaking for himself, he had developed the theory
of the ideal Democracy: right and might without bayonets
or bishops, and every man his own King through co-
operation. With the spectacle of a blood-soaked Europe
before his eyes, Carlyle, a year after the American's departure, was still snorting with contempt at the memory
of this spiritual Quakerism. That was the year of his tour
of inspection of famine-stricken Ireland. One of his companions reported that accompanying Carlyle was like

travelling with an incarnation of a thunder-cloud or with
the prophet Jeremiah under a fierce attack of dyspepsia.
Carlyle, his eyes on the starving, incompetent Irish, told
how Emerson had voiced a belief that every man's self-
will ought to be cultivated; that men would grow virtuous
and submissive to just authority without coercion.
Amazing! And furthermore, while Emerson had admitted that there were some men in the world who were
able to govern the rest, yet he held that, should such a
man be found, instead of being put in the seat of authority
he ought to be restrained in fetters as a dangerous and
destructive agency. Carlyle with skilful mimicry described just how Emerson looked as he spoke thus pre-
posterously — he pictured his sharp, perking little face and
told how he kept bobbing it up and down and exclaiming
'Yissir, yissir!' in answer to all expostulations. Poor
Emerson! Yet, admitted Carlyle, he bore with great good
humour the utter negation and contradiction of his precious
theories.

But in spite of all this, there is no real justification for
the remark attributed to Macaulay that the two men found
each other out on the occasion of the second visit and as a
result ceased to care for each other. When there had been
a passage of time, when the broad Atlantic once more lay
between them, it was not impossible to put on again the
gleaming mantle of friendship, although close scrutiny of
it might reveal an ugly patch or two. Friendship may
be founded on things other than the shifting sands of
personal opinions.

On the first resumption of correspondence between Concord and Chelsea, a faint whiff of coldness could be felt
in Emerson's salutations. And Carlyle's sensitive nature
was quick to detect it. The fact troubled him to the
depths of his being. In his heart he knew there was some

cause for offence. Contritely he wrote, 'O, forgive me,
forgive me all trespasses,— and love me what you can!'
And he signed himself, 'Yours ever, T. Carlyle.' Trespasses indeed; and some were still to follow. There were
the *Latter-Day Pamphlets*. The very first of these had
pontificated that nothing worthy would come of the
American Republic. 'What great human soul, what great
thought, what great noble thing that one could worship,
or loyally admire, has yet been produced there? None:
the American cousins have yet done none of these things.
"What have they done?" growls Smelfungus, tired of the
subject: "They have doubled their population every
twenty years. They have begotten, with a rapidity beyond recorded example, Eighteen Millions of the greatest
bores ever seen in this world before,— that hitherto is their
feat in History."' Carlyle had first employed those words
while talking with Cobden, at whose unqualified eulogies
of the American nation he had become somewhat irritated.
The phrases, alas, had pleased their creator and tickled his
sense of humour, so he flung them recklessly to the Universe. Yet when the wails of stuck pigs, as he termed the
resultant uproar, burst about his ears, he was both shocked
and grieved. These *Latter-Day Pamphlets*, he admitted,
were proving to be little more than a purge for his own
bile, the rascally publishers having seen to it that they
alone reaped the financial harvest — leaving the unwary
author to receive the kicks. And, more serious even, the
realization smote him that his spleen perhaps had alienated
his friend. 'Has not the man Emerson, from old years,
been a Human Friend to me? Can I ever forget, or think
otherwise than lovingly of the man Emerson?' He begged
for a sign, a token, that there was still a brother-soul left
alive in the world and a kind thought surviving in Concord. He saw well enough, he admitted, what a great

deep cleft divided him from Emerson; what differences
existed in his own way of looking at the world and the
way of his friend. But—he added—he saw where the
rock-strata, miles deep, united again. Did not Emerson
perceive this too? Carlyle longed for reassurance.

And Emerson's heart melted. His next letter breathed
again the perfume of an old affection. How could one
hold out against Carlyle? For all his ill-tempered rant-
ing, for all his sternness amounting to ferocity, he was at
heart such a child! There came from him such gleams
of tenderness, so bright and so warm, that it was impossible
not to love him with all one's heart.

Emerson was again ready to entrust his young men to
Carlyle. 'If you find him inhospitable to American ideas,
and perhaps to Americans,' he told one of them, 'you
must not be surprised.' But the letter of introduction
which accompanied this warning proved to be a passport
and a talisman. When he received the visitor, Carlyle
spoke of Emerson with gentleness and affection. In his
bilious moods he may have said splenetic things of the one
American whom he really loved. He may have resented
Emerson's refusal to accept his leadership and subscribe
to his ideas. He may have noticed a rivalry, and perhaps,
for the sake of what he regarded to be the truth and
because of his assumption of the right to monopolize it,
he may have watched jealously and with alarm Emerson's
growing ascendancy among Englishmen who had once
been his own followers. Yet he remained essentially true
and loyal. He was Emerson's friend, and Emerson was
his. As the latest visitor whom Emerson had introduced
at Cheyne Row prepared to take his departure, Carlyle
placed in his hands, for delivery in Massachusetts, a photograph of himself bearing an affectionate inscription. It
was duly brought to the Concord house. There were

other letters and gifts from England, but these Emerson put aside. He kept the photograph in his hand.

'It was Carlyle himself who sent me this?'

'Yes, you see the inscription and the date.'

'But you did not ask him for it — it was his own thought?'

Emerson was reassured by his caller that the gift came as the result of a spontaneous impulse. His face lighted up. He held the picture with a grasp that was almost a caress.

'Thank you,' he said, 'you could have brought me nothing I should so much value.'

But there was another earthquake which was to open a fresh chasm between the two men — the American Civil War and Carlyle's defence of the Confederacy and slavery. Yet even over this cruel abyss, friendship sought to build a bridge.

Carlyle had always found great difficulty in comprehending why there should be such a great to-do over the nigger-question, as he defined it. He admitted readily enough that once he had spouted the jargon of the Abolitionist — but that phase of his youth had soon passed. Had not Heaven appointed some to be slaves; some to be free? It was beyond the power of Parliament to meddle with such matters. Man's mission on earth was to do his work. Since the white man was physically unfitted for labour in the torrid zones, God, in his infinite wisdom, had created the black man for that service. The black man should be compelled to perform the task intended for him. Thus reasoned Carlyle in his *Occasional Discourse on the Nigger Question*, published late in the year 1849 — the year after Emerson's visit.

When the American Civil War burst into flame, Carlyle was filled with astonishment and sorrow, then with a kind of bitter mirth. Here indeed was a smoky chimney which had caught fire! His self-betraying facility for phrases impelled him, shortly, alas, before the bloody slaughter of Gettysburg, to insert a brief squib in *Macmillan's Magazine*. It bore the heading: *ILIAS (Americana) IN NUCE* — an Iliad in a nutshell. New Englanders read it at the very same time that they scanned with fearful eyes the casualty lists of the battle.

'*Peter of the North (to Paul of the South)*. "Paul, you unaccountable scoundrel, I find you hire your servants for life, not by the month or year as I do! You are going straight to Hell, you ———!"

Paul. "Good words, Peter! The risk is my own; I am willing to take the risk. Hire you your servants by the month or the day, and get straight to Heaven; leave me to my own method."

Peter. "No, I won't. I will beat your brains out first!" (*And is trying dreadfully ever since, but cannot yet manage it.*)

T.C.'

Emerson's friends crowded about him, urging him as a sacred duty to utter a public denunciation. But Carlyle's friend stood serene and silent as a rock until the angry seas grew calm. He did, however, privately write the Scotsman a patient but firm protest. When Carlyle received it, he puzzled for a long while over it, his heart filled with misgivings. In the letter, Emerson begged his friend to leave off cavilling at the petty failures of humanity and at the bad manners of Americans and their playing the dunce's part. That rôle, Emerson remarked, could hardly fail to be the leading one in the tragi-comedy of human affairs. But would not Carlyle look up from these trifles, and leap to the suggestions and finger pointings of the Gods, which, above the restrictions of literal understanding, fed the hopes and guided the wills of men?

And Carlyle, thus admonished, began to scrutinize the murk more closely, his eyes seeking to define the shapes concealed in smoke. Gradually he altered his conceptions. At last he shook off his dream of a beautiful patriarchal life in the Southern States. He had longed that somewhere in the world a fruitful society might be founded, where there would be a great army of honest and competent toilers, each labourer, throughout his span of days, provided for by his benevolent and wise overlords: the workers in turn causing the earth to blossom like the rose. Word had come to him that the South was such a land.

The mirage gradually faded.

After the letter prompted by Carlyle's hostility to the North, Emerson found it increasingly difficult to communicate with his old acquaintance. What could he say to him? On hearing belated news of Jane's death, a disaster from which Carlyle never fully recovered, he wrote in condolence, but a weary letter from Mentone, where Carlyle was seeking recuperation, went unanswered, and there was the hush of a three years' silence. Emerson's eyes were failing: that, and other obstructions made correspondence difficult.

So might things have rested, had not circumstances otherwise conspired. Mrs. Charles Lowell, of Cambridge, Massachusetts, sent Carlyle a copy of the memorial volume of the Harvard students who fell in the war. He read it carefully. He was prepared to confess that he had been mistaken in his judgment as to the triviality of the contest. When Emerson's friend Charles Eliot Norton was in London in 1869, Carlyle was ready to make a gesture of amends. He suggested that the books which he had assembled for the writing of his *Life of Frederick the Great* be given to the Harvard Library. Norton was delighted.

Emerson and the other interested Americans must at once be informed. When Carlyle wrote to Concord of the proposal, Emerson, chiding his heart for what he felt had been a brutish silence, hastened to dispatch a letter to the old, familiar address. Again the correspondence revived, for a space, to fragrant life. The friends were growing old, yet time and the deeds of men were inconsequential in the presence of that companionship.

THE ROAD FROM CRAIGENPUTTOCK

Meanwhile another young man, stepping into the part which Sterling and Clough, each in his own way, had played, became in a sense a link between the friends. This was William Allingham, Emerson's correspondent of Bally-shannon, Ireland.

Sterling, Clough, Allingham — they had shared alike the experience of having sought Emerson by letter. Their lives bridged the years. Their names were mileposts on the road from Craigenputtock.

Allingham was only five years' Clough's junior, but he outlived him by twenty-eight years, a circumstance which placed these two men at least on opposite sides of the invisible line which separates generations. Had he lived, John Sterling would have been eighteen years Allingham's senior. Thus where Sterling was the friend of Carlyle's early middle years and Clough the friend of his prime, Allingham grew to be the companion of his old age and survived after the sage of Chelsea was dead.

It was inevitable that Carlyle should regard Allingham, so much younger than he, in a somewhat different light from that in which he had seen the two youths who had been his earlier companions of the earth and spirit. And this differing attitude was accentuated by the very nature and character of the young man himself. To see him trotting beside Carlyle as he strode through London was like watching a little Irish terrier jogging beside a huge, deep-jowled mastiff. And the rough Scotsman recognized in Allingham a weaker, an appealing fellow creature: one, he felt, who needed protection and guidance, but who, through the charm of his Celtic personality, well repaid the pains of the effort. 'Little Allingham' was his affectionate, half-contemptuous mode of referring to his friend, and indeed in Carlyle's bearing there was something of the love and condescension which a mighty human being shows in his treatment of a privileged, not very robust pet dog.

Slight and small-boned, William Allingham was shy and gentle, yet of a gregarious turn. Of course there was more to him than Carlyle's eyes were ready to discover, but Allingham was perfectly willing, most of the time, to forgive his much older friend's sometimes deliberate astigmatism. After all, one could hardly be expected to be taken seriously as an independent entity if one did not look the part. Allingham had a little moustache, which accentuated the slightness of his frame, and an irregular goatee — a triumphant achievement of his early manhood. This facial adornment was presently allowed to spread until it became a close cropped, Meredithian beard. Yet even these props to virility could not render him imposing. He bore a slightly damaged look. There was an odd cast in his deep-set, large, sad eyes. But other qualities — vivaciousness, imagination, and even a faint gleam of defiance — were discernible on closer study of those dream-ridden eyes, eyes of a peculiar and alluring shade of greyness. It was difficult to resist his appeal and impossible not to like him. To a supersensitive nature, his appearance

brought an emotion akin to pain.   Pale and thin, he looked
an easy prey to consumption.   And his health was, indeed,
delicate.

Perhaps this quality of frailness was what first won Jane
Carlyle's heart.   She had a peculiar tenderness for those
whom she felt to be afflicted.   For them she sheathed her
barbed wit and became kind, tender, and encouraging.
Mrs. Carlyle liked to give William solicitous advice not to
overtax his high-strung nervous system.   She was sorry
for him, and amused by him.   She was amused at his mode
of dress — he liked to wear clothes which reflected the
flamboyant tastes of his friends Dante Gabriel Rossetti and
William Morris — and when, one day, he appeared in a new
hat of extraordinary design, Jane, charmed with it, clapped
it on her own head to show him how it looked.   She liked
his Irish humour.   She genuinely admired him.   His
characterization of a book of Ruskin's as claret and butter-
milk delighted her, and she enjoyed repeating the remark,
declaring of Ruskin that after all nothing else could be
expected from the writings of a man who went to sleep
every night with a different picture by Turner propped
up on a chair beside his bed so that the first light of morning would bring him something inspiring to feed his soul.
And Allingham had good manners.   He had the tact to
present a bracelet to the wife of his distinguished friend,
and Jane was graciously pleased to wear it.

Though her husband, who had little use for poetry,
minimized the degree of his young friend's talent, Jane
refused to hear such criticisms.   'Dear Mr. Allingham, be
a Poet by all means, for you have a *real gift* that way.'
She read every line of his first book and was especially
moved by one poem which reminded her of her mother
who was dead.   She told Allingham that his poem had
made her cry, and that he was to consider this a tremendous

compliment. 'If you knew what remarkably dry eyes I read with generally — nay, live with generally — you would attach some importance to this manifestation of feeling!' Even Carlyle listened docilely while Jane read aloud from the little volume, and what is more, he did so without a word of critical objection and with several of praise. He had always great respect for his wife's tastes.

Friendship with the Carlyles had begun for Allingham during a vacation in London. This was shortly after the time of Emerson's British lecture tour, when the young Irishman, tied down by his duties as a Customs official at Donegal, through letters had asked for and gained the American's interest and good will. Exile in Ireland forced him to seek this means for nourishing his mind, and through correspondence with various writers he had made several precious acquaintanceships.

But though his home and livelihood lay in Ireland, London drew him like a magnet. Why not pull up stakes? seek a writer's calling in this centre of the Universe? When he reached his thirtieth year he acted on his impulse, resigning his post in the Customs Service. He already knew London well. He had many good friends there and felt sure of opportunities of various kinds to make his way with his pen. There was little risk in the enterprise and it offered incalculable advantages. If his health could bear the strain — and he determined to live quietly and regularly — he ought soon to find himself the possessor of a steady income.

Several positions, on various periodicals, were offered to him, and his prospects were indeed good. But it did not take him long to find out that a career in journalism — the only opening for a writer who required means for living — was not at all to his liking. Carlyle helped him to this discovery. A hack writer must give himself up to all sorts

of desultory and ephemeral work. He must truckle to
editors and publishers and swallow countless vexations.
No, it would not do. He would lose all freedom. Better
return to the quiet exile of the Customs Service and make
the best of that. And Carlyle entirely agreed. When
Allingham came to say good-bye, the Scotsman told him
that he was effecting a blessed escape from the profession
of literature. 'You'd have gone from bad to worse,' he
said, 'now you can do your day's work, and if you have
anything to say or write, do so; and if no man will have
it, you can say, "Well, thank God, I can do without
selling it."'

And there remained the holidays in London. The
intimacy with Carlyle could still flourish.

So for the next few years, summers usually found
William Allingham knocking at the familiar door in
Chelsea. The sage changed but little as the seasons rolled
past. In the beginning the young Irishman could scarcely
believe that his friend must grow truly old. When he saw
Carlyle just returned from two delightful months of solitude in Scotland, Allingham could not help comparing him
to a rugged peasant farmer of the North. He was so
brown — almost ruddy — and the respite from literary work
had left him in the best of spirits. But work on the huge
project of a history of Frederick the Great presently dis-
sipated the good humour. In his disturbed moods Carlyle,
refusing all comfort, would grumble eruptively at the
world, his eyes flaming. Allingham noticed, however,
that he retained most of his vigour through the ordeal of
composition, although patches of white appeared on his
not always shaven massive lower jaw, and his hair turned
perceptibly greyer.

Allingham knew how to disarm his friend. Usually his
presence could relax that grim face into a smile, and Carlyle

would turn gracious and mellow, his manner cordial and full of an appealing sweetness: his hearty laughter shattering his direst remarks into harmlessness. Allingham would sluice the talk into some channel of literary interest which contained nothing to raise the old man's pugnacity, and the two companions would sail tranquilly into sheltered waters. The books and writers which charmed Carlyle's youth renewed their enchantment in his old age.

Carlyle, not quite sure of the magic which his Irish friend exercised — nor even fully aware of its existence — admitted that Allingham's company was better than no company at all. He would often invite him on walks, or to chat in the garden or parlour. Allingham fixed that parlour and its inmates, that little garden, on the sensitive screen of his imagination till he could recall the images at will to his mind. In the garden there was a little copper beech where Carlyle, when the sun was hot, smoked his pipe in the welcome shade. And Allingham could also evoke a vision of him sitting there under the summer stars, puffing clouds into the quiet air. Three or four lilac bushes, a pear tree, and an ash tree grew in tolerant association: and a jasmine blended in fraternal accord with the ivy that clambered over the walls.

The young man's place in Cheyne Row became almost filial, and he was moved as by a son's thoughtfulness. When they tramped together, he was frequently alarmed by his friend's heedless method of crossing the busy streets. Surely he would some day meet his death thus! Once determined on advance, Carlyle would forge ahead regardless of obstacles, carrying his stick like a lance so as to poke it into a threatening horse's nose if there were need. They walked in rain or fair weather, the little man jogging beside the Norse giant as he strode to Hyde Park, Bayswater, or some other destination that he favoured.

On one occasion, when they had left the house as a yellow gleam of sunlight shone through the rain, Carlyle talked reminiscently of his writing. His books, he said, had always given him much trouble. He had brought them into the world with labour and sorrow, and now that they were done, he must reckon them but small trash after all. But usually the old man grew cheerful and jocular under the influence of the open air. He enjoyed telling his companion quaint or amusing anecdotes of the Scottish people. They were a degenerate race now, he exclaimed, roaring with laughter. Yes, degenerate! Why, in ancient days, the old-fashioned lairds used to get drunk for ten days at a stretch! Or he would speak whimsically, understandingly, of the peasants. There was old Susy, a blacksmith's daughter, who knew nothing of mathematics, yet could do quadratic equations in her head. She solved her problems, she said, by '*thwarting*' them. He told of a Scottish iron worker who was a great arguer: used to say, 'Tak' ayther side ye like, an' I'll doon ye!' Also a tale of two Scotchmen who found themselves confronted by Ailsa Craig. The pair stared in amazement at the great sea-precipices, then one said to the other, 'Eh Jock, Nature's deevilish!'

Once they talked of dreams. 'Do you dream much?' inquired Allingham, who in sleep lived in a beautiful world of fantasy — of lovely woods and flowers, of elves and fairies that danced by moonlight. 'Dreams!' exclaimed Carlyle, 'my dreams are always disagreeable — mere confusions — losing my clothes and the like, nothing beautiful.' At another time, Carlyle told how with a friend he had gone to Whitechapel to see some of the dens there. A few policemen went along to make sure that no harm came to the visitors. The party seemed to give no offence, but one woman, tipsy, said to a bobby, 'You're showing

us to the Gentlemen, but if they want to see the greatest
rascal in London they'll take a look at yourself, you —— !'
Carlyle did not finish her sentence, but added, presently,
that in all probability the woman was not far from the
truth.

He mentioned Allingham's occasional writings. Yes, he
had read his 'Ramble in New Forest,' in the recent issue
of *Fraser's*. It was the only thing worth noticing in the
entire magazine — very pretty and pleasant. But Allingham was wasting his time; he should be at work on his
history. Carlyle was possessed by the notion that his
young friend should become the chronicler of Ireland.

Meanwhile Allingham, stationed now here, now there,
as circumstances required, continued to serve as a member
of Her Majesty's Customs Service. Some vacations, instead of seeking his usual Mecca — London — he spent in
travel. At Weimar, when he visited Goethe's house, he
was curious to observe on the shelves of the dark, narrow
library an early volume of Carlyle's: his translation of
German Romances. When he opened the book, he found
the pages uncut. But the fly leaf bore, in Carlyle's hand,
a descriptive sketch of the house at Craigenputtock where
he had lived while he was in correspondence with this
greatest of German writers.

Allingham made a second attempt, in 1862, to settle in
London. This time he came not as a professional writer
but as a custom official stationed at the city docks. But
the atmosphere of the wharves proved to be debilitating
and uncongenial. His health failed him and he was forced
to pull up stakes to seek a less trying climate. He was
given a post at Lymington in Hampshire. Sad at heart,
he left London. Carlyle sought to cheer him. 'You will
be near Tennyson,' he said. But even this prospect could
not raise the spirits of the Irish poet, much as he admired

the Laureate, whom he had met some years before. In his present mood, disgusted as he was at his delicate health, he felt he did not wish even for the best of company.

Carlyle, however, was right. Tennyson liked Allingham, and even admired his poetry. He could appreciate the sensitive Irishman's understanding of nature; he enjoyed the delicacy of his descriptions of elves and flowers, waterfalls and brooks. Allingham's head would have been quite turned if he could have heard the older poet, several years before Tennyson came to know him personally, reading aloud from the Irish writer's first book among the water lilies of the lake at Coniston. Soon the two poets entered on an intimate and congenial friendship. Often they talked of Carlyle. Allingham was amused to find Tennyson quite as annoyed as himself by Carlyle's blind spots. Yet it was not hard to forgive the rough Scotsman. His ignorance of the qualities that go to make poetry, even though he had read thousands of lines of it, was so appalling and so pitiable that one could readily enough excuse him for his lack of perception. Tennyson mentioned how he had started reading the *Frederick* and had persevered till he came to the contemptuous line: 'they did not strive to build the lofty rhyme.' At that, he had snapped the book shut and flung it into a corner.

In 1870 Allingham was offered a position as sub-editor of *Fraser's Magazine*. Despite past misfortunes in his experiments with London, and in the face of Carlyle's previous warning, he accepted the post. And Carlyle himself was most friendly, and offered encouragement. Apparently Carlyle's favourite goddesses, the Destinies, were willing to smile at last. The third attempt to be a Londoner met with better fortune. Allingham remained a resident of the city, and from that time on became Thomas Carlyle's almost daily companion.

The Scotsman was still harping on his pet theme that his friend should do a history of Ireland. A little descriptive sketch which Allingham had written for the *Ballyshannon Almanac* had convinced the author of *Frederick* that here was a real talent going to waste. The Irishman's fragile poetry he hardly noticed. All that was needed, felt Carlyle, was much patient delving. Allingham should first read everything procurable that concerned his native land, then meditate unweariedly, month by month, year by year, the riddles, the obscurities, the contradictions which books offered till the whole great mass resolved itself into an intelligible perceivable matrix. That was the just prescription for the historian; that should become Allingham's task! Carlyle spoke of it with enthusiasm. Why did he dissipate his energies on verse? Why did he persist in shifting about so, and pulling up his tether, while nothing got itself accomplished? Surely what poetry there was within him could find its true release and expression through the channels of history. And Allingham did waste much precious time in an attempt to live his life as Carlyle wished to plan it for him. Patiently he burrowed into chronicles of Ireland, baptizing himself like a dull-plumaged sparrow in the dust of the scholar's road. But at last he gave up the chore as uncongenial to his nature.

Yet Carlyle would not cease prescribing. One day, as the two sought shelter from the rain under a plane tree in Hyde Park, where they had been walking, the old man, oblivious to the downpour, talked vehemently, on and on, about emigration. Then stopping all at once, and turning on Allingham, he urged him to write something on it. 'I'll take down anything you dictate on the subject,' replied Allingham, who was quite aware of his own limitations as a social scientist. Whereupon Carlyle burst into laughter at himself and his friend. Indeed, their relationship was rarely darkened by passing clouds of misunderstanding or vexation. Allingham was always happy to be near the grumbling, lovable old lion. Only once, before the third remove to London, had he entertained serious misgivings about the friendship. He had called, one evening, at Cheyne Row. There stood Carlyle, lowering in the passageway. 'Go away, sir!' he exclaimed in an angry voice, 'I can do nothing with you!' What could it mean? The little Irishman slunk off. His reflections were many and black. When he told Froude of the catastrophe, Froude replied darkly that the old man was given to strange moods. Heavy at heart, Allingham left the city. Two weeks later came a letter from Carlyle. Froude, he said, had inquired if it were really true that Allingham had been turned abruptly away from the door. 'No, for certain, never!' Carlyle expostulated. He was shocked at the thought. And he was nonplussed. However could such a misconception have arisen? Finally he recalled the circumstances. He remembered an unrecognized interloper who had knocked at an inopportune time as Carlyle was about to leave for an engagement. He had taken this human figure for one of the thousand impertinent intrusives who besieged the Chelsea house with begging letters and petitions. Naturally — the rebuff! 'Forgive my *old eyes* which no longer see clearly beyond a few yards.' No, assuredly no! The man Allingham could never be driven from that door! Allingham's company would have been right welcome for the walk up to town! 'How I have tormented myself!' exclaimed the poet, vastly relieved.

Residence in London much improved his chances to study the old man, and he made the most of his opportunities. Yet his analysis was never done in any spirit other than that of love, understanding, and respect. He admired the honesty and strength of Carlyle's rugged personality; he forgave and overlooked his faults. More and more Carlyle liked to poke fun at painting and poetry. This was tedious and vexatious. It was best to close one's ears to such jibes. Yet of course one did sometimes feel thoroughly provoked; feel like exclaiming, 'You have said your say, and I'll say my say, not yours over again, great as you are!' Yet what was to be gained by a counter explosion? Argument was quite useless. Once Allingham had begun quoting Shakespeare's tombstone epitaph, lines which Carlyle himself enjoyed repeating: 'Good Friend, for Jesus' sake forbear —' At this point, Carlyle interrupted. No, it was 'Sweet Friend,' he insisted. Nothing could be said to shake the Gibraltar of his conviction. Allingham obtained a photograph of the stone with the inscription clearly legible. In the quietest possible way, as the two were sitting on a tree trunk in an interlude of walking, he showed the record to Carlyle. The Scotsman looked at it, but said nothing. Not long afterwards, he was again misstating his beloved old formula as if nothing had happened. Discussion of the epitaph had arisen apropos of biographers. Carlyle, like Shakespeare, wished his dust undisturbed. When Allingham suggested an autobiography, Carlyle exclaimed, 'I would as soon think of cutting my throat with my penknife when I get back home!' Yet before he died he did attempt writing something of the sort. Himself a biographer, he anathematized the tribe of biographers: but such was Allingham's spell that when Carlyle's niece, Mary Aitken, remarked, 'People say Mr. Allingham is to be your Boswell,' he replied, 'Well, let him try it. He's very accurate.'

Carlyle was the least judicial of men. He wished to hear only what fed his prejudices. Allingham remembered his many futile efforts to interpret the genuine Ireland and the real Irish to his friend. He recalled other significant episodes replete with perverseness or inconsistency. There was an encounter between Carlyle, Sir Charles Dilke, and Hepworth Dixon. They had come to solicit Carlyle's vote for Dilke. But the Scotsman declared shortly, 'I never gave a vote in my life.' When the pair left, he expatiated resoundingly on Parliament and its absurdity. How could any man, he wondered, desire to sit night after night in an ill-ventilated room, listening to twaddle?

Allingham was well aware of his friend's intolerance. Years ago, he had objected to Carlyle's sneering reference to John Keats: 'If a man *can* be killed by a review, let it be done.' Carlyle, mused Allingham, is a sturdy, big-boned man. Let him be thankful and considerate. '*Carlylus Tyrannus*' was the phrase he coined for that side of his friend's character. In 1870, he wrote to Emerson, of whom he often thought in tranquil Concord, 'My chief companion is Carlyle. . . . I hear from him much to agree with and no little to disagree from — try to keep my necessary protests within the narrowest limits — feel constant regard and veneration — and get on pretty comfortably with my dear benevolent old tyrant. He often has a friendly word to say of you.'

Allingham's reflections on Emerson and Carlyle were frequently blended. He could never forget Emerson. He thought of him with a personal warmth. Soon after the lecturer's departure in 1848, Allingham, at Bally-shannon, had read transcriptions of the British lectures. And as he had wandered, during that period, by the sea-shore, it was good to look over the Atlantic to America, where lived the man who had the faculty to give high and pleasant thoughts. And Emerson had given more than thoughts: he had given praise and friendship — his own and other men's. He understood Allingham's poems, and had recited 'The Touchstone' as part of his oration in Concord on the day of John Brown's execution at Harpers Ferry for the ill-fated, ill-advised, but courageous and inspired Jamestown raid which had been so important a factor in precipitating the American Civil War.

Emerson himself had learned how he scattered seeds of friendship in England to bring a rich harvest to the young poet exiled at Ballyshannon. By letter Allingham had reminded him of the first cast of the sower. 'Coventry Patmore, Henry Sutton, Thomas Woolner (the young sculptor) . . . with a host of other excellent acquaintances, have sprung (a friendly Cadmaean crop) out of the few written words which passed between you and me when you were in England. I sent you "The Pilot's Daughter" (whence it comes that I pleased myself with putting it in the front of my volume) which you showed to Patmore and to Clough. Sutton was also named by you, and to him, some months after, I was consequently impelled to write.' Thus had begun a long series of friendships.

When an American edition of Allingham's poems was published, it bore in the author's preface a tribute which must have made Emerson blush. 'To my own imagination America is for many reasons the most interesting of countries, and especially because of a certain living Writer,— one of the men in whose rank no country has many, living or departed.' And Allingham quoted in the book the vital words of this man who was his friend: 'Let us take heed to what surrounds us. Today is a king in disguise.' When a little anthology compiled by Allingham appeared in 1860, under the title of *Nightingale Valley*, it contained seven of Emerson's poems. Indeed the Irishman was as familiar with Emerson's writings, and with Thoreau's and Hawthorne's, as if he had grown up in Boston. While he believed that Emerson's prose was so royally precious as to outvalue his verse, Allingham nevertheless felt it his pleasant task to help establish a juster balance. How different from Carlyle's was the personality revealed in those few poems. They were full of flowers: scented fern and agrimony, clover, catch-fly, adder's tongue, violets and bilberry bells! One day Allingham, walking with Carlyle through Battersea Park, paused to admire some tall foxgloves. But Carlyle would not glance at them. 'Old Mother Nature is profuse in her gifts!' he remarked, and passed by. This insensibility to the beauty of growing things was one of the oddest oddities in Carlyle: it was depressing. The Irish poet could not understand it.

Once, after a stroll (Carlyle no longer always walked vigorously), as he shook hands in farewell, Carlyle said, 'You won't walk many more times with *me*.' The thought filled Allingham with sadness. He did not wish to think of inevitable death awaiting Carlyle. He did not like to hear him say, of an acquaintance lately dead, 'Ah yes, he's out of this confused puddle that we must still go floundering in a while longer.' Association with Carlyle produced such confusing emotions! Allingham may at times have wondered, in spite of Carlyle's hearty laugh, in spite of his vigorous though often misdirected encouragement, just how good or bad for one's spirit companionship with him might be. With such a philosophy ringing in one's brain, how could one love living? He found himself, at times, supremely unhappy — quite dissatisfied with existence. 'Life slips by — to what purpose?' The blank page to which he committed this reflection could give him no answer. Yet one thing he did come to believe: knowledge and love of Emerson was enough to make one count oneself fortunate in life.

It would be fascinating, he mused, to see his two sages together.

In 1872 he chanced to meet Edward, Ralph Waldo's son, when the young American was on a visit to England. With Edward, Carlyle, and Mary Aitken, Allingham dined one day at John Forster's in the autumn of that year. And then the news had exploded. Emerson (his house had recently burned and he had suffered considerably from the shock) was coming — was being sent to Europe by his well-wishers to recuperate his health!

To Carlyle, the news was like the rending of a veil: it was like the raising of a curtain on an old, familiar play in which the actors themselves had subtly changed.

He made his friend, with all sincerity and warmth, the offer of the former lodging at Cheyne Row. But he did not expect him to accept: and his surmise was correct. Although Emerson was not to abide under his roof, he looked forward with anticipation to his coming. He would be glad to see him in the flesh again.

And when Emerson knocked at the familiar door (Jane no longer there to greet him now) the Scotsman, strong in character as ever and in manner, but yet so aged-looking, flung wide his arms and embraced his friend.

They saw each other several times during Emerson's limited days in London. 'Carlyle called today,' Emerson informed Allingham. The Irish poet who had made his appeal to the travelling lecturer twenty-five years before and the American who remembered well enough the friendly and joyful interlude of the resultant correspond-ence had at last met. 'Carlyle called today. His humour runs into everything, hearty laugh, excellent company — has always something memorable to say.'

Allingham studied his two men with loving curiosity. Yes, they recognized each other as no common mortals: they liked each other, and praised each other. They also sensed those elements of personality which were antipathetic to each, and guessed at those opinions wherein lay their greatest differences. Carlyle thought Emerson too much in the air; Emerson thought Carlyle too much on the ground. As an angel to a genie, as light to fire, was Emerson to Carlyle. Emerson held up a mild steady lamp, while Carlyle brandished a huge, fuliginous torch. One cried, 'Come up! Try your wings! Seek with me the dawn-glow of the East!' The other cried, 'Stride beside me on the solid mantle of earth!' Each, in his inner being, honoured the other's voice. The friendship endured because of its own peculiar qualities, and because each man, the Ocean's breadth lying between them, looked over affectionately to the other and idealised him. Perhaps both, in the wisdom of their years, guessed this secret of their bond.

Emerson, greatly restored in health, was about to leave for the States. When Allingham, at three in the afternoon of April 28, went to Number 5, Cheyne Row, he found Carlyle preparing to sally forth to his American friend's lodgings in Down Street to bid him farewell. Allingham, delighted at the prospect of seeing them together under such circumstances, was full of eagerness to be off. But there were unaccountable delays. Carlyle fiddled with a new clay pipe, the long stem of which had somehow become clogged. Fifteen minutes at least slipped by while the old man poked at the stubborn shaft with a brass wire. No use: it would not be cleared. So he sent for another pipe. When it came, there was nothing to do but sit down and smoke it. He rarely smoked while walking. At last they got under way, Carlyle setting out to Hyde Park by Queen's Gate and westward along the broad walk near the Serpentine. This was a rather circuitous approach to the objective, but a favourite route with the Scotsman. Presently they would reach their destination. Allingham grew more and more excited in the expectation of seeing Emerson again, this last time with Carlyle.

As he marched along, Carlyle argued over Milton's poetry, contradicting Allingham's notion as to the meaning of a particular passage. Yes, Emerson was a mild, pure, gentle spirit, he remarked presently, with an abrupt change of the subject.

At Hyde Park Corner the old man stopped short and looked at the clock.

'You are going to Down Street, sir?' said Allingham, with apprehension.

'No, it's too late.'

'The place is close at hand.'

But the hint was of no avail.

'No, no, it's half-past five.'

The chance was gone.

EPILOGUE

EIGHT years fled away. Carlyle dwelt in his lonely house, his thoughts turning often to the approaching moment of his death. He saw little of the world that was about to pass him by. 'It is very curious,' he murmured, 'the head is still the same, only the interest in things is nearly gone.' When he spoke, it was often in so low a tone as to be scarcely audible. Near him, in the drawing-room, was Jane's work-box, and other reminders of her vanished presence. His memories returned frequently, lovingly, to Craigenputtock. He and Jeannie were young then : it was good to recall the courage with which she had faced the future. It was good, even, to remember the gigantic sad tranquillity of the moors. Those heather-decked ridges knew the spell of happiness, too. And closely associated with that period of difficulty and hope was the visit of the stranger from America when the young Scotsman, though confident of his powers, was longing for a sign and received it through Waldo Emerson's pilgrimage. 'Give my love to Emerson,' said the old man, in the last year of his life. 'Give my love to Emerson. I still think of his visit to us in Craigenputtock as the most beautiful thing in my experiences there.'

Emerson, his house restored by kind friends at Concord, lived in a serene, dream-like world. His memories were fading. Yet though the years might rob him, they could not make him old. When acquaintances, still smarting from the vitriol of Carlyle's words during the civil war, attacked the Scotsman, Emerson's defence was quick and vigorous. No! Carlyle was a very good friend of the Americans! Satire indeed is his knack, and rough humour, but his aims are as good as gold. Was not the gift of Frederick books at Harvard a symbol?

The wish creating the belief, Emerson told of a visit he once received from Carlyle at Concord and of the pleasures it gave them both. He pointed to Carlyle's picture, smiled, and said, 'That is my man, my good man!' These were almost his last words.

ACKNOWLEDGEMENTS

MANY persons have aided in the writing of this book. When I recall their courteous helpfulness and see in these pages the product of their labours, I feel a sense of guilt in having imposed so on the kindly willingness of interested people to be of service in carrying out my purpose. The book is theirs. Not in big things alone, but in little also — often more of a nuisance to those concerned — I have met gracious thoughtfulness and assistance. The librarians of Free Public Libraries in British towns where Emerson lectured never failed to respond to my inquiries concerning materials. I am grateful to several not only for such help, and for readiness to extend to me the facilities of their institutions, but in addition for that hospitality which one student can grant another. I wish especially to thank the officials of the Reference Library, Manchester, for placing at my disposal Alexander Ireland's collection of Emersoniana and for providing me with comfortable quarters for study. To Dr. H. K. Meikle, of the National Library, Edinburgh, Scotland, I owe thanks for many personal courtesies as well as for services rendered in his capacity as Keeper of the Manuscripts. The administrators of Dr. Williams's Library, London, permitted me to draw on the manuscript collection of Henry Crabb Robinson which is in their care. In America, the staffs of the Sterling Library, Yale University, and of the Harvard College Library, put themselves to much trouble on my behalf in furthering my requests for material.

I wish to acknowledge warmest gratitude to Mr. Edward Forbes, and to other members of the Emerson family, for liberality, kindness, and patience. Professor Ralph L. Rusk, of Columbia University, has shown unfailing willingness to place at my disposal the rich stores of material and information which he has assembled in the preparation of his edition of Emerson's correspondence. To Miss Phoebe Carlyle I am thankful for a visit to Craigenputtock. Miss Maude Ashurst Biggs, of Idbury Manor, Kingham, Oxford, and Mr. Ernest Hall, of Liverpool, descendants of persons who were Emerson's hosts on his visits to Britain, made available to me evidence valuable in estimating the response to Emerson in the nineteenth century. My friend Stanley T. Williams I thank for sharing with me in spirit the journey to Craigenputtock. Mrs. Louis V. Pirsson has made possible the use of the portrait of Emerson which serves as frontispiece for the book. I take pleasure in the thought that two short sections of *The Lonely Wayfaring Man*, in slightly different form, first came out in the pages of the *American Scholar*.

Harold Goddard, Robert E. Spiller, and Elizabeth Cox Wright, my colleagues at Swarthmore, assisted by reading my manuscript and offering valuable suggestions which I have incorporated into the text. To the last-named I am especially grateful for hints contributing to the final arrangement of sections in the book.

C. D. Smith and Virginia Scudder, by their painstaking help, aided me through the tasks of typing and proof-reading. Only one's wife, who invariably bears the brunt, can know and mitigate these trials. To my dear friend Kent Roberts Greenfield I owe the greatest debt of all. His enthusiasm for Emerson, and for what I have here attempted to do, has carried me through the work of composition.

BIBLIOGRAPHY

THROUGH the courtesy of the Emerson Memorial Association, it has been possible to base this book in part on Emerson's manuscript diaries. These have supplied details not found in the published *Journals*, edited by E. W. Emerson and W. E. Forbes (Boston, 1909-1913), or appearing in modified form in *English Traits* (Boston, 1856), or elsewhere in Emerson's writings. Thus my accounts of his visits to Landor (pp. 7-10), Coleridge (pp. 13-17), Carlyle (pp. 18-29), and Wordsworth (pp. 29-30), have been vivified from this source. For example, the record of Emerson's call on Landor appears in the *Journals* in somewhat abridged form, and later, with similar alteration, in *English Traits*. The same is true of the visits to Coleridge and Carlyle. The *Journals* omit most of the account of Emerson's visit to Wordsworth because Emerson used much of the material again in *English Traits*. Yet this omission does Emerson some injustice. His account of the meeting, as set forth in *English Traits*, gives the distinct impression that he found Wordsworth's recital of verses amusing, and a tone of condescension is perceptible in his description. There is no trace of this slightly contemptuous attitude in the youthful diary written immediately after the meeting. Emerson's amusement was apparently an afterthought which came to him in 1848 or later, when he was reshaping the records of his two European journeys for his book on England. The diaries for 1847-1848 are equally illuminating. From them come Mrs. Carlyle's remark, 'I go up and down like an ichneumon, eating crocodiles' eggs' (p. 57), and Emerson's comment: 'In Carlyle, a large caprice' (p. 60). The manuscript diaries have also been invaluable in establishing a chronology of Emerson's experiences on his British visits.

Through the kindness of the Emerson Memorial Association, the Widener Library, and Professor R. L. Rusk, and through other channels as well, it has been possible to enrich my account from hitherto unpublished letters by Emerson. Thus the extract on page 2 referring to his wife's fatal illness is from an unpublished letter dated 31 January [1831]. The long

199

quotation on page 10 is from a letter, only part of which has previously been printed, to George A. Sampson, which Emerson began at Rome, 20 April 1833, and finished at Florence. These extracts are given through the courtesy of Professor Rusk. The letter to Landor (p. 11) is from the MS. in the Victoria and Albert Museum, London, England. It is dated 28 May 1833. The quotation on page 58 is from an unpublished letter, Emerson to Margaret Fuller, dated 28 February 1847. On page 60 I have used a few sentences from unpublished letters, Emerson to his brother William, dated, respectively, Manchester, 28 January 1848, and 9 March 1848. The description of Emerson's visit to Harriet Martineau (pp. 127-135) is derived in part from an unpublished letter to Margaret Fuller dated 2 March 1848.

I have also used unpublished letters and diaries by other hands which refer to Emerson. On page 58 I quote from a letter written by Thomas Carlyle to his sister Jean, dated Cheyne Row, Chelsea, 28 October 1847. This letter, heretofore unpublished, I have printed, with an explanatory comment, in *The Saturday Review of Literature* for 14 September 1935. The strong letter on pages 152-153, which I quote almost in its entirety, has never before appeared in print.

In the episodes dealing with Emerson and Henry Crabb Robinson (pp. 135-144), I have drawn heavily on Robinson's voluminous MS. diaries and letters in Dr. Williams's Library, London. About two-thirds of the material which I have quoted has not before been printed. The rest has appeared, often in garbled and misleading form, in Sadler's edition of the *Diary, Reminiscences, and Correspondence of Henry Crabb Robinson* (London, 1869).

The testimonial, hitherto unpublished, which I refer to on page 135, is in the Forster Collection in the Victoria and Albert Museum, London. It reads as follows :

To Ralph Waldo Emerson Esq.

London April 1848

Dear Sir

We, the undersigned, being desirous of the gratification of hearing from you a course of lectures in London, hereby unite in respectfully requesting you to comply with our wishes, (which we feel confident are participated in by a large number of persons) by appointing a time for the purpose, in order that the requisite arrangements may be made.

The description of Carlyle as the incarnation of a thunder storm (p. 170) is from an unpublished letter, W. E. Forster to Emerson, dated 27 November 1849. The quotation on page 188 is from an unpublished letter by William Allingham to Emerson dated 9 October 1870. That on page 189 is from a letter dated 12 October 1851, which has been printed only in part in *Letters to William Allingham*, edited by H. Allingham and E. B. Williams (London, 1911).

I am deeply indebted, as are all biographers of Emerson, to J. E. Cabot's admirable *Memoir of Ralph Waldo Emerson* (Boston, 1887), to the *Journals* and their editors, and to the *Correspondence of Carlyle and Emerson*, edited by C. E. Norton (Boston, 1883). Alexander Ireland's *Ralph Waldo Emerson: his Life, Genius and Writings* (second edition, London, 1882) has also been of great help as has M. D. Conway's *Emerson at Home and Abroad* (Boston, 1882). But where I have used already printed material, a large proportion has come from rather obscure sources — pamphlets, newspapers, journals, books out of print. I can illustrate with some examples. Thus the conversation between Wordsworth and Samuel Rogers (p. 16) is recorded by Ellis Yarnall in *Wordsworth and the Coleridges; with other Memories Literary and Political* (New York, 1899). The letter from Wordsworth criticizing Emerson's prose (p. 30), as I give it, is a composite from two sources. Christopher Wordsworth's *Memoirs of William Wordsworth* (Boston, 1851), II, 390, quotes this letter to Wordsworth's American friend Professor Reed, dated 16 August 1841, but substitutes dashes for the names of Emerson and Carlyle. William Knight, in his *Letters of the Wordsworth Family* (Boston, 1907), III, 229, gives the same letter, supplying the proper names, but omits the last, most scathing sentences. The anecdote (p. 40) of Alcott, Carlyle, and the vegetables was told to Mrs. J. T. Fields by Henry James, returned from a visit to London where he had been much in the company of the Carlyles (Cf. *Memories of a Hostess*, by Mrs. J. T. Fields, edited by M. A. DeWolfe Howe [Boston, 1922], p. 75). Carlyle's conversation with Alcott (p. 41) comes from 'Emerson and his Friends,' by F. B. Sanborn in the *Literary World*, vol. XI, no. 11, p. 179 (22 May 1880). The accounts of Carlyle's disagreement with Emerson over Cromwell (pp. 59-60) and of Emerson's Manchester dinner (pp. 101-112) come in great part from an obscure little book of 48 pages, entitled *Emerson; his life and writings*, published in London in 1855. An interesting annotated copy of it, from which I have drawn, is to be found in the Alexander Ireland collection of Emersoniana in Manchester, England. The name on the title page, 'January Searle,' was the pseudonym of G. S. Phillips, a young and ardent admirer of Emerson, who saw much of the American during the period that Emerson was on his lecture tour of 1847-1848 in the North of England — a fact revealed by the MS. notes of Alexander Ireland. Emerson's remarks to Clough on shipboard, on page 71, are to be found in *James Russell Lowell and his Friends*, by E. E. Hale (Boston, 1899), pp. 136-137. Emerson told the anecdote to Lowell. Much of the information on the friendship of Emerson and Clough is derived from Clough's correspondence with Emerson, still available only in a limited edition edited by R. L. Rusk and H. F. Lowry.

The account of the Grand Soirée of the Manchester Athenæum is derived chiefly from the *Manchester Guardian* of 20 November 1847. I have made frequent use of contemporary local newspapers. The quotations on page 77 are, respectively, from the *Manchester Examiner* for 2 November 1847 and the *Athenæum Gazette* for 10 November 1847. That near the foot of page 77 comes from the *Annual Report* of the Manchester Athenæum for the year 1847. Among other newspapers quoted are the *Manchester Courier* (p. 96), the *Nottinghamshire Guardian* (*Ibid.*), and the *Dundee Advertiser* (p. 100). Contemporary periodicals have also been of great value as sources. For instance, C. S. Venable's review of Froude's *Life* of Carlyle, in the *Fortnightly Review* for November 1884, furnished several original anecdotes, such as that given on pages 147-148 — the Carlyles' relief that a visitor was not Emerson — and that on page 171 on the origin of Carlyle's remark on America's sole production : eighteen millions of bores. Venables, as an intimate of Carlyle and admirer and friend of Emerson, was in a position to know obscure details concerning the two men. The conversation recorded on pages 172-173 is from the *Times Literary Supplement*,

London, 29 May 1903. Most of Gilfillan's writings, quoted from on pages 96-107, are now out of print, as are William Allingham's, whose *Diary* (London, 1907), furnished much of the material on Carlyle and Emerson in the last chapter.

What follows is a chapter by chapter bibliography of the sources which have been most serviceable to me.

PRELUDE

Cabot's *Memoir* furnishes the details for the years immediately preceding Emerson's first visit to Europe and for the visit itself. I have availed myself of its guidance throughout this section, supplemented by other books of reference mentioned in my general comment on sources. Emerson's own essay on 'Love' furnishes clues to his feelings at the time of his marriage with Ellen, and the correspondence edited by Professor Rusk reveals more fully than before the intensity of Emerson's affection for his first wife. The letter quoted on page two of *The Lonely Wafaring Man*, telling of Ellen's illness, is dated 31 January [1831], as I have indicated in my prefatory comment to this bibliography. The extract appears through the courtesy of Professor Rusk. Emerson's words on the purposes which led him to travel are to be found in *English Traits*, while Charles's letter on his brother's health is given by Cabot. The *Literary World* for 22 May 1880, contains an informative essay by W. B. Hill on 'Emerson's College Days' and his interest in British reviews and contemporary literature. F. T. Thompson has a detailed article on Emerson's early readings in Carlyle in *Studies in Philology*, volume 24, pp. 438-453 (1927). The published *Journals* are an excellent guide to Emerson's travels through Europe, giving information which I have supplemented from the unpublished diaries and note-books.

Details of Landor's life in Italy are to be found in John Forster's *Walter Savage Landor* (London, 1876). Emerson's useful essay on Landor, based on his manuscript journals, is in *The Dial* for October 1841. Charles J. Woodbury, in his *Talks with Ralph Waldo Emerson* (New York, 1890), records Emerson's amazement at Landor's dropping his 'h's'. For Emerson's statement of his disappointment in Landor: 'I love real men . . . topics which interest me,' see the introduction to this bibliography.

The date of Emerson's visit to Coleridge at Highgate is given in the unpublished diaries as 5 August [1833]. An account of Coleridge under Dr. Gillman's roof may be found in Lucy E. Watson's *Coleridge at Highgate* (London, 1925). 'You mean . . . white hair?' is from Emerson's note-books. I have here taken the liberty of turning indirect discourse to direct. Harriet Martineau's account of her visit is given in her *Autobiography* (London, 1877). As indicated in the preface to my bibliography, the conversation between Wordsworth and Rogers after their visit to Coleridge comes from Ellis Yarnall's *Wordsworth and the Coleridges* (New York, 1899). When David Scott called on Coleridge in 1832, he was warned by the Gillmans not to remain longer than half an hour. (W. B. Scott's *Memoir of David Scott* [Edinburgh, 1850]). Coleridge's friend, S. C. Hall, in his *Book of Memories of Great Men and Women* (London, 1871), makes the statement that Emerson may have been a visitor unwelcome to Coleridge. Carlyle's famous account of Coleridge at Highgate, useful in forming a picture of the old poet, is in his *Life of John Sterling* (London, 1851).

J. A. Froude and D. A. Wilson are the biographers to turn to for information on Thomas and Jane Carlyle. I. W. Dyer's *Bibliography of Thomas Carlyle's Writings* (Portland, Maine, 1928) is indispensable to any student of Carlyle. The numerous published volumes of the correspondence of the Carlyles are very helpful, and I have drawn freely on them. There are full accounts of the Carlyles at Craigenputtock in Froude's *Thomas Carlyle, a History of the First Forty Years of his Life* (London, 1882) and in the second volume of Wilson's biography, *Carlyle to 'The French Revolution'* (London, 1924). Carlyle's remarks on the loneliness of Craigenputtock without company, and his lament on the scarcity of 'articulate-speaking mortals' I take from his *Letters to John Stuart Mill, John Sterling and Robert Browning*, edited by A. Carlyle (London, 1923). The journal entry for 24 August is from Froude. Carlyle's characterization of Emerson as a 'lonely, wayfaring man' is reported by several biographers, in slightly different versions. That which I use comes from Alexander Ireland's *Ralph Waldo Emerson*, second edition (London, 1882), on which I have drawn for several other details of the visits to Landor, Coleridge, Carlyle, and Wordsworth. A review of the Carlyle-Emerson correspondence, by A. Ireland, in the *Academy* for 7 April 1883 (pp. 231-233), also furnishes valuable information. Emerson's reference to Carlyle as a childlike, brilliant man is from a letter he wrote to Alexander Ireland on 30 August 1833, shortly after the visit to Carlyle. Emerson's hope that Carlyle would never leave 'these hills of wild freedom' is from the same source. Various persons, including Tennyson, have been made the heroes of the story about the silent night of pipe-smoking. I find the rôle ascribed to Emerson in a rare, quaint little book, undated, in the Sterling Library, Yale University, entitled *Tobacco in Song and Story*. In *English Traits* Emerson speaks of his talk with Carlyle on immortality. M. D. Conway's article in *Harper's Monthly* for May 1881 (pp. 888-912), reporting his interview with Carlyle on Emerson's visit, besides containing interesting comments by its author, sheds more light on the conversation of Emerson and Carlyle.

I have taken 'a plain, elderly . . . goggles' from Emerson's description of Wordsworth in *English Traits*, which, almost solely at this point, is more expressive than the original journals. For Emerson's estimate of Wordsworth's poetry, and Wordsworth on Emerson's prose, see the foregoing general note on sources.

CHAPTER I

In those portions of this chapter which deal with Carlyle, I have drawn, as before, on Froude and Wilson. Emerson's correspondence with Carlyle, begun on 14 May 1834, is an essential guide to the relationship of the two men. Carlyle's remark, 'It is now some three-and-twenty months . . . craft of literature,' is from Froude's *Thomas Carlyle, a History of his Life in London* (London, 1884). Jane's letter to her husband, announcing receipt of money from the sale of the American edition of Carlyle's *French Revolution*, may be found in *Letters and Memorials of Jane Welsh Carlyle*, edited by Froude

(London, 1883), while Carlyle's delight on hearing the news is recorded in a letter quoted by Froude in his *Life* of Carlyle in London. While Jane Carlyle's letters furnish the primary clues to her character, information on her is obtainable from many sources, among which I shall here mention: *The Life of Jane Welsh Carlyle*, by Mrs. Alexander Ireland (London, 1891); *Literary Recollections and Sketches*, by Francis Espinasse (London, 1893); *Conversations with Carlyle*, by Gavan Duffy (London, 1892); *Some Personal Reminiscences of Carlyle*, by A. J. Symington (Paisley, 1886); and *Memories of Old Friends*, by Caroline Fox (London, 1882). These books, of course, also throw light on Thomas Carlyle, and I have drawn on them freely. Carlyle's letter to Mill in praise of Emerson, dated 8 December 1837, is from his published correspondence with Mill (previously cited). The Carlyle-Emerson correspondence furnishes a general record of the visitors from America who came to Carlyle's door.

A. Bronson Alcott; his Life and Philosophy, by F. B. Sanborn and W. T. Harris (Boston, 1893), is a serviceable guide. Many references to Alcott occur in Emerson's published *Journals*. *Bronson Alcott at Alcott House, England, and Fruitlands, New England*, by F. B. Sanborn (Cedar Rapids, Iowa, 1908), is also a valuable guide. 'What shall we say . . . wise Englishman?' is quoted from Emerson's published *Journals*. The account of Alcott's visit to the Carlyles, and the vegetarian breakfast, is drawn from *Memories of a Hostess*, by Mrs. J. T. Fields, edited by M. A. DeWolfe Howe (Boston, 1922), as previously mentioned. Carlyle's walk with Alcott through Piccadilly and his remark to him are recorded in F. B. Sanborn's 'Emerson and his Friends,' the *Literary World* (22 May 1880). Sanborn also gives Carlyle's letter to Alcott, 'You leave . . . to me,' in his *The Genius and Character of Emerson* (Boston, 1885).

Carlyle's comment on *The Dial*, 'It is edited . . . etc. . . . etc.' is from *New Letters of Thomas Carlyle*, edited by A. Carlyle (London, 1904), as is his characterization of the periodical as an *un*born soul.

Memoirs of Margaret Fuller Ossoli (Boston, 1852) and her *At Home and Abroad* (Boston, 1856) are useful records. Her friendship with Harriet Martineau, and its inception, are recorded in the latter's autobiography. Emerson's published *Journals* make numerous mentions of her. Froude, in his *Thomas Carlyle, A History of his Life in London* (London, 1884) quotes Carlyle's description of Margaret as a 'strange lilting lean old maid.' Only Miss Jewsbury's letters are given in *Selections from the Letters of Geraldine Endsor Jewsbury to Jane Carlyle*, edited by Mrs. Alexander Ireland (London, 1892), but from her echoes of Jane's remarks it is not difficult to perceive Mrs. Carlyle's feelings with regard to Miss Fuller.

Mrs. Carlyle's encounter with 'a precious specimen of the regular Yankee' is given in full in *Letters and Memorials of Jane Welsh Carlyle*, edited by Froude (London, 1883). Her comment on the drawling speech of Americans, and her flight from a tea for them, are recorded in *Letters to her Family*, edited by Leonard Huxley (London, 1924). Her self-characterization as 'a brimstone of a creature' is to be found in *Early Letters of Jane Welsh Carlyle*, edited by D. G. Ritchie (London, 1889). Symington, in *Some Personal Reminiscences of Carlyle* (Paisley, 1886), speaks of Jane's ability to sway her husband's estimates of persons. 'But, Mr. Carlyle . . . that poor man' comes from M. D. Conway's *Thomas Carlyle* (New York, 1881), while the episode of the coffee is told by H. J. Nicoll in his *Thomas Carlyle* (Edinburgh, 1881). *The Critic and London Literary Journal*, in its issue for 1 August 1851, has an article on Emerson in England, 1847-1848, by Lucian Paul, from which is taken the comment, referring to the period shortly before Emerson's arrival in 1847, 'Whether is Carlyle or Emerson the greater man?' with further remarks on Emerson's growing popularity. Francis Espinasse, in his *Literary Recollections* (London, 1893), speaks of Jane's 'wife-like jealousy' of Emerson 'as a sort of rival of her husband.' Her remark that not much good was to come from Emerson's writings was reported by Caroline Fox in her *Memories of Old Friends* (London, 1882). Her comment on Dilberoglue's admiration for Emerson's writings is taken from *New Letters and Memorials of Jane Welsh Carlyle*, edited by Alexander Carlyle (London, 1903).

CHAPTER II

The authoritative guide to the friendship of Alexander Ireland and Emerson is, of course, the former's book, *Ralph Waldo Emerson, his Life, Genius, and Writings* (second edition, London, 1882), but modesty forbade Ireland to say much concerning himself in it. The obituary notice of Ireland in the *Manchester Guardian*, 8 December 1894, goes far to supply details. There is also an informative article by M. D. Conway, 'Alexander Ireland and Emerson,' in the *New York Evening Post*, 19 January 1895. I have found useful various essays by Ireland, and reviews of Emerson's works, notably that appearing in the *Athenæum Gazette*, Manchester (10 November 1847). During the course of his life, Ireland gathered a large collection of Emerson memorabilia, including lecture programmes, manuscripts, newspaper clippings, photographs, and books. I have found this collection of great assistance throughout. Its fullness is indicative of Ireland's regard for his American friend. 'It fixes more firmly . . . are solid' is from Ireland's *Emerson*.

For a study of Emerson's British lecture tour, see T. Scudder, III, 'Emerson's British Lecture Tour, 1847-1848,' *American Literature*, volume VII, pp. 15-36 and 167-180 (March and May, 1935). It is in two parts, the first dealing with the preparations for the tour and the nature of Emerson's audiences, the second with Emerson as a lecturer and the reception of the lectures. For a chronology of the tour, see *PMLA*, volume LI, pp. 243-248 (March 1936). Emerson's letter expressing reluctance concerning lecturing in England is dated 28 February 1847, as mentioned in my general note on sources. It is quoted here through the courtesy of Professor Rusk. I have used Emerson's manuscript diaries and records of engagements to trace his course during the 1847-1848 visit to Europe. The *Liverpool Mercury* for 29 October 1847, gives the time of Emerson's debarkation as Friday evening, 22 October 1847, thus correcting an insignificant error by the editors of the published *Journals* who mention the day of the week as Saturday.

Sources of general information on the Carlyles are as indicated in the bibliography for Chapter I. Espinasse in his *Literary Recollections* quotes Carlyle's description of Emerson as 'a flowing poetic man.' Jane's difficulties with Emerson's bed are described in her *Letters and Memorials*. *The Carlyles' Chelsea Home*, by Reginald Blunt (London, 1895), and the *Illustrated Catalogue* issued by the Carlyle House Memorial Trust serve as guides during the period of the occupancy of the house. David Masson, in his *Memories of London in the 'Forties* (Edinburgh, 1908), makes mention of Carlyle's smoking habits and his favourite mixture of tobacco. Francis Espinasse, in *Literary Recollections*, gives an excellent characterization of Jane and Thomas in their living room, and the painting by Robert Tait, also helpful to me, bears out Espinasse's description. As I have previously shown, Jane's remark, 'I go up and down . . . eggs,' is from Emerson's manuscript journal. Carlyle's letter to his sister Jean is in the National Library, Edinburgh, Scotland. Emerson's comment on the Carlyles' life together, as well as other quotations from him in the following pages, may be found in his published *Journals*. The account of Carlyle's displeasure over Emerson's failure to respond to his enthusiasm for Cromwell is from *Emerson, his Life and Writings*, by G. S. Phillips (London, 1855). Phillips wrote under the pen-name of January Searle and his little book has long been out of print. 'In Carlyle, a large caprice,' comes from Emerson's manuscript journal. As mentioned earlier, Emerson's characterization of the ordeal of reading lectures as 'pounds of flesh' is from a letter to William Emerson dated 9 March 1848. The quotation which immediately follows this one is from a letter to William dated 28 January 1848. Both are given here through the courtesy of Professor Rusk.

The record of the friendship of Emerson and Sterling is contained in *A Correspondence between John Sterling and Ralph Waldo Emerson*, edited by E. W. Emerson (Boston, 1897). Carlyle's *Life of John Sterling* (London, 1851) is excellent, and has been of great service. Emerson's *Journals* make numerous mentions of Sterling. *Strafford*, by Sterling, was published in London in 1843.

Emerson's surprise on receiving letters from unknown British correspondents is revealed in a letter home dated Manchester, 28 December 1847. The letter is given in Cabot's *Memoir*.

William Allingham, a Diary (London, 1907) furnishes a very complete record which has been invaluable to me. *Letters to William Allingham*, edited by H. Allingham and E. B. Williams (London, 1911), has likewise been of service for my sketches of Allingham and others. There are frequent references to Allingham in the correspondence of the Carlyles. Hunt's proposal to introduce Allingham to Carlyle, an offer which evoked Allingham's exclamation, 'Gracious Powers ! ! !' is to be found in Allingham's *Diary*. Emerson's advice to Allingham, 'The more lonely . . . days' and quotations immediately following are taken from *Letters to William Allingham*.

In writing on Clough, I have found the following books most useful : *Prose Remains of Arthur Hugh Clough, with a Selection from his Letters, and a Memoir*, edited by his wife (London, 1888); *Emerson-Clough Letters*, edited by H. F. Lowry and R. L. Rusk (Cleveland, 1934) ; *The Poems of A. H. Clough, with a Memoir*, edited by C. E. Norton (Boston, 1862) ; the edition of Clough's poems, with a memoir, brought out by F. T. Palgrave and published in London in 1885 ; and *The Letters of Matthew Arnold to A. H. Clough*, edited by H. F. Lowry (London and New York, 1932). An article by Clough's friend C. E. Norton in the *Atlantic Monthly* for April 1862, was also helpful. Arnold's lecture on Emerson in *Discourses in America* (London, 1885) makes mention of the American's influence among the young men of Oxford, and Froude, in his *Life of Carlyle in London*, tells how the Oxonians were struck by his resemblance to Newman. Clough's first letter to Emerson is quoted from *Prose Remains*. Froude's letter to Emerson on the latter's visit to Oxford is given through the courtesy of the Emerson Memorial Association. Part of this letter has appeared in print before in a note to *English Traits* in the Centenary edition of Emerson's *Works* (Boston, 1903). The account of Emerson's stay in Paris with Clough may be found in the published *Journals*. The episode of Clough's farewell to Emerson, and the conversation quoted, comes from *James Russell Lowell and his Friends*, by E. E. Hale (Boston, 1899).

There are numerous traces of Emerson's influence on young men. Among sources helpful to me I shall mention those that follow. In *Harper's Weekly*, volume 26 (1882), M. D. Conway, in an article on Emerson in England, writes of Emerson's widespread influence on younger persons there, and, in the *New York Evening Post* for 19 January 1895, comments further on the subject, comparing Emerson and Carlyle. An article in *Douglas Jerrold's Shilling Magazine* (volume VII, pp. 322-331 [1848]), written by George Cupples, shows great enthusiasm for Emerson as a leader of youth. The Emerson Memorial Association has a letter from James Hutchinson Stirling, the eminent Hegelian, addressed to Emerson, 26 May 1866, which says, in part:

'Your works form large part of my circulating current: I have "Nature," the "Method of Nature," "Man Thinking," "History," "Self-reliance," "Heroism," & their fellows virtually by heart; it was on these I fed — it was by these I grew. Carlyle came first, but, by & by, I used to prattle of him to myself as but the eagle (of imaginative intellect say) that flew away with me to the rock Emerson — rock (shall we say again?) of moral thought. So I felt on seeing you both together in Exeter Hall at the Lecture on Domestic Life in that short course in which I had the privilege to participate in London.

'Then I have been among those who knew & loved you, as the Carlyles, Jerrold, John Stores Smith, Miss Barland, Samuel Brown's family, Phillips, Cupples, &c. . . . Lastly, I have had intercourse with many "for whom history has no tablets" — simple students — humble men — into whom, nevertheless, your works had penetrated with due effect — raising them into quietude & sincerity & thought.'

One of the clearest statements defining Emerson's attraction is that of R. C. Hall, in the *Weekly Albion* (26 May 1883). Hall heard Emerson lecture in Liverpool and Manchester. The *Pall Mall Gazette* (1 May 1882) and the *Manchester Guardian* (29 April 1882) bear further testimony. See also the article in *American Literature*, volume 8, pp. 22-36 (March

1936), 'Emerson in London and the London Lectures,' by T. Scudder, III.

The *English Review*, volume XII (1849), published an article condemnatory to Emerson, entitled 'The Emerson Mania.'

CHAPTER III

Unless otherwise indicated, all details of the Annual Soirée of the Manchester Athenæum are taken from the *Manchester Guardian* for 20 November 1847. For a useful, painstaking study of the development and nature of Mechanics' Institutes and similar organizations, see Robert Chambers, 'Mechanics' Institutes,' *Papers for the People*, III, 197-228 (Philadelphia, 1851). The annual *Report* (1848) of the Manchester Athenæum gives the figures of the proceeds of the Soirée.

I have drawn most heavily on the following three sources for Emerson's Manchester dinner for his friends: *Emerson, his Life and Writings*, by January Searle [George Searle Phillips], (London, 1855); *Ralph Waldo Emerson, his Life, Genius, and Writings*, by Alexander Ireland (second edition, London, 1882); *Literary Recollections and Sketches*, Francis Espinasse (London, 1893). As before, Emerson's published and unpublished journals aided as guides to his movements.

A source of information on Emerson, Joseph Neuberg, and Carlyle is an article in *Macmillan's Magazine*, volume 50 (August, 1884).

I have drawn on J. M. D. Meiklejohn's *Life and Letters of William Ballantyne Hodgson* (Edinburgh, 1883) for information, and also used the description of Hodgson as a disciple of Emerson in the article by Lucian Paul on Emerson in the *Critic and London Literary Journal* in its issue for 1 August 1851.

Alexander Ireland, in his *Ralph Waldo Emerson*, has a description of Phillips which I found useful, since Phillips naturally did not describe himself in characterizing those at Emerson's dinner. Emerson's remarks on Gill, Channing, and Thoreau are taken from Phillips's book. Sutton's *Evangel of Love* was published in 1847.

CHAPTER IV

The letter in the *Manchester Courier* protesting against Emerson's 'bold enunciations' appeared in the issue of 10 December 1847. The quotation from the *Nottinghampshire Guardian* is from the issue of 24 November 1847.

George Gilfillan: Letters and Journals, with Memoir, by R. A. and E. C. Watson (London, 1892); David Macrae's *America Revisited and Men I have Met* (Glasgow, 1908); and Gilfillan's disguised autobiography, *The History of a Man* (1856), have supplied most details concerning Gilfillan, while his own books have furnished his responses to Emerson. Those used included *A Gallery of Literary Portraits* (Edinburgh, 1845), *A Second Gallery of Literary Portraits* (Edinburgh, 1850), *A Third Gallery of Literary Portraits* (Edinburgh, 1854), and *Christianity and our Era* (Edinburgh, 1857). The quotation, 'a fluctuating progress . . . orthodoxy' is from Gilfillan's *The History of a Man*. . . 'Paradise Manse . . . thrown-back head' is from *George Gilfillan*, by R. A. and E. C. Watson. The conversation between Gilfillan and his wife concerning the advisability of inviting Emerson to participate in family worship appears in David Macrae's *America Revisited and Men I have Met*, as does the remark on the appeasement of the Celestial Powers. The two quotations, 'a single objectionable sentence' and 'It was translated . . . passing through it' are from the *Second Gallery of Literary Portraits*. Gilfillan's record of his meeting with Emerson is in his diary as given by the Watsons. Alexander Ireland, in his *Ralph Waldo Emerson*, quotes the anecdote, from an American newspaper clipping in his collection, concerning the supplicating quality of Emerson's glance. Gilfillan's letter to Allingham occurs in *Letters to William Allingham* (London, 1911). The quotation, 'rapt, simple, dreaming enthusiast,' is from the *Third Gallery of Literary Portraits*. 'Emerson of America . . . rather than clear' comes from Gilfillan's *The History of a Man*. 'When we think . . . our shores' is from the *Second Gallery*. 'We have heard . . . forgiveness' appears in the *Third Gallery*. 'Trust thyself?

. . . above thee' is from Gilfillan's *The Grand Discovery ; or, The Fatherhood of God* (London, 1854). 'I have been looking . . . broken glass' is quoted by R. A. and E. C. Watson in their *George Gilfillan*. 'The great lessons . . . self-reliance' is from Gilfillan's article in *Tait's Edinburgh Magazine* for January 1848, as is 'What a want of confidence . . . faith !' The final quotation from Gilfillan's diary is given by the Watsons.

Biographical details concerning Miss Jewsbury are drawn chiefly from *Selections from the Letters of Geraldine Endsor Jewsbury to Jane Welsh Carlyle*, edited by Mrs. Alexander Ireland (London, 1892), and from Edmund Mercer, *Geraldine Endsor Jewsbury*, a pamphlet reprinted from the *Manchester Quarterly*, October 1898. Miss Jewsbury receives frequent mention in the correspondence of the Carlyles.

M. D. Conway, in *Emerson at Home and Abroad* (Boston, 1882), supplies details concerning the Brays and Emerson's visit to them. 'If the law . . . other ?' is taken from that source (Conway copied the words from Mrs. Bray's guest book) as is the conversation between Emerson and Mary Ann Evans. Miss Evans's declaration : 'I have seen Emerson . . . seen.' comes from *George Eliot's Life*, by J. W. Cross (London, 1885), as does her later opinion, 'My heart . . . years ago.'

For details on George Stephenson, and for his meeting with Emerson, I have consulted the standard biography by Samuel Smiles, *The Life of George Stephenson* (Centenary edition ; London, 1881). Holmes's remark on Emerson's aloofness is in his *Ralph Waldo Emerson* (Boston, 1885).

The most adequate source of information on David Scott is the *Memoir* written by his brother, William Bell Scott, and published in Edinburgh in 1850. All quotations from Scott's diary are taken from it. Two excellent descriptions of Scott's appearance occur, respectively, in Gilfillan's *The History of a Man* and in Dr. Samuel Brown's *Essays, Scientific and Literary* (Edinburgh, 1858). I have drawn on both. Margaret Fuller's estimate, 'What he does . . . great desire' is in *The Memoirs of Margaret Fuller Ossoli* (Boston, 1852). The dinner with Scott and DeQuincey at Mrs. Crowe's is described in Emerson's published *Journals*. Scott's quoting from

Festus is told of in Dr. Samuel Brown's *Essays*. Emerson's letter to Scott, 'I carry . . . where and when' is from M. D. Conway's *Emerson at Home and Abroad*.

CHAPTER V

Emerson's remarks on Scotland and Scotsmen are in the published *Journals*. The published *Journals* and those in manuscript have been used in this chapter to establish Emerson's travels and chronology.

Information on Miss Harriet Martineau has been drawn chiefly from the following sources: Harriet Martineau, *Autobiography* (London, 1877), and *Harriet Martineau*, by Mrs. F. Fenwick Miller (Boston, 1885). Because she was a very active woman with a wide acquaintance, she received frequent mention in the published correspondence of the period. Her opinions of the United States and of Emerson are drawn largely from her *Retrospect of Western Travel* (London, 1838) and *Society in America* (London, 1837).

Carlyle's characterization of Miss Martineau as blown up with self-conceit and the most wearisome of women is from an unpublished letter to his mother, dated Chelsea, 16 November 1846. The manuscript is in the National Library, Edinburgh, Scotland. Crabb Robinson's amazement at Miss Martineau's mode of life, 'she rises at six . . . till 2 —!!!' is from *The Correspondence of Henry Crabb Robinson with the Wordsworth Circle*, edited by Edith J. Morley (Oxford, 1927).

For the description of Emerson's call on Wordsworth with Miss Martineau I have drawn chiefly on *English Traits*. Biographical details for Wordsworth are from *William Wordsworth, his Life, Works, and Influence*, by George McLean Harper (New York, 1929, third edition).

With regard to the testimonial requesting that Emerson lecture in London, see the prefatory remarks to this bibliography. For a study of Emerson and his lectures there, see T. Scudder, III, 'Emerson in London and the London Lectures,' *American Literature*, volume 8, pp. 22-36 (March 1936). A detailed contemporary account of the lectures which I have freely drawn on is to be found in the article by Lucian Paul on Emerson in *The Critic and London Literary Journal* (1 August 1851).

For information on sources for Henry Crabb Robinson, see the introductory section of this bibliography. Unless otherwise noted, all quotations from Robinson or paraphrases of his opinions of Emerson and his writings are from the manuscripts in Dr. Williams's Library, London.

The comment, 'Do you think . . . understand better?' is quoted by Emerson himself in the published *Journals*.

Miss Martineau's letter seeking to explain Emerson to Crabb Robinson, to which I have several times referred, is dated 8 June 1848. It is in Dr. Williams's Library.

The incident concerning Lord Morpeth's objection to parts of Emerson's lecture on 'Natural Aristocracy' is revealed in a footnote to *English Traits* (Centenary Edition, 1903). For sources on the Carlyles, see this bibliography under the Prelude and Chapter I. 'Nobody comes . . . followers of mine' is quoted from Espinasse's *Literary Recollections*. Jane Carlyle's remark on her lack of affection for Emerson may be found in *Letters of Jane Welsh Carlyle to Joseph Neuberg*, edited by T. Scudder, III (Oxford, 1931). 'When the bell . . . relief' is in a review of Froude's *Thomas Carlyle, the History of his Life in London*. The article is by G. S. Venables and appeared in the *Fortnightly Review* of November 1884. I have found two sources for the story of Carlyle's walk with Emerson through London. They are Richard Garnett's *Life of Thomas Carlyle* (London, 1887) and J. W. Cross's *George Eliot's Life* (London, 1885). The versions differ slightly. The comparison of Carlyle and Emerson at Exeter Hall, including the quotation, 'do any recognize me here?' is from an article by J. Hutchinson Stirling in the *University Independent*, of Glasgow University, second series, No. 3 (7 April 1874). Espinasse's anecdote of Carlyle's rejoinder, 'Merchant! you figure well,' is in his *Literary Recollections*.

The account of the visit to Stonehenge is derived from Emerson's unpublished diaries, *English Traits*, and Carlyle's correspondence. 'I plant cypresses . . . wrong' is taken from *English Traits*.

Carlyle's letter to his sister Jean Aitken is from the manuscript in the National Library, Edinburgh, Scotland.

CHAPTER VI

See the bibliography of Chapter II for sources for Clough. In addition to using material there cited, I have drawn on Emerson's *Journals*.

The title of Clough's poem of the Oxford reading party in the Highlands underwent several changes; the form here given is as it first appeared.

CHAPTER VII

For a list of materials used for the Carlyles, look in this bibliography under the Prelude and Chapter I. Other sources are indicated below.

'Oh, he sits . . . *sneers*' is from *Recollections of Seventy Years*, by F. B. Sanborn (Boston, 1909). Emerson's conversation with Carlyle on the hope for Democracy in America is recorded in *Letters from Ralph Waldo Emerson to a Friend*, edited by C. E. Norton (Boston, 1899). In *Literary Recollections*, Espinasse speaks of Carlyle's amazement at such doctrines. W. E. Forster, Carlyle's travelling companion in Ireland, made the remark comparing Carlyle to a thundercloud. It is taken from a manuscript letter dated 27 November 1849, W. E. Forster to Emerson, in the keeping of the Emerson Memorial Association. Gavan Duffy was the observer of Carlyle's mimicry of Emerson and recorded the episode in his *Conversations with Carlyle* (London, 1892). The first of the *Latter-Day Pamphlets* was that on 'The Present Time.' 'What great . . . History' is taken from it. G. S. Venables, in the *Fortnightly Review* for November 1884 (pp. 598-599), gives the genesis of Carlyle's remark on the eighteen millions of bores. The episode of the young visitor sent by Emerson to Carlyle, with the recorded conversation, 'If you . . . surprised,' 'It was . . . value,' is from the leading article, 'Ralph Waldo Emerson,' in the *Times Literary Supplement*, 29 May 1903. Carlyle's *Occasional Discourse on the Nigger*

Question was first published, under a slightly different title, in *Fraser's Magazine* for December 1849. The squib in *Macmillan's Magazine* appeared in the issue for August 1863. Mrs. J. T. Fields, 'Glimpses of Emerson,' *Harper's New Monthly Magazine* (February 1884), tells how Emerson's friends tried to make him turn against Carlyle, and of his refusal. In M. D. Conway's *Thomas Carlyle* (New York, 1881) are set forth Carlyle's ideas on the Southern Confederacy. *Letters of Charles Eliot Norton*, edited by Sara Norton and M. A. De-Wolfe Howe (Boston, 1913), tell of Carlyle's gift of books to the Harvard Library.

Sources of general information on William Allingham are as given in the bibliography for Chapter II. *William Allingham, a Diary* (London, 1907) has been used throughout Chapter VII. 'Dear Mr. Allingham . . . that way' is taken from *Letters to William Allingham* (London, 1911), as is 'If you knew . . . feeling.' Carlyle's advice against a literary career, 'You'd have gone . . . selling it' comes from Allingham's *Diary* as do all the following quotations from Carlyle, unless otherwise noted. Carlyle's letter concerning the unintended slight to Allingham is from the *Letters to William Allingham*. The manuscript of Allingham's letter to Emerson, 'My chief companion . . . say of you' is in the keeping of the Emerson Memorial Association. The letter is dated 9 October 1870. The second letter, 'Coventry Patmore . . . to write,' from the same collection, is dated 12 October 1851. It has been printed in part in *Letters to William Allingham*. Emerson's remarks to Allingham on Carlyle's call are in Allingham's *Diary*, as is the conversation between Carlyle and Allingham at the time of the incompleted farewell call.

EXPLICIT

M. D. Conway's *Autobiography, Memoirs and Experience* (Boston, 1904) furnishes a glimpse of Carlyle in the last year of his life, and Carlyle's greeting to Emerson is taken from that source.

C. E. Norton, in a letter to Carlyle dated 26 July 1880, told of Emerson's belief that he had received a visit from Carlyle

at Concord.   The letter is in Norton's correspondence edited
by Sara Norton and M. A. DeWolfe Howe.   'That is my
man, my good man!' is taken from *Emerson in Concord*,
by E. W. Emerson (Boston, 1889).

INDEX

A

Acland, Dr. Henry, 69
Ainsworth, W. H., 79
Aitken, James, 153
Aitken, Jean, sister of Carlyle, 57-58, 152-153
Aitken, Mary, niece of Carlyle, 187, 191
Alcott, Amos Bronson, 38-41, 42, 55, 111
Alison, Archibald, 77, 79, 80, 82
Allingham, William, 65-68, 103-104, 176-193
Allston, Washington, 14
Ambleside, 127, 128, 132, 133, 135
America, United States of, 13, 14, 17, 26, 28, 30, 33, 34, 35, 38, 41, 42, 43, 50, 52, 55, 62, 70, 130, 150-151, 152, 153, 158, 162-163, 171, 188, 189
'American Scholar, The,' by Emerson, 36
Amesbury, 150, 151, 152
Amours de Voyage, by Clough, 164-167
Antiquarian Society, London, 140
Argyle, Duke of, 136
'Aristocracy,' Emerson's lecture on, 143
Arnold, Matthew, 69
Arnold, Dr. Thomas, 68
Ashburton, Lady, 162
Athenaeum Gazette, 77
Atlantic Monthly, 163, 164

B

Bacon, Francis, Lord, 59, 80
Bailey, Philip James, 87, 125
Baird, General Absalom, 46
Ballantyne, Thomas, 42, 93
Ballyshannon, 65, 176, 188, 189
Ballyshannon Almanac, 185

Baring, Lady Harriet, 46
Barnard, Henry, 37, 38
Birmingham, 90, 94, 95
Bishopstoke, 152
Blackwood, Robert, 79
Blake, William, 139
Boccaccio, 6
Boston, Massachusetts, 2, 3, 7, 34, 51, 82, 115, 131, 154, 160, 161, 189
Bothie of Toper na Fuosich, by Clough, 154-158, 159, 164 ff.
Bowring, John, 79, 80
Brackley, Viscount, 79
Bradford, 127
Bray, Charles, 111, 112
Bray, Mrs. Charles, 111-112
Bright, John, 52, 74, 79
British and Foreign Unitarian Association, 128-129
British Institution, 120
British Museum, 93
Brown, John, 189
Brown, Dr. Samuel, 125
Browning, Robert, 41, 66
Buller, Charles, 47
Burke, Edmund, 80
Byron, 3, 5, 11
Byron, Lady, 136

C

Cambridge, Massachusetts, 160, 161, 175
Cambridge University, 61
Carlyle, Mrs. James, mother of Thomas Carlyle, 29, 38
Carlyle, Jane, 18, 19, 25, 32, 33, 34, 35, 40, 43-49, 50, 56, 57, 66, 108, 109, 110, 145, 146-148, 175, 178-179, 191, 194
Carlyle, Dr. John, brother of Thomas Carlyle, 19, 20, 57
Carlyle, Thomas, 3, 4, 10, 16, 18-20, 23-25, 26, 27, 28-29, 31, 32-38, 39-

Carlyle, Thomas (*Cont'd*)
41, 42, 43, 44, 45-46, 47, 48, 49, 51,
54-55, 56-60, 61-62, 63, 65, 66-67,
68, 70, 71, 72, 87-88, 92, 93, 98,
105, 108-109, 110, 129, 135, 136-
137, 139, 140, 144-146, 147-153,
157, 161-162, 168-177, 178, 179,
180-183, 184-188, 190, 191-193,
194, 195
Céard, Nicholas, 12
Chalmers, Dr. Thomas, 52
Channing, Ellery (American poet),
91, 161
Channing, Dr. W. E., 14, 15
Chapman, John, 144, 145, 146-147
Charleston, South Carolina, 161
Chelsea, 37, 40, 45, 54, 56, 65, 145,
170, 180
Chesterfield, 113, 115
Cheyne Row, 32, 35, 41, 44, 56, 99,
144, 145, 146, 147, 172, 181, 186,
191, 192
Child, Lydia Maria, 37
Christianity and our Era, by Gil-
fillan, 105-106
Civil War, American, 81, 173-176,
189, 194
Clough, Anne Jemima, 69
Clough, Arthur Hugh, 68, 69-71,
137, 154-167, 176, 189
Cobden, Richard, 77, 79, 80, 82, 171
Coleridge, S. T., 3, 4, 13-17, 24, 50,
51, 139, 141
Collier, John Payne, 141
Concord, 28, 38, 41, 42, 55, 58, 61,
87, 105, 112, 116, 127, 160, 161,
168, 169, 170, 171, 172, 176, 188,
189, 194, 195
'Concord Centennial Address,' by
Emerson, 36
Conduct of Life, by Emerson, 106
Confessions, by Rousseau, 112
Coniston, 184
Connecticut, 21, 37
Corn Law reform, 74, 80
Cornwall, Barry, pen name of
B. W. Procter, 135
Coventry, 111, 112

Craigenputtock, 18, 20, 22, 23, 32,
33, 35, 36, 54, 56, 62, 68, 148, 149,
152, 176, 183
Crawshay, George, 64
Cromwell, Oliver, 56, 59-60
Crossley, James, 85
Crowe, Mrs., Emerson's hostess at
Edinburgh, 125
Cruikshank, George, 79, 80, 82
Cumberland, 128

D

Dal Verme, Conte, 12
Dante, 6
Darnley, J. R., 121
Darwin, Charles, 45, 59
Darwin, Erasmus, 45, 58, 59
Dawson, George, 94
Decameron, Boccaccio's, 6
Deerbrook, by Harriet Martineau,
129
DeQuincey, Thomas, 3, 51, 125
Dial, The, 42, 55
Dickens, Charles, 6, 66, 76, 77, 79,
135, 138
Dilberoglue, Stavros, 49
Dilke, Sir Charles, 188
Disraeli, Benjamin, 76
'Divinity School Address,' by
Emerson, 36
Divinity School, Cambridge,
Massachusetts, 1
Dixon, Hepworth, 188
'Domestic Life,' Emerson's lecture
on, 143
Donegal, 65, 179
Dryden, John, 159
Dumfries, 18, 21, 24, 57
Dumfrieshire, 27, 57
Dundee, 97, 99, 101, 102, 104, 107,
127
Dunscore, 18, 21, 22

E

Ecclefechan, 29
Eckermann, 43

Edinburgh, 18, 20, 50, 52, 79, 97, 120, 122, 123, 124, 126

Edinburgh Review, 4

Education Department, British Council Office, 162-163

Eliot, George, pen name of Mary Ann Evans, 112-113

'Eloquence,' Emerson's lecture on, 101, 143

Emerson, Charles, brother of R. W. Emerson, 3, 10

Emerson, Edward, son of R. W. Emerson, 191

Emerson, Mrs. Ellen Louisa (Tucker), first wife of R. W. Emerson, 2, 24, 28, 64

Emerson, Mrs. Lidian, second wife of R. W. Emerson, 112

Emerson, Mary Moody, aunt of R. W. Emerson, 3

Emerson, Ralph Waldo, early ill health, 1, 3, 5, 10 ; ordination, 2 ; marriage, 2 ; illness and death of first wife, 2 ; resignation of pastorate, 3 ; determination to travel and first trip to Europe, 1832-1833, 3 ff. ; visits Landor, 6-11 ; in Venice, 11 ; in Milan, 12 ; crosses Switzerland, 12 ; in France and Paris, 1833, 12-13, 155-156 ; arrives in England, 13 ; visits Coleridge, 13-17 ; tours England and Scotland, 17 ; visits Carlyle at Craigenputtock, 18-29 ; and Carlyle, 25-26, 28-29, 32, 168-173, 192, 194-195 ; on Carlyle's *Sartor Resartus*, 29 ; visits Wordsworth, 1833, 29-30 ; opinion of Wordsworth's 'Ode on Immortality,' 30 ; leaves for America, September 4, 1833, 31 ; writes Carlyle letter of comfort after destruction of first volume of *French Revolution*, 34 ; instrumental in publication of Carlyle's books in America, 34-35 ; sends Carlyle *Nature*, 'Concord Centennial Address,' 'The American Scholar,' 'The Divinity School Address,' 'Literary Ethics,' first series of *Essays*, 36 ff. ; first British edition of *Essays*, 37 ; sends friends to call on Carlyle, 37 ff., 172 ; Emerson, Alcott and Carlyle, 38-41 ; edits *The Dial*, 42 ; introduces Margaret Fuller to Carlyle, 42-44 ; increasing British reputation, 48-49, 68-70 ; influence on young men, 50 ff., 64-65, 72-73, 189, 190 ; and Alexander Ireland, 50-54 ; second visit to England, 1847-1848, 54 ff. ; with Carlyles in London, 55-60, 144-153 ; lectures in North of England and Scotland, 60-61, 64, 90, 95, 96, 97, 100, 101, 115, 179, 188 ; and John Sterling, 61-64 ; correspondence with William Allingham, 67-68, 189 ; lectures in London, 68, 135-137, 141-144, 149 ; visits Clough in Oxford, 68-70, 156 ; with Clough in Paris, 70, 155-156 ; and Francis Espinasse, 71, 88-89, 93-94, 95 ; entertained in London, 74, 140, 142 ; speaks at Grand Soirée of Manchester Athenæum, 74-86 ; temporary residence in Manchester, 86 ; Manchester dinner for his friends, 87-95 ; and George Gilfillan, Dundee, Scotland, 96-108 ; and Geraldine Endsor Jewsbury, Manchester, 109-111 ; visits Charles Bray at Coventry and meets George Eliot, 111-113 ; excursion to Stratford, 112 ; and George Stephenson, Chesterfield, 112-117 ; and David Scott, Edinburgh, 117-126 ; dines with DeQuincey, Dr. Samuel Brown, and David Scott at Mrs. Crowe's, Edinburgh, 125 ; portrait painted by David Scott, 125-126 ; visits Harriet Martineau in Lake District, 127, 133-135 ; calls on

Emerson, Ralph Waldo (*Cont'd*) Wordsworth, 134-135; and Henry Crabb Robinson, London, 135-144; dines with Antiquarian Society, London, 140-141; John Chapman's farewell party for Emerson, 144; residence at Chapman's in London, 145; visits Stonehenge with Carlyle, 150-153; leaves for America, July 15, 1848, [70-71], 152, 156-157, 165; and Clough, Concord and Boston, 154-167; lecturing in America, 160; on Democracy and America's future, [85, 150-151], 169-170; Macaulay's comment on the Carlyle-Emerson friendship, 170; receives gift of photograph from Carlyle, 172-173; Emerson, Carlyle, and the American Civil War, 173-176, 194-195; receives report on Carlyle from Allingham, 188; contrasted with Carlyle by Allingham, 188, 190-192; recites Allingham's 'The Touchstone' at service for John Brown, 189; his poetry included in *Nightingale Valley* by Allingham, 189-190; third visit to England, 1872-1873, 191; sees Carlyle for last time, 191; final thoughts of Carlyle, 194-195

Emerson, William, brother of R. W. Emerson, 2, 60

England, 5, 10, 13, 17, 34, 50, 53, 54, 55, 60, 61, 64, 65, 68, 74, 76, 81, 83, 84, 86, 108, 150-151, 158, 163, 173, 189

English Lake District, 127-128, 131-135

English Review, 73

English Traits, by Emerson, 30

Espinasse, Francis, 48, 71, 88, 89, 92, 93, 95, 149, 169

Essays, by Emerson, 36, 37, 43, 48, 61, 64, 88, 110, 124, 125, 137, 138

Essays, by Montaigne, 51, 64

Evangel of Love, by Henry Sutton, 91

Evans, Mary Ann, see *George Eliot*

Exeter Hall, London, 135, 143, 149

F

Faraday, Michael, 69

Festus, by Philip James Bailey, 87, 125

Field, Edwin, 139

Florence, 5 ff., 11, 120

Forster, John, 135

Fourier, Charles, 142

Fraser, James, 34

Fraser's Magazine, 29, 33, 183, 184

Frederick the Great, by Carlyle, 87 ff., 175, 180, 184, 195

French Revolution, by Carlyle, 19, 32, 33, 34-35, 46, 169

Froude, J. A., 69, 70, 137, 186

Fuller, Margaret, 42, 53, 125

G

Gallery of Literary Portraits, by George Gilfillan, 97, 102; *Second Gallery*, 104-105; *Third Gallery*, 105

Geneva, 12, 120

George's Chapel, Dundee, 99, 100

German Romances, Carlyle's translation of, 183

Germany, 88

Gettysburg, battle of, 174

Gibbon, Edmund, 80

Gilfillan, George, 97-102, 103-107, 108

Gilfillan, Mrs. George, 100-101

Gill, T. H., 90, 94, 95

Gillman, Dr. James, 14

Glasgow, 97, 127

Goethe, 25, 43, 66, 68, 143, 183

Golden Treasury, Palgrave's, 69

Greeley, Horace, 43

Greenough, Horatio, 7, 8, 161

H

Hallam, Arthur, 61
Hampshire, 183
Harpers Ferry, 189
Harvard University, 175, 195
Hawthorne, Nathaniel, 161, 189
Hazlitt, William, 51
Helen, the Carlyles' maid, 45
Herbert, George, 92
'Heroes and Hero Worship,' Carlyle's lectures on, 144
Highgate, 13, 14, 16, 50
Hodgson, W. B., 88, 92
Holmes, Oliver Wendell, 116
Houses of Parliament, London, see *Parliament*
Huddersfield, 88
Hunt, Leigh, 65-67

I

'ILIAS (*Americana*) IN NUCE,' by Carlyle, 174
Imaginary Conversations, by Landor, 7, 11, 51
Inglis, Sir Robert, 141
Ireland, 60, 64, 65, 66, 169-170, 176, 179, 183, 185
Ireland, Alexander, 50-54, 55, 60, 88, 89, 93, 94, 95, 110
Italy, 5 ff., 10 ff., 20, 57

J

James, Henry, 38
Jamestown raid, 189
'January Searle,' see *George Searle Phillips*
Jeffrey, Francis, Lord, 121
Jewsbury, Frank, 109
Jewsbury, Geraldine Endsor, 44, 108-111
Jewsbury, Maria, 109
Johnson, Dr. Samuel, 80

K

Keats, John, 6, 59, 65, 188

Kendal, 127
Kirkcaldy, 35

L

Lamb, Charles, 76
Lancashire, 52, 58, 86, 93
Landor, W. S., 3, 4, 5, 6, 7-10, 11, 24, 51
Latter-Day Pamphlets, by Carlyle, 54, 145-146, 171
Laurence Bloomfield, by William Allingham, 67
'Laws of Thought,' Emerson's lecture on, 141
Leeds, 127
Life of Schiller, by Carlyle, 4
Life in the Sick-Room, by Harriet Martineau, 129
Literary and Philosophical Institution, London, 135
'Literary Ethics,' by Emerson, 36
Liverpool, 31, 54, 69, 131, 157, 165
London, 13, 20, 26, 27, 35, 37, 41, 43, 47, 54, 55, 57, 65, 74, 79, 122, 135, 136, 140, 149-150, 152, 161, 162, 168, 175, 177, 179, 180, 183, 186, 191
London University, 143, 158
Longfellow, H. W., 37, 135, 161
Lowell, Mrs. Charles, 175
Lowell, James Russell, 161
Lucas, Frederick, 58, 59
Lucas, Samuel, 59
Lymington, in Hampshire, 183
Lytton, Bulwer, 135

M

Macaulay, T. B., 121, 170
Maccall, William, 93
Machiavelli, 7
Macmillan's Magazine, 174
Mahon, Lord, 141
Manchester, 42, 48, 49, 52, 53, 55, 60, 64, 67, 78, 80, 81, 86, 87, 88, 90, 93, 108, 109, 110, 149

Manchester Athenæum, Grand Soirée, 74, 76-86
Manchester Courier, 96
Manchester Examiner, 52, 76, 77
Manchester Guardian, 76, 77, 78, 81
Manchester-Liverpool railway, 115
Manchester Mechanics' Institute, 53
Manchester School of Liberals, 52, 59, 74
Manchester Times, 60, 76
Martineau, Harriet, 14, 30, 43, 127, 128-133, 134, 135, 137, 138, 139, 141, 142
Massachusetts, 1, 21, 82, 85, 172, 175
Mechanics' Institutes, 53, 58, 74-76, 99
Mentone, 175
Michel Angelo, 7
Midlands, The, 53
Milan, 12, 120
Mill, John Stuart, 20, 33, 34, 36
Milnes, Richard Monkton, 58, 59, 136
Milton, John, 193
Montaigne, 51
Monybuie, 23
Morning Star, 59
Morpeth, Viscount, 76, 136, 143
Morris, William, 178

N

Napoleon, 12
Nature, by Emerson, 36, 52, 62
Neuberg, Joseph, 64, 87, 147
New England, 1, 18, 21-22, 25, 27, 41, 42, 159, 160, 161
New Hampshire, 21, 27
New York Tribune, 43
Newcastle, 64, 114
Newman, J. H., Cardinal, 68
Nightingale Valley, edited by W. Allingham, 189-190
Northampton, Lord, 139
North American Review, 159

Norton, Charles Eliot, 160-161, 175
Nottingham, 64, 68, 87, 91, 147
Nottinghamshire Guardian, 96

O

Occasional Discourse on the Nigger Question, by Carlyle, 173
'Ode on Immortality,' by Wordsworth, 30
Odyssey, Homer's, 101
Old North Church, Boston, Massachusetts, 2
Oliver Cromwell's Letters and Speeches, by Carlyle, 54
Oriel College, Oxford, 68, 155, 158
Ossoli, Mme., see Margaret Fuller
Owen, Richard, 69, 142
Oxford University, 68, 69, 137, 154, 155, 156, 158, 159, 162

P

Palgrave, Francis, 69
Pantheism, 98
Paradise Manse, Dundee, 99
Paris, 12-13, 70, 120, 155-156
Parker, Theodore, 161
Parliament, 122, 148, 188
Patmore, Coventry, 68, 163, 189
Perth, 101, 127
'Peschiera,' by A. H. Clough, 166
Phillips, George Searle, 88, 89, 92, 93, 94, 95
Philosophy of Necessity, The, by Charles Bray, 111
Piccadilly Circus, London, 40
Pickwick Papers, by Dickens, 60, 79
'Pilot's Daughter, The,' by William Allingham, 189
'Plato,' lecture on, by Emerson, 90, 95
Plutarch's Lives, Dryden's translation of, 159
Poe, E. A., 97
Procter, B. W., see Barry Cornwall

Punch, 82
Putnam's Magazine, 159

R

Rachel, star of the *Théâtre de la République*, 58
'Ralph Waldo Emerson,' by George Gilfillan, 96-97
'Ramble in New Forest,' by William Allingham, 183
Retrospect of Western Travel, by Harriet Martineau, 130
Robinson, Henry Crabb, 74, 129, 132-133, 137-144
Robinson, Thomas, brother of H. C. Robinson, 138, 139
Rogers, Samuel, 16, 74
Rome, 6, 120, 121, 122
Rose Hill, Coventry, home of Charles Bray, 111
Rossetti, D. G., 178
Rothwell, Richard, 121
Rousseau, J. J., 112
Royal Academy, London, 122
Royal Scottish Academy, 122
Rugby School, 68
Ruskin, John, 178
Russell, Le Baron, 34, 38, 46
Rydal Mount, 134
Rydal Water, 128, 132

S

Salisbury, 150
Sartor Resartus, by Carlyle, 29, 33, 34, 38, 46, 169
Scotland, 17, 57, 60, 61, 64, 74, 87, 96, 97, 102, 121, 127, 180
Scott, David, 117-126
Scott, Robert, father of David Scott, 117
Scott, Mrs. Robert, 117
Scott, William Bell, brother of David Scott, 64
Sedgwick, Miss Catherine Maria, 38
Self-Reliance, by Emerson, 137-138

Severn, Joseph, 121
Shakespeare, 112, 187
'Shakespeare,' Emerson's lecture on, 100
Shelley, P. B., 5, 65, 97
Slavery, abolition of, 37, 99, 173-174
Smith, Adam, 93
Society in America, by Harriet Martineau, 130
Spedding, James, 58, 59
Speech by Emerson before Manchester Athenæum Grand Soirée, 81-85
'Spirit of the Times,' Emerson's lecture on, 100
Stephenson, George, 112-117
Sterling, John, 61-64, 150, 162, 176
Stonehenge, 150, 151-153
Strafford, by John Sterling, 63
Stratford, 112
Sumner, Charles, 37, 161
Sutherland, Duchess of, 136
Sutton, Henry, 68, 87, 91, 92, 94, 95, 189
Swanwick, Frederick, 115, 116
Swedenborg, 139
Switzerland, 11, 12

T

Table Talk, by Coleridge, 17
Taggart, Thomas, 138
Tait's Edinburgh Magazine, 96, 98, 104
Talford, Thomas Noon, 76
Tapton House, Chesterfield, home of George Stephenson, 115
Tennyson, Alfred, Lord, 55, 61, 157, 183-184
Thoreau, H. D., 87, 91, 189
'Touchstone, The,' by W. Allingham, 189
Turner, J. M. W., 178

U-V

United States, see *America*
University Hall, London, 158

Venables, George Stovin, 58, 59
Venice, 11, 120
Villa Gherardesca, 6

W

Walden Pond, 158, 161
Wall, James Walter, 12
Watt Institute, Dundee, 99, 100
Wedgwood, Hensleigh, 45
A Week on the Concord and Merrimack Rivers, by H. D. Thoreau, 91
Weimar, 183
Wheeler, Stearns, 38
Wilhelm Meister, by Goethe, 25, 29

Wilkinson, Thomas, 139, 143
William of Wykeham, 152
Wilton, 152
Wiltshire, 153
Winchester, 152
Windermere, 128, 132, 134
Woolner, Thomas, 189
Wordsworth, Dora, 29, 135
Wordsworth, W., 3, 4, 13, 15-16, 17, 29-30, 51, 70, 128, 132, 134-135, 139, 143

Y-Z

Yorkshire, 88
Zoe, by Geraldine Endsor Jewsbury, 108